CHOPIN

CHOPIN

THE RELUCTANT ROMANTIC

Jeremy Siepmann

VICTOR GOLLANCZ

LONDON

First published in Great Britain 1995
by Victor Gollancz
An imprint of the Cassell Group
Wellington House, 125 Strand, London WC2R OBB

© Jeremy Siepmann 1995

A catalogue record for this book is
available from the British Library.

ISBN 0 575 05692 4

Phototypeset in Great Britain by
Rowland Phototypesetting Ltd, Bury St Edmunds, Suffolk
Printed and bound in Great Britain by
Mackays of Chatham PLC, Chatham, Kent

This book is dedicated to my wife

Contents

List of Illustrations

Jane Wilhelmina Stirling.

Chopin on his deathbed.

Death mask of Chopin, made by Auguste Clésinger.

Chopin's left hand, cast by Auguste Clésinger.

The Chopin monument at Monceau Park.

Acknowledgements

My first debts, of course, are to my subjects – notably Chopin and George Sand, whose letters and recollections provide the core of any Chopin biography. On the musical side, I owe an incalculable debt to my teachers Hans Neumann, Peter Feuchtwanger and Alan Walker, who opened my ears to the greatness of Chopin's music very many years ago now. More immediately, I acknowledge with heartfelt thanks the generous and stimulating contributions to the present volume made by Emanuel Ax, Alfred Brendel, Michael Roll, Carl Schachter, Howard Shelley, Melvyn Tan, Mitsuko Uchida and Tamas Vasary, whose joint thoughts on Chopin deserve a book of their own. Professor Tadeusz Chmielewski, President of the Warsaw Chopin Society, Hanna Wroblewska-Straus, Director of the Chopin Museum, Aleksandra Czapiewska of the Polish Cultural Institute, Michel Lummaux of the French Embassy in London, and Marc Cioffi, Conservateur of the Maison de George Sand, Nohant, were friendliness and helpfulness itself. Professor Jim Samson, too, could hardly have been more helpful or obliging, nor could Giulia Hetherington, who assisted me in the picture research. Above all, however, I must acknowledge the contribution of my wife, and my editor Richard Wigmore, whose combination of patience, flexibility, knowledge and creative suggestion has been of invaluable help to me at every stage of the book's development.

Preface

Alone among his musical contemporaries, Chopin has never suffered even a brief period of eclipse. Unlike Liszt, Berlioz, Mendelssohn and Schumann, his music has enjoyed uninterrupted (indeed, ever increasing) popularity from the time of his youth to the present – and this despite an originality that can still administer shocks. But popularity has its own perils. Of the many books on his life and works, many tell us as much about their authors and the prevailing values of their age as they do about their subject. Admittedly, the bare outlines of his life are a gift to the Romantic imagination: the endearing prodigy in the largely parochial Poland of the early 1800s; the conquests of the dazzling virtuoso in Vienna and Paris; his much-publicized affair with the cross-dressing novelist George Sand; his obsessive dandyism; his frail constitution and early death at thirty-nine. Less well aired, because of its psychological subtlety, is the contradictory inner turmoil of a man who felt largely out of sympathy with the very age that he has long been said to have personified: the only composers whom he admired unreservedly were Mozart and Bach, and his interest in literature – one of the hallmarks of the Romantic movement – pales into insignificance when compared with most of his friends and contemporaries. Still less familiar are his accomplished mimicry and his often sharply satirical sense of humour, a characteristic largely ignored by generations of biographers and pianists alike.

The vast literature that he spawned divides broadly into two categories: straight (and often fanciful) biographical writings in which the music itself tends to get short shrift, and sophisticated musicological studies aimed primarily at scholars and musical practitioners. A smaller body of work sets out to combine studies of the man and his music in a manner comprehensible to the intelligent layman who may have no formal knowledge of musical jargon or techniques. Of these, most are out of print or have never appeared in English translations. There has been no new biography in English since Adam Zamoyski's of 1979, which contains little in the way of musical exposition (the author makes no claim to being a musician). Meanwhile Chopin research has proceeded apace. The time would seem to be right, then, for an up-to-date biography, drawing for its background on all the important Chopin research of the past twenty years. While containing substantial musical commentary – not least on the intriguing history of the mazurka, the polonaise and the concert waltz – the book is specifically addressed to a general audience and, in its strictly biographical function, presumes no formal musical knowledge on the part of the reader.

The ratio of biography to musical elucidation heavily favours the former. The music is not treated in a separate section of the book, as in the standard life-and-works format, but rather in a sequence of interludes, alternating with the biographical chapters so that the reader may opt for a continuous narrative and return to the specifically musical discussions later on. My aim throughout has been to relate the character of the man and his music to the spirit not only of the time but of the places in which he lived and worked, and to reflect his lasting influence on the near century and a half after his death.

I have tried, as consistently as possible, to present the biographical material (containing abundant quotations from letters, diaries, news-papers and so on) in such a way as to hold the attention even of the tone-deaf. While never 'cooking the facts', as it were, and while avoiding the kind of imaginative scene-setting that blights so many biographies, I have attempted to give the book some of the immediacy of a novel by allowing its protagonists, in large measure, to relate the story in their own words. These give a far richer and more fascinating portrait of both the characters and their time than any amount of subjective 'interpretation'.

A noteworthy feature of the book is the sequence of Appendices, which trace the prevailing trends in Chopin playing since the advent of recording and explore some of the eternal challenges to the interpreter with some of the finest Chopin players of our time – and one, Alfred Brendel, who decided many years ago *not* to play Chopin. This necess-arily compact symposium should be enough to show that the long and changing Chopin tradition is still very much alive. I hope it will also demonstrate the extent to which performing styles and outlooks can diverge, not only in successive ages but simultaneously.

NOTE A name followed by an asterisk denotes a brief biographical entry in the Personalia.

CHOPIN

— 1 —

Prophetic Beginnings
1810–1825

Like a spy, he was not what he seemed. There was no one more obviously aristocratic, yet he came from peasant stock; there was no one more evidently wealthy, though he was often close to poverty; there was no composer more revolutionary, yet he was conservative to the point of priggishness; there was no man more generous or accommodating, yet Robert Schumann said of him: 'he will give you anything, except himself.' That self has proved tantalizingly elusive for more than a century and a half. The 'real' Chopin steadfastly refuses to stand up, although a fair likeness can be built from the many fragments and hints that he has left us, just as the likeness of a painting can emerge from the pieces of a jigsaw puzzle. But only if they can all be found to fit. Almost every aspect of Chopin's life can be argued over, with no promise of consensus. Not even on the subject of his birthday are his biographers agreed. A baptismal certificate at Brochow Church, near the small Polish village of Zelazowa Wola, states plainly that he was born on 22 February 1810. According to the parish register:

> Nicholas Chopin, the father, aged 40 years and dwelling in the village of Zelazowa Wola, showed to us a child of the male sex which was born in his house on the 22nd day of the month of February in this present year [1810] and informed us that it was his wish to give the child the two names Fryderyk Franciszek.

Yet his own mother, in a letter from 1837, cites 1 March as his birthday, which is the date unquestioningly accepted by himself, his sisters, his schoolmates and his pupils. Is it credible that his own mother did not know the date on which her first and only son was born? And what of their friends and neighbours? The discrepancy is especially noteworthy in view of the Chopin family's almost compulsive observation of birthdays and name-days generally.

Interestingly, Nicholas Chopin claimed not to know the date of his own birth (now fixed as 15 April 1771, although long believed to have been 17 April). As the family name suggests, he came from French stock and was born at Marainville, in northeast France, to a family of vine-growers and wheelwrights. Unusually for a boy of that background, he learned to read and write and came to the attention of a Polish administrator, who, on returning to his homeland in 1787, offered to take the sixteen-year-old with him. The boy accepted and turned his back on France and family for ever. Whether through shame for their illiteracy or for other, more delicate reasons, he never spoke of his French family to his own children, and when Frédéric became the toast of Paris in the 1830s he was quite unaware that he had two aunts, labouring in the vineyards not far away.

From the moment of his arrival in Poland, Nicholas Chopin determined to become a Pole, later referring to his birthplace as a foreign land. When offered a chance to return on a visit in 1790, he declined. Even had he wished to see his family, he was not about to risk conscription into the French Army, a near certainty since the outbreak of the Revolution. Ambitious to advance himself in society, he worked his way up from being a clerk in a tobacco factory to serving as tutor to a variety of noble Polish families, his pupils including at one time the ill-fated Maria Walewska, later to become the mistress of Napoleon.

He could hardly have come to Poland at a more interesting or uncertain time. Fifteen years before, the kingdom had effectively been dismembered by the so-called First Partition, engineered by Frederick the Great, in which a third of Poland's land was divided up between her three powerful neighbours, Russia, Austria and Prussia. A Second Partition in 1793 exacted further losses, in this case mostly to Russia. A year later a national uprising was led by Tadeusz Kosciuszko,* who had cut his revolutionary teeth in 1776 fighting against the British in the American War of Independence. Failing to enlist the support of the French Revolutionaries for the Polish cause, he now led his people, unaided, in a crusade against the Russian occupation. Having evaded conscription by his motherland, Nicholas Chopin rushed to his adoptive country's aid, joining the Warsaw National Guard and rising to the rank of lieutenant before being invalided out in 1794, when the Poles were defeated by the superior Russian forces. The entire country was now occupied, and was again divided up between the three autocracies in the Third Partition of 1795. The land they controlled, however, was in a desperate state.

In many ways this most troubled of European countries was only now emerging from the Middle Ages. Not even in Tsarist Russia, with whom its history is so intimately linked, was the contrast of wealth and poverty, luxury and suffering, more starkly or shockingly etched than in Poland. In the countryside, a loaf of bread was an almost unimaginable delicacy. At the time when Nicholas Chopin was growing from boy to youth in pre-Revolutionary France, few Polish villages even possessed an oven. The weaver's loom was a rarity, and the spinning-wheel was as yet unknown. Many peasants lived and died without ever seeing such basic conveniences as knives, forks and spoons. Their homes were often little more than hovels. Nor did the surrounding countryside offer much relief from the prevailing scene of desolation. Sparsely populated (averaging fewer than fifty persons to the square mile), the great plain of Mazovia, stretching from Cracow to Warsaw, was a vast expanse of flatlands, much of it overgrown with untamed forest – mostly pines and firs, interspersed with beech, birch and undernourished oaks. Occasionally the woods gave way to open pasture land, but even here, despite the natural richness of the soil, crops were few and generally ill-attended. Such travellers as passed through the region, like the English clergyman William Coxe* in the late eighteenth century, were near unanimous in their impressions. 'The natives were poorer, humbler and more miserable than any people we had yet observed; whenever we stopped, they flocked around us in crowds, and asking for charity, used the most abject gestures. . . . The Polish peasants are cringing and servile in their expressions of respect.'

The degradation of Poland at the time of Chopin's birth, however, was by no means at an end, nor was it confined to the peasantry. Another observer, writing as late as 1812, paints a still bleaker picture:

> Nothing could exceed the misery of all classes. The army was not paid, the officers were in rags, the best houses were in ruins, the greatest lords were compelled to leave Warsaw from want of money to provide for their tables. . . . I saw in Warsaw two French physicians who informed me that they could not procure their fees even from the greatest lords.

Could these be the people whose traditions fired Chopin's imagination? Whose dances and songs enabled him to create a truly national music, admired and applauded throughout the civilized world? From that point of view, Heinrich Heine's* impressions, gathered a generation after Coxe, ring truer:

It cannot be denied that the Polish peasant often has more head and
heart than the German peasant in some districts. Not infrequently
did I find in the meanest Pole that original wit which on every
occasion bubbles forth with wonderful iridescence, and that dreamy
sentimental trait, that brilliant flashing of an Ossianic feeling for
nature whose sudden outbreaks on passionate occasions are as invol-
untary as the rising of the blood into the face.

But by Heine's time much had changed. In 1812, when Chopin was
two, Napoleon had declared war on Russia, advancing on Moscow at
the head of an 'army of twenty tongues', 80,000 of whom were Poles,
grasping once again at the chance of escape from their Russian overlords.
With Napoleon's defeat, all thoughts of Polish autonomy were dashed,
and in 1815 the Congress of Vienna again consigned the country to the
rule of its mighty neighbours, Russia's share now extending westwards
to include Warsaw, which had previously been subject to Prussian control. In principle, the treaty could have been worse, for although the
Tsar was proclaimed King of Poland, his Polish dominions were to be
granted a modern, liberalized constitution. The settlement was proclaimed permanent and inviolable, and Poland was to maintain its own
army, schools and administration. Cynics, however, were soon confirmed in their suspicions. Contrary to widespread expectations, the
Tsar failed to name as his viceroy the diplomatic, influential, highly
experienced (and Polish) Prince Adam Czartoryski, who had formerly
served as Russian Minister for Foreign Affairs, and instead of appointing
Kosciuszko as supreme commander of the army, he gave the post to
his brother, the Grand Duke Constantine, whose only virtue in Polish
eyes was that he had a Polish wife. Yet even under these disappointing
circumstances, the country's fortunes took a distinct upward turn, and
Warsaw in particular prospered as never before.

Despite the above quoted claim that 'the best houses were in ruins,
and the greatest lords compelled to leave Warsaw from want of money',
there were a substantial number of aristocratic and noble families whose
opulent life-style had persisted throughout the worst of Poland's
troubles. Prominent among these were the Czartoryskis, the Radziwills
and the Potockis, all of whom were to play a substantial part in Chopin's
life, from the time of his childhood onwards. And their ostentation
made no concessions to the prevailing poverty around them. A writer
of the time has left a vivid description of a Polish count:

He was clad in the uniform of the palatinate: a doublet embroidered
with gold, an overcoat of the finest Tours silk, ornamented with

fringes, and a belt of gold brocade from which hung a sword with a hilt of Morocco. At his neck glittered a clasp with diamonds. His square white cap was surmounted by a magnificent plume, composed of tufts of heron's feathers, of which each feather costs a ducat.

From another writer we hear of 'ambassadors riding through towns on horses loosely shod with gold or silver, so that the horse-shoes lost on their passage might testify to their wealth and grandeur'. Nor was expense spared in the dressing of the horses, 'with their bridles and stirrups of massive silver, and their caparisons and saddles embroidered with gold and purple flowers'. Whatever else may be said of them, the nobility of Poland were not meek, but to many of their poorer compatriots they seemed already to have inherited the earth.

Perhaps the greatest common bond between the indigenous Poles was their Christianity – more specifically, their Roman Catholicism. From princes to ditch diggers, they were sustained by their belief that the sufferings and privations of this world would be rewarded in the next. The one possession they universally had in common was a crucifix, affixed to the wall above a vessel of Holy Water. In the meantime, such commerce and industry as could be found in Poland was almost exclusively dominated by foreigners and Jews, who took a different view of earthly life. Although settled in Poland for many generations, the Jews maintained a conspicuously separate culture, differing from their neighbours in language, dress and standard of living. While amounting to less than 10 per cent of the population, they controlled a wholly disproportionate share of the country's resources, effectively monopolizing trade, keeping inns and taverns, serving as stewards to the nobility, and involving themselves in business at every level. Indeed – and this was then unique to Poland – they even took an active part in agriculture, labouring in the fields like any other peasant.

If the wealth and grandeur described earlier were not rare among the Polish nobility, neither were they general. Many aristocrats were living in straitened circumstances. Among these was the Skarbek family of Zelazowa Wola, a village about 32 miles (53 kilometres) from Warsaw, with whom Nicholas Chopin found employment as the children's tutor in 1802. Their estate was pleasant but small: a manor house, no more than a comfortable bungalow with a modest annexe at either side, set in the heart of a little wood, divided by the little Utrata river. Also living on the estate at that time was the Skarbeks' housekeeper, Justyna Krzyzanowska, a lively, pretty, capable girl aged twenty whose family had fallen on hard times. In the years ahead, tutor and housekeeper drew steadily closer, and on 2 June 1806, four years after their first meeting, they were married and moved into one of the annexes. The little house is still there, nestled amid chestnut, poplar, oak and willow trees, but the river, while still flowing, has fallen victim to the pollution which serves as a signature of the twentieth century. In the Chopins' time there was a stork perch by the chimney, designed to attract these large birds, held by the country people to be harbingers of luck. And of children. One year after moving in, Justyna gave birth to their first daughter, Ludwika. Frédéric, their only son, was born in 1810 (on that, at least, all are agreed) and was followed by two more sisters, Isabella in 1811 and Emilia in 1812.

All four of the Chopin children were exceptionally talented. Like the sisters of Mozart and Mendelssohn, the eldest, Ludwika, was herself a gifted and accomplished musician, being both a fluent pianist and a competent composer, while Emilia, the youngest, showed astonishing precocity as a writer. Isabella was not so creative as her siblings but was extraordinarily cultured and discerning from an early age, and was perhaps the first to grasp the true nature of her brother's gifts. As the only son and brother in the family, Frédéric was regarded by his father with a deep affection and pride, and by his mother and sisters with a love and delight that bordered at times on open reverence. In addition to his musical talents, he was a born mimic and a budding caricaturist, whose drawings betrayed an ironic, even satirical streak, which remained with him for life.

The children grew up in an atmosphere of great industry and aspiration, but leavened with humour and untainted by the stultifying parental ambitions that so often make a curse of natural blessings. The church played no more than a conventional role in family life, although Justyna was noted for her piety. Ethics and a high moral code, on the other hand, were central. Nicholas preached a gospel of thrift and moderation in all things, but without the strictures of the puritan. Both parents were musical. Justyna played the piano, Nicholas the flute and violin, and chamber music lent added joys to the relaxed conviviality of family life. From infancy, Frédéric was deeply affected by music, and at the age of four or five he became an avid pupil of his mother and eldest sister. By the time he was six it was plain that he had a prodigious gift. He could tackle with ease and assurance works whose difficulty was out of all proportion to his age, and was already showing a pronounced gift for improvisation, the source of his greatest happiness throughout his life. He quickly exhausted all the guidance his mother and sister could give him, and before he was seven his musical development was entrusted to an acquaintance of his father's, a Bohemian immigrant by the name of Adalbert Zywny.

In appearance, Zywny might have sprung straight from the pages of the young Chopin's sketch pad. Tall, dishevelled and toothless, he signalled his allegiance to the past in general, and to the eighteenth century in particular, by wearing a close-fitted, yellowing wig, offset by a long, green, quilted frock coat, tasselled knee boots, a yellow velvet waistcoat and an outsize red-checked handkerchief, permanently stained with tobacco. Preceding him wherever he went was the strong and unmistakable aroma of snuff, mingled with a more elusive scent (in lieu of bathing, which he deplored, Zywny's only concession to personal hygiene was to daub himself liberally with vodka). Beneath the comic opera façade, however, he was both intelligent and cultured and soon became a fixture in the Chopins' social life. Long after he had ceased giving lessons to Frédéric, who rapidly outdistanced him, there was hardly a family occasion from which he was excluded. From Zywny Chopin acquired a lifelong passion for Mozart and Bach, whose music played a seminal role in the development of his own style, and a thorough knowledge of works by Haydn, Hummel and Ries, though none by Beethoven (still very much alive), of whom his master disapproved. Interestingly, neither Zywny nor Joseph Elsner, who succeeded him, had any formal schooling as a pianist, a fact which may have had a formative influence on the unprecedented originality of Chopin's approach to the keyboard. In any case, we have it on the authority of his father that the mechanics of piano-playing hardly detained him for an hour. He was one of those freaks of nature who seem to be born masters of an activity which in itself could hardly be more unnatural. Yet so determined was the child to overcome all obstacles that, according to one well-seasoned if uncorroborated story, he took to going to bed with bits of wood wedged between his fingers in the hope of increasing their span while he slept.

Within a year of starting lessons with Zywny, who introduced him to all of the musical establishment in Warsaw, Frédéric had already attained a degree of local celebrity and was inevitably being talked of as a second Mozart. Before his eighth birthday he had composed two polonaises and a military march (the latter being scored for band by an employee of the Grand Duke Constantine and performed in front of the Saxon Palace). On the publication of his second polonaise, in G minor, he received his first printed notice, in the Warsaw *Review* of January 1818:

The composer of this dance, only eight years of age, is a real musical genius. . . . He not only performs the most difficult pieces on the piano with the greatest ease and extraordinary taste, but is also the composer of several dances and variations that fill the experts with amazement, particularly in view of the author's youth. If this boy had been born in Germany or France, his fame would probably by now have spread to all nations. May the present notice remind the reader that geniuses are born in our country also, and that they are not widely known only because of the lack of public notice.

A month later, on 24 February, Chopin made his formal début as a pianist in a concerto by the Bohemian Adalbert Gyrowetz, who numbered Mozart among his admirers and whose best works were often confused with Haydn's. Predictably, he caused a sensation. When asked by his mother, who had been prevented by illness from attending, what the audience had liked best, the little boy is said to have replied: 'My English collar, Mama.' It has the ring of truth about it, reflecting both his innate modesty and his lifelong obsession with dress. From this concert dates his mutual (and again lifelong) love affair with the Polish aristocracy, of whom he instantly became the darling. Henceforward, their patronage was to have a formative effect on the development of his character and outlook, hardly less pervasive in its influence than that of his family and teachers.

The attentions of one particular aristocrat, however, he might well have preferred to do without. The Grand Duke Constantine Pavlovitch, Supreme Commander of the Kingdom of Poland, was no Pole, but the brother of the Tsar: feared and hated in equal measure for his barbarous cruelty and the open contempt that he displayed for the Poles under his command. Given to periods of hysterical derangement (posthumously diagnosed as schizophrenia), he was known to go on random shooting sprees through the streets of Warsaw before sinking into a deep melancholy and calling for music to soothe his troubled soul. The music and playing of the child Chopin seemed to pacify him especially, and he regularly sent his carriage, drawn by four white horses, each bearing a Cossack rider in full uniform, to collect the boy and convey him by royal command to the Belvedere Palace. Here Chopin entertained the Duke, conversing with him intermittently and staying on to play with his son, of whom he rapidly became a favourite. Thus from the age of eight, he acquired the manners and assurance of the nobility while never forsaking his national or family roots. In the autumn of 1818, he notched up another royal conquest when he played for the Dowager Empress

Maria Feodorovna, to whom he presented two polonaises, composed and personally inscribed to her (both works, alas, ha¹ lost).

Far from being a frail, sheltered genius, prey to excessive sensibilities and sequestered from his less gifted contemporaries, Chopin was always popular among his schoolmates. Predominantly cheerful and given to laughter, he delighted in childish pranks and his ever-developing feats of mimicry and caricature were the delight of his friends and family alike. Indeed, as he grew older, a number of professional actors protested that he was born for the theatre and that his talents were wasted on music. He and his sisters were forever improvising little dramas, and in celebration of their father's name-day in 1824, Frédéric, now fourteen, collaborated with Emilia on a one-act comedy, *The Mistake; or the Pretended Rogue*, written entirely in verse. Despite the general education on which his father insisted, however, Chopin was never wholly at ease with words. As he had put it in another name-day tribute, composed when he was only eight,

> It would be easier for me to reveal my feelings if they could be expressed in musical sounds, but since the finest concerto could not do justice to my devotion to you, I must use simple words straight from my heart to convey to you the homage of my tender gratitude and filial attachment.

The year 1823 marked a turning-point in Chopin's life, heralded by the long overdue cessation of his lessons with Zywny. Despite his musical prowess and his burgeoning celebrity, his parents were agreed on the subject of his education, and from the autumn of that year until the summer of 1826 music yielded by parental decree to Latin, Greek, mathematics, literature and science. Before his official enrolment, however, a new window, of incalculable importance, was opened for him on the nature of his musical destiny. That spring, the Chopins received from Mme Skarbek an invitation to spend the summer at Zelazowa Wola. This was Chopin's first holiday in the country, and it cemented his inborn sense of Polishness with sounds and images that were to stay with him for life. Returning to his birthplace after thirteen years, he had no memory of the manor, the park, the mill or the river, let alone the sounds of the countryside, but he was entranced by what he found, and soon contributed new enchantments of his own. At Mme Skarbek's suggestion, her piano was carried outdoors in the evening and placed in the shade of the spreading chestnut trees. After dinner, as the residents of the manor and their guests gathered round, Chopin, eyes raised heavenwards (his now habitual attitude at the piano), played to them. The memory of these pastoral recitals was engraved on the minds of all who heard them. And there, in the presence of nature, Chopin felt his Polishness to be complete.

When he returned to Warsaw he was proud to wear the regulation student uniform and cap. In his long, close-fitting jacket, buttoned high at the neck and belted at the waist, he was a Pole for all to see. In time to come, his uniform discarded, he would be a Pole for all to hear. In the meantime, he would study Poland's past, imbibing her proud spirit through her history, her literature and art. Music apart, there was nothing that so keenly held his interest. Diligent and dutiful, if not naturally industrious, he learnt mathematics, Greek and Latin, geography and science, with indifference but determination. What his friends and teachers best remembered was his humour and his wit. On a number of occasions, his irreverent impersonations won him the spontaneous applause of classmates and teachers alike. If they were able to forget his genius, his precocity and his continued cultivation by the rich and powerful, it was at least in part because he himself was able to forget. Much has been made of Chopin's snobbery, but the charge is unsustainable. He moved among the aristocracy not as a social-climbing *arriviste* but as one of them. Nor did he ever scorn the middle-class from which he came, or the peasantry in whom he found the heart of Polishness. He never condescended. He had a gift for friendship and a sense of loyalty that lasted him a lifetime, and never more so than in his student years. Indeed, to a degree unusual in the history of genius he had a need for intimacy which amounted almost to a tragic flaw, the more so for the deepening reserve with which it coexisted.

Until his thirteenth year his closest friendships were within the family. With the conjunction of the Lyceum and his father's boarding house (a necessary concession to financial pressures), he found the friends through whom he found himself: Jan Matuszynski, later to become a doctor, Jan Bialoblocki and Julian Fontana, both excellent pianists, and most importantly of all, at this stage of his life, Titus Woyciechowski (again, a musician), with whom he fell innocently but passionately in love. Like Zywny and others, these friends were welcomed into the bosom of the Chopins' family life, ever teeming with creative activity. Emilia and Frédéric together had organized a club called the Literary Entertainment Society, which met in the evenings and was devoted to reciting their own works. Frédéric was president, Emilia was secretary; the remaining membership consisted of the boarders. Lacking his sister's outstanding flair for language, Chopin immersed himself, as well, in the design and making of sets and costumes for their frequent dramatic productions, of which he was always the (usually comic) star.

However dutifully he may have applied himself to his general education, music remained the focus of his life. In the aftermath of his lessons with the still beloved Zywny, Chopin had begun to study, informally at first, with Warsaw's most distinguished musician, Joseph Elsner, the recent founder of the Warsaw Conservatory. Like both Zywny and Nicholas Chopin, he was an immigrant. Born in Germany in 1769 and educated there, he had lived a restless, peripatetic life until settling in Warsaw in 1799, when he proceeded to become more Polish than the Poles. Of his thirty-two operas, thirty are in Polish, as are all of his twenty-five songbooks, and only one of his several published treatises is concerned with a non-Polish subject. As a teacher he was quick to recognize Chopin's individuality and drive and made no attempt to force his education into a rigid, traditional framework. Among the earliest of Chopin's works to be produced under Elsner's guidance are the exotically pitched Polonaise in G sharp minor and the so-called 'Swiss Boy' Variations (his most sophisticated work to date), both composed in 1824. It was a year memorialized for him by two worthy but dull books: Karol Anton Simon's *Short Guide to the Rules of Harmony in a Manner Easy to Learn* (this prescribed by Elsner, who knew from the beginning that Chopin's attitude to rules would always be deeply ambivalent), and the volume awarded him at the end of his first year at the Lyceum, a stupefyingly inappropriate tract entitled *An Outline of Statistics for the Use of County and District Schools*. On the flyleaf it bore the inscription: *Moribus et diligentiae Fryderyk Chopin in examine publico Licei Varsoviensi die 24 Julii 1824*. More memorable and significant by far, however, was the summer holiday that followed, spent in the countryside village of Szafarnia, to the northwest of Warsaw.

We now begin to encounter evidence of that delicate health which was to blight so much of Chopin's adult life and cast shadows over much of his music. His hosts at the manor house, the family of his friend Dominik Dziewanowski, were warm and welcoming and took pains to ensure that he followed to the letter the regimen prescribed for him. Accordingly, his meals were regularly supplemented with half a litre of linden extract, six glasses of roasted acorn coffee, a daily infusion of pills to encourage weight gain and an exclusive ration of white rolls, baked especially for him.

To the souvenirs of the previous summer's visit to his birthplace was now added a kaleidoscope of impressions richer than anything he had yet encountered. There was hardly an aspect of the country life that did not engross him, from the gossiping of the hens and the war between the ducks and geese to the squabbling of the servants and the toiling of the peasants in the fields. He enjoyed, too, the gregarious generosity of the landed gentry. The arrival of guests, unexpected or invited, was invariably a cause for celebration. Tables and chairs would be set up beneath the linden tree in front of the house, refreshments flowed, and lively conversation followed. In turn, the family regularly called on neighbours, some of whose houses were virtual shrines to a Poland long gone. Sabres and family portraits hung on the walls, old mahogany furniture glittered with gilded Empire ornament, full of ostentation and an outworn pride. Chopin, too, was cordially received wherever he went, and as he enjoyed travelling he soon became familiar with the whole region – the only part of Poland, outside Warsaw, that he ever knew. The most memorable discovery, though, the most awesome spectacle, as ever in the country, was the harvest.

Nor could Chopin fail to be struck by the consolatory and work-enhancing songs of the toilers in the field, wafting back to him across the open plain. Here as never before he came to value the virtues of tradition. The music made by these simple, hardened peasants was a birthright which even the most heinous despot could not take away from them. Here Chopin encountered for the first time the full impact of the oral tradition, unchanged yet always changing through many generations. Here for the first time, in the flatlands of Mazovia, he was conscious of hearing the authentic voice of Poland. As a consequence, he now prepared to make a special harvest of his own. Before the plans were much advanced, however, he discovered a third strain, which combined with the music of the peasants and the Warsaw aristocracy to give him all he needed for the creation of a truly national art music – a style that would leave the operas of his teacher Elsner way behind. But that was still to come. For the moment, there was a lot of catching up to do.

The humorous and uncomfortably self-conscious newsletters he dispatched to his parents in Warsaw in the guise of bulletins from the fictitious *Szafarnia Courier* give some measure of the gulf that still separated Chopin the fourteen-year-old boy from Chopin the pianist-composer. At the same time, we find him already absorbing influences that were to nourish his imagination for the rest of his life.

Szafarnia Courier, 3 September 1824

HOME NEWS

On 1 September, as Mr Pichon [a pseudonymous anagram of Chopin] was playing his piece *The Little Jew* [better known today as the Mazurka in A minor, op. 17, no. 4], Mr Dziewanowski called his Jewish cattle-hand and asked him what he thought of the young Jewish virtuosos. Young Moses came to the window, poked his hooked nose into the room and listened. Then he said that if Mr Pichon cared to play at a Jewish wedding he could make at least ten florins. Such a pronouncement encouraged Mr Pichon to study this kind of music as hard as he could.

FOREIGN NEWS

As he was passing through Nieszawa, Mr Pichon heard a village Catalani [a reference to the famous Italian soprano Angelica Catalani,* who had presented him with a gold watch in 1820] singing at the top of her voice as she sat on a fence. His attention was at once caught, and he listened to both song and voice, regretting, however, that in spite of his efforts he could not catch the words. Twice he walked past the fence, but in vain. He could not understand a word. Finally, overcome by curiosity, he fished out of his pocket three *sous* and promised them to the singer if she would repeat her song. For a time she made a fuss, pouted and refused, but tempted by the three *sous*, she made up her mind and began to sing a little mazurka from which the present editor, with the permission of the authorities and censorship, may quote as an example one verse:

> See, the wolf is dancing there behind the mountains:
> He's breaking his heart because he hasn't got a wife.

It was the first of many song-collecting expeditions, giving the lie to Béla Bartók's unfounded assertion that Chopin had no first-hand knowledge of Poland's indigenous music.

As term time approached, Chopin returned to Warsaw to prepare for his second year at the Lyceum. In his fifteenth year he began to show an interest in the opposite sex which, uncharacteristically, he did little to conceal. As the writer Eugenius Skrodzki recalled many years later:

A few hundred students went in and out of the university buildings. That is the reason why I can no longer identify the girl who deeply preoccupied Chopin when he was a fifth or sixth grade student at the Lyceum. He seemed too serious and mature for his age, clad in his uniform, which he sometimes wore unbuttoned – strictly against regulations. I used to spend summer evenings in the acacia row of the Botanical Gardens. Usually a group of girls would appear, most of the time chaperoned, but sometimes without an escort. Chopin would turn up. They would all sit down on a bench and Fryderyk's hazel eyes would light up. I could hear loud talk and soft sighs, then teasing, joking and laughter. . . . I would see Fryderyk strolling alone with one of the girls. I, still a child, would bring him worms and May bugs, ask him about them, and I would pick flowers for the girl. Fryderyk used to smile and give me a handful of caramels extracted from his pocket.

One day the stern professor, Fryderyk's father, appeared in the garden. Recognizing me, he began to question me. 'Tell me,' he said, 'my dear boy, does my son Fryderyk happen to be here?' I could tell from his expression that he was intending to scold Fryderyk. I lied. 'No – I haven't seen him.' 'But he does come here, doesn't he?' asked the father, looking at me severely. 'I haven't seen him' – and feeling my face turn purple, I turned away and started to play ball. Fryderyk's father lingered for a minute, grumbled, tapped his cane on the ground, and then left. When I was sure he had gone, I ran to find Fryderyk and told him what had happened. He winced, blushed, and said to me, 'You did well, Gene, you did well,' and he pulled out a handful of caramels.

Perhaps surprisingly to anyone intimately acquainted with his music, Chopin now took up the study of the organ, an instrument seemingly alien to his natural keyboard style and to his highly restricted taste in music. During his second year at the Lyceum he became the school's official organist, and by the summer of 1825, now fifteen years of age, Chopin was appointed Sunday organist at the Church of the Visitation, which drew much of its choir from the Lyceum.

At the same time he was becoming increasingly interested in the world around him, and, particularly where Poland was concerned, in its past and possible future. His holiday in Szafarnia had combined with the natural heightening of awareness which comes with adolescence to give a new immediacy and a new complexity to his consciousness of being a Pole. He now listened with the keenest attention to the conversations that had long been a staple of his family's social life. With his father's friends and colleagues, as in the homes of the gentry and nobility, he felt relaxed, confident and, most important of all, respected in ways normally reserved for adults. Regular visitors to the Chopin home included scientists, musicians, poets, actors, some of them well known, all of them lively. From their arguments and reminiscences, he gained a steadily deepening sense of the country to which he had been born and of its history of suffering and injustice.

Ever since the Congress of Vienna in 1815, the Tsar's agents in Poland had consistently ignored treaty obligations; the Polish Diet had been largely consigned to oblivion, and the much touted liberal constitution was all but forgotten. For all that Tsar Alexander liked to style himself 'the liberator of Poland', his rule, especially as administered by his brother, served only to fan the flames of discontent. A number of underground organizations, symptomatic of the revolutionary tide then sweeping over most of Europe, preached a gospel of sedition and courted danger by printing and distributing officially suppressed literature. Inevitably, the police infiltrated many of these societies, and the conspirators were imprisoned and worse. No sooner were they removed, however, than others took their place. As ever, the most vocal dissidents were to be found among students. Nicholas Chopin, being in daily contact with both the Lyceum and the university, viewed the developing crisis with deep concern. Like all revolutionary movements, this one threw up its figureheads and heroes, among whom none stood taller than Walerian Lukasinski, a major in the popular Fourth Infantry Regiment, who had founded a secret patriotic society in 1821. In 1824 Lukasinski was arrested and charged with high treason. Imprisoned and tortured for two years, during which time he consistently refused to betray his associates, he was sentenced by a court-martial to ten years' hard labour. Under the circumstances he got off lightly. Like all arrested suspects, his head was shaved, chains were fixed to his legs and in an act of public humiliation he was forced again and again to push wheelbarrows filled with stones before the lines of the Russian military who administered regular beatings. Small wonder that he became a hero of the resistance. As Warsaw shook beneath a mounting wave of arrests and prohibitions, Nicholas Chopin, like most of his colleagues, grew daily more despondent. With each tightening of Russia's grip on the city, the prospect of foreign aid, indispensable if Poland was ever to triumph, ebbed quietly away. The crisis passed, though the spies only redoubled their efforts, and in the ensuing months life returned to something like normality.

In the spring of 1825, twelve months after the Lukasinski affair, the Tsar, hoping to placate some of his restive subjects, elected to visit

Warsaw for the long-deferred opening of the Polish Diet. The immediate effect of his announcement was encouraging. The grim mood that had gripped the capital evaporated, for the moment. Visitors flocked to the capital, the parks and public squares resounded to the strains of military bands, theatres buzzed with the preparation of spectacular productions especially designed to reflect the impending visit, musical performances of many kinds proliferated, and the great houses of the rich and noble were groomed for a sequence of sumptuous balls. In all this fever of activity there was undoubtedly an element of escapism, but it betokened, too, a reawakening of hope. Unusually, the Tsar announced that he would grant audiences to social and political leaders and receive petitions from their disaffected constituents. This unexpected access of liberalism was due in part to the monarch's late immersion in matters of the spirit. Spurred, apparently, by guilt over the assassination of his father, he was a fervent supporter of the Russian Bible Society, which he had helped to found, and it was whispered that his knees were callused through hours of prayer.

It may have pleased the Tsar to discover that not all of the revolutionaries of Warsaw were political. Among the exceptions was a septuagenarian academic who featured regularly on the Chopins' guest list and was a particular favourite of Frédéric's. Jacob Fryderyk Hoffman, a botanist by training, had invented a new instrument, the tortuously titled Aeolomelodikon, with which he confidently expected to revolutionize the world of music. Similar to a harmonium, it had a deeper, fuller tone, enhanced by a complicated network of copper tubes and controlled by a battery of pedals, by means of which the volume and resonance of the notes could be varied with a subtlety and power unknown even to the organ (it was the promoters' proud claim that the instrument could drown a large chorus and fifty-piece orchestra with a single blast). This was soon succeeded by an instrument of still greater ingenuity, combining the principal elements of harmonium and piano within a single case and bearing the slimmer, more ingratiating name, Aeolopantalon. To the great disappointment of Professor Hoffman, his revolution failed to materialize. After an initial flurry of curiosity, Warsaw quickly reverted to its established favourites. While elsewhere in Poland it was a sign of good breeding to play the Spanish or English guitar, the flute or the clarinet, in the capital, partly of course by dint of its greater wealth, the ultimate signs of respectability were the possession of a piano and the ability to play it. Indeed for a city of its size and placement, it was among the most musical in Europe. In Warsaw alone there were more than thirty factories devoted to musical instruments, of which four produced pantalons and pianos, there were sixty full-time music teachers, nine music-cum-musical book shops and five concert halls. It was in none of these, however, but in the city's protestant Evangelical Church that the Tsar made his acquaintance with the Aeolomelodikon, and the attraction for him was not so much the instrument as the fifteen-year-old boy who was playing it. After the performance, the Tsar, as a token of his enjoyment and esteem, presented Chopin with a diamond ring. The honour coincided with another, which the young composer valued more.

On 2 June, deliberately timed to coincide with the visit of the Tsar, Messrs Brzezina & Co. brought out in Warsaw Chopin's Rondo in C minor, op. 1, the first of his works, as its number suggests, to receive commercial publication. Eight days later, composer, piece and instrument were united at a charity concert at which Chopin also improvised at length. This marked the first occasion on which his name was carried to the outside world. A critic for the *Allgemeine Musikalische Zeitung* of Leipzig reported to his readers back in Germany,

> Young Chopin distinguished himself in his improvisation by a wealth of musical ideas, and under his hands, this instrument, of which he is a great master, made a deep impression.

More useful to Chopin, however, was the presence of Prince Antoni Radziwill, himself a composer, and a man of the world whose opinion was to prove decisive in the shaping of Chopin's future. Strange to say in the light of his remarkable achievements, it had still not been determined that Chopin should make music his career. From this point on, the die was cast.

— 2 —

Town and Country
1825–1829

A month or so after his conquest of the Tsar, Chopin completed his first year at the Lyceum, a last-minute burst of studious activity ensuring that he carried off the form prize. Then, with scarcely a day in which to catch his breath, it was back to the countryside. As the now familiar fields and glades of Szafarnia hove into view, the fatigue induced by long nights of cramming drained away and with every new breath of country air he gained in exhilaration. Here, to a degree and in a spirit not possible in Warsaw, he rediscovered the soul of Poland. If it was in large part a Poland of his own fancy, it mattered not a whit to him. It had all the enchantment and intemperate joy of early love, and he felt himself suffused with an almost mystical energy. He took to horseback like the proverbial duck to water, riding frequently and with fresh vigour. Uncharacteristically, he joined in the hunt and bore the trophies of his marksmanship with pride.

> My health is as good as a faithful dog, and today I'm off to Plock, tomorrow to Rosciszew, the day after to Kikol etc. . . . The air is fine, the sun is shining beautifully, the birds are twittering; there isn't any brook or it would be murmuring, but there is a pond and the frogs are piping delightfully! But the very best of all is the blackbird performing all kinds of virtuosity under our windows; and after the blackbird, the Zboinskis' youngest child Kamilka, who is not yet 2 years old. She's taken a great fancy to me, and lisps 'Kagila loves oo'. And I loves oo a billion times, Papa, Mamma, just as she loves me; I kiss your hands!

To his friend Bialoblocki he wrote in less lyrical vein, but with an almost infantile jocularity and self-mocking bravado that characterized many of his friendships at this time.

Oh, Mme de Sévigné would not have been able to describe my delight on receiving your letter! I should sooner have looked for death than for such a surprise. It would never have entered my head that such an inveterate paper-smudger, a philologist who keeps his nose in his Schiller, would take up his pen to write to a poor booby as slack as his grandfather's horsewhip; to a person who has scarcely read a page of Latin yet; to a pigling who, fattening on hogwash, hopes to arrive at, anyway, a tenth part of your beefiness. All this is only an *exordium*; now I come to the real matter; and if you wanted to frighten me with your Pulawy and your hare, I intend to take down such an inexperienced sportsman with my Torun and *my* hare (which was certainly bigger than yours!), and my four partridges, which I brought down the day before yesterday. What did you see in Pulawy? What?! You saw only a tiny part of what my eyes rested on in full. Did you, at Sybillie, see a brick taken from the birthplace of Copernicus? I have seen the whole house – a little profaned at present. In the corner of the very room where that great astronomer was born now stands the bed of some German who after eating too many potatoes probably emits many zephyrs [goes on to rhapsodize about the Torun cakes and cookies] . . . Oh how I want to see you! I would go two weeks without playing to see you really, because mentally I see you every day.

Indeed Chopin seems to have come close to forgetting the piano altogether on this second country idyll. Again he was entranced by the sounds of nature and intrigued by the music of the peasantry, but as before, it was the rituals of the harvest which left the most colourful impression.

One evening as we sat at dinner, finishing the last course, we suddenly heard in the distance a chorus of falsetto voices; old peasant women whining through their noses and girls squealing mercilessly half a tone higher, all to the accompaniment of a single violin, and that only a three-string one, whose alto voice could be heard repeating each phrase after it had been sung through.

The boys got up from dinner and went outside. Approaching the house was a column of peasants. At their head was a quartet of young girls carrying the traditional wreaths and swathes of harvested crops. On reaching the house, the harvesters sang a lengthy sort of ode, including verses addressed to each of the people then staying at the manor. When the turn came round to Chopin, he blushed crimson as they sang of his weedy appearance and his well-noted interest in one of the peasant girls.

The girls bearing wreaths were welcomed into the house, only to be drenched with water by some stable boys who had hidden in the hall with buckets. Barrels of vodka were rolled out, candles were set up along the porch, and the old violinist swung into a vigorous mazurka. Chopin himself, blushes already forgotten, opened the dancing with a young cousin of his hosts, and carried on with other girls, through a sequence of country dances, until he was ready to drop. The warm, starry night was already well advanced by the time Chopin and his friend Dominik were summoned to bed and the peasants moved on to another village to continue their revels.

Among the first fruits of his Szafarnian experience on his return to Warsaw in the autumn were two mazurkas, one in G, the other in B flat, whose authentically rustic roots confounded the capital's connoisseurs and earned him his first critical rebuke, for offending their ears by 'violating all the rules of musical grammar'. Worse violence was to come, though in this case it was political not musical.

On 1 December 1825 Tsar Alexander I died at Taganrog in mysterious circumstances which have never altogether been explained. For several decades rumours persisted in Russia that the Tsar had not died at all but had fled to Siberia, where he became a hermit, dying of natural causes forty years later under the assumed identity of Feodor Kusmitch. In order to allay these rumours, the Russian government finally had the Tsar's coffin opened in 1865. It was found to be empty.

Alexander's sudden exit from the stage unleashed a maelstrom of political unrest. In 1825 Russia was the last bastion of old-fashioned stability in Europe, though even she was not immune to change. The collapse of feudalism had sent out shock waves that resounded through the continent for centuries, but the prevailing political system in Russia was maintained. Whatever his individual leanings, the Tsar ruled by decree (there was no other kind of law), and being heir to the empire of Byzantium was recognized as the supreme defender of Christian Orthodoxy. In the history of Russian autocracy, Alexander had been relatively liberal. As the founder of the Holy Alliance, he embraced the principle of interdenominational Christianity, he lent a sympathetic ear to an increasing groundswell of support for the idea, much influenced by Adam Smith,* of emancipating the serfs, and he introduced an element of constitutional reform, particularly in the governing of the Baltic provinces, which occasioned considerable if short-lived optimism amongst his far-flung subjects, not least in Poland. On Alexander's death, the natural heir to the throne was his brother the Grand Duke

Constantine, who in 1822 had secretly abdicated his place in the succession, leaving the way open to his younger brother Nicholas. In the resulting confusion, a group of liberal-minded army officers, supported by many nobles in southern Russia, conspired to overthrow the monarchy. The plot was badly coordinated and hopelessly divided in its objectives. Some of the conspirators aspired to the establishment of a republic, others to the replacing of Tsarist autocracy with government by committee, several advocating the immediate emancipation of the serfs, while many sought to preserve the social order, fearing a general uprising of the serfs. On the day of Nicholas's coronation, more than 3,000 soldiers, acting on the orders of the rebel officers, erupted into the Senate Square, where, after putting up a heroic resistance, they were crushed by superior fire-power, having been betrayed by spies from the secret police. A similar uprising was suppressed by government troops in the Ukraine. In the retributive bloodbath that followed, five of the conspirators were hanged, many others were tortured and publicly flogged, and hundreds were sentenced to lifelong exile in Siberian labour camps. Many of these were subsequently hailed as martyrs and cited as the true founders of the Russian Revolution which finally triumphed in 1917. From the December uprising on, the new Tsar, Nicholas I, was implacably opposed to all forms of liberalism. 'Revolution,' he declared, 'is at the very gates of Russia, but I swear that while I have a breath of life left in my body it shall not enter here.' And he was as good as his word.

The Decembrist Conspiracy had widespread repercussions. The search for subversives reached every corner of the Russian Empire. In Warsaw hundreds were arrested and imprisoned. When the dungeons of the Carmelite monastery proved insufficient to accommodate them, the cellars of the city hall and of the Bruhl Palace were commandeered to take the overflow. The year 1826 dawned in Warsaw to the accompaniment of continuing arrests, acts of state (and random) violence, and an atmosphere of rampant despotism. As ever, students were heavily engaged in arguments and counter-plots, and the Lyceum and university seethed with a dangerous mixture of idealism and outrage. Nor would the public at large be cowed. Hundreds attended the memorial masses which were held for the victims of a massacre at Praga, and more than 2,000 gathered for the funeral of the great patriot Stanislaw Staszyc, who had left all of his land to the peasants. This living demonstration of Polish martyrdom and solidarity made a deep impression on the young Chopin, although he remained, in any active sense, apolitical throughout his life. It burned its way into the very heart of his creative imagination, serving at once to refine and to limit its focus.

The grimness of the political scene only enhanced for Chopin the redemptive powers of music, and while he worked diligently enough at his academic studies it was to music alone, both his own and other people's, that he gave his whole attention. Like many musicians, and most of the best, Chopin could be unsparing in his criticism of colleagues, but from the very beginning of his social awareness he showed both generosity and humility towards those whom he genuinely admired. He seems, too, to have been wholly without that competitive streak which motivates so many successful performers. A case in point is his rhapsodic account, to his friend Bialoblocki, of 'a certain Mr Rembielinski who has come to Warsaw from Paris'.

> He has been there 6 years and plays the piano as I have never yet heard it played. You can imagine what a joy that is for us, who never hear anything of real excellence here. He is not appearing as an Artist, but as an Amateur. I won't go into details about his quick, smooth, rounded playing; I will only tell you that his left hand is as strong as the right, which is an unusual thing to find in one person. There would not be space on a whole sheet to describe his exquisite talent adequately. You would simply not believe how beautifully he plays.

Chopin's appraisal of Warsaw's musical life is particularly significant considering his inexperience of life in any other city. While he undoubtedly drew great satisfaction from his local celebrity, he was fully aware, at fifteen, that there were tests to which his talents and accomplishments would never be submitted so long as he remained in Poland. If his great modesty was both attractive and genuine, it was also wisely based. He quickly befriended the lately returned Rembielinski and paid him the ultimate compliment of incorporating some of his compositions into his own pianistic repertoire. Indeed, despite his innately conservative tastes, Chopin played a great deal of contemporary music, much of it, perhaps even the majority, by distinctly second-rate composers. This is neither a slur on his powers of discrimination nor an indictment of his time. It is the perennial state of affairs, if only because greatness is by definition rare, and usually exclusive. Of any generation, only a handful will earn the blessings of posterity, being seen to have transcended the limitations of their age. As Chopin once said in reference to his own composition: 'patience is the greatest teacher, and time the best censor.' In the Warsaw of the middle 1820s, there was little gold but much dross, nowhere more so than in the case of piano music. The craze of the day, however, was Italian opera, which ruled the roost to the virtual exclusion of everything else. Fully five years after its triumphs elsewhere in Europe, Carl Maria von Weber's most famous work, *Der Freischütz*, was only now getting its first production in Warsaw, and that after months of rehearsal. Chopin was sceptical of its chances.

> When I think of Weber's aim in this work, of the plot which is so German, of the work's strange romanticism, its unusual and abstruse harmonies which are particularly suited to the German taste, I fear that the Warsaw public, used as they are to Rossini's light songs, will praise him, at first, not from conviction but simply to be able to repeat what the experts say about him and because everybody elsewhere has been praising him.

A strangely cynical and sophisticated thought for a provincial teenager. Chopin was under no illusions about the public.

On 27 July 1826, Chopin's three-year stint at the Lyceum came to an end. Like his friends Titus Woyciechowski and Jan Matuszynski, he won an honourable mention and celebrated by dashing off that evening to see a performance of Rossini's *La Gazza Ladra* with his schoolmate Wilhelm Kolberg (whom he honoured by composing, with astonishing rapidity, a Polonaise in B flat minor, using a theme from the opera, which he formally entitled 'Farewell to Wilhelm Kolberg'). The next day, accompanying his mother and sister Emilia, he left Warsaw for the Silesian spa town of Bad Reinertz in a last-ditch attempt to rescue Emilia from the tuberculosis that now held her mercilessly in its grip.

For all his acute and often heartless observations of human foibles, Chopin is generally disappointing as a travel writer. His letters, with few exceptions, suggest a curious indifference to the natural world around him. Reinertz, unsurprisingly, was one of the exceptions. To the sixteen-year-old whose only acquaintance with the countryside to date had been the flat grasslands of the Mazovian plain, the mountainous Silesian landscape was both exciting and frustrating.

> I go for regular walks in the surrounding hills; indeed I'm often so enchanted with the views of the valleys below that I'm reluctant to come down; and when I do, as often as not, it's on all fours. . . . Near Reinertz there is a mountain with rocks known as Heu-Scheuer, from which there are apparently wonderful views; but the air on the summit is not good for everyone. Unfortunately I'm one of those patients to whom it's forbidden, but never mind. I've already been up another mountain called Einsiedeli, where there's a hermitage. To

reach it, you have to go to the top of one of the highest hills around here, and then climb up about 150 steps in a straight line, cut almost vertically out of the stone, to the hermitage from which there's a magnificent view all over Reinertz. . . . As for the customs of the place, I am already so used to them that nothing worries me. At first it seemed strange to me that in Silesia the women work more than the men; but as I don't do anything myself, it's easy for me to acquiesce in that. There were a lot of Poles here, but many have now gone. I got to know them all. There's plenty of fun to be had, and even the most distinguished German families join in all the games. There is, however, one thing lacking, for which not all the beauties of Silesia can compensate me: a decent instrument. There isn't a single good piano to be found, and the instruments I've seen cause me more distress than pleasure. Fortunately, this martyrdom shouldn't last much longer.

And there were two occasions on which he'd been prepared to endure it in good grace. On the day of his arrival at the spa, two young children had been orphaned by the sudden death of their father, a Bohemian cloth-merchant who had travelled to Reinertz in hopes of a cure. Chopin readily agreed to give a concert for their benefit, this leading quickly to another, 'by popular demand'. What he played is unknown, but it might well have included the three écossaises which date from the same period – charming, playful, elegant little trifles, enjoyable to listen to and fun to play (although geographically a little wide of the mark: the dances are English, not Scottish, in origin). Seventy-one years later, long after his death, a commemorative plaque was installed at the site of these impromptu if limited triumphs and a memorial to Chopin was established in the surrounding parkland. In 1826, however, despite his evidently prodigious gifts and the success of his appearances in Warsaw, not only was Chopin largely unknown, it still remained uncertain just what course his education should take on his return to Poland. His father, ever cautious and a firm believer in the value of a general education, favoured the university. Frédéric himself, although his thoughts on the matter are not recorded, almost certainly preferred the specialist training on offer at the Conservatory. As befits the ambiguity that runs like a thread through the whole of his life, it was decided that he should do both. In September he enrolled as a full-time student at the Principal Music School (the academic wing of the Warsaw Conservatory) while agreeing, at his father's insistence, that he would at least attend lectures at the university. The agreement seems not to have extended much beyond filial obedience, and in the event Frédéric gave serious attention only to a course on Polish literature, taught by a man whose principal pastime was the collection and study of folk music. His musical development was now wholly supervised by Elsner, whom he was to acknowledge as his principal mentor for the rest of his formal education.

Chopin now came face to face with the yawning gaps in his musical education. Imbued by Zywny with a devotion to Bach and Mozart, he now embarked on the systematic study of counterpoint, to which he devoted six hours a week under Elsner's guidance. As might be expected, his music soon began to reflect the influence of his teacher.

Academic and conservative by nature, Elsner quietly deplored the thriving industry of Italian (and specifically *bel canto*) opera. Noting Chopin's own inclinations in that direction, he provided a counterbalance by acquainting his brilliant but impressionable young student with the works of the really substantial composers of the day, headed (in Elsner's view) by the Austrian Hummel★ (a pupil of both Mozart and Haydn), the Bohemian Ignaz Moscheles★ and the lyrical Irish poet of the keyboard, John Field. From Field, Chopin took the newly minted form of the nocturne and lifted it to a level of art hardly even hinted at in Field's polished but rather insipid work. From Moscheles, he may have derived some of the inspiration for his own trail-blazing études; but it was on the model of Hummel, far more than on either Mozart or Beethoven, that he fashioned all of his much-maligned orchestral works.

In addition to his contrapuntal studies, he undertook a three-year grounding in 'musical theory, thorough-bass and the techniques of composition, considered in their grammatical, theoretical and aesthetic aspects', the final year being devoted to what the school unalluringly described as 'practical exercises' (these including the compulsory composition of Masses in both Latin and Polish, trios, quartets, septets, sonatas, fugues and large-scale works for chorus and orchestra). Unexpectedly, Chopin here lagged behind some of his classmates, a fact attributed by some to a chronic streak of indolence. One should beware, however, of hasty judgements. In his middle-teens Chopin was rapidly discovering his own true voice as a composer. With increasing precision he knew the path he wished to tread, and like any efficient organism he absorbed what was useful to him and sooner or later discarded the rest. To his credit, Elsner recognized the distinction between genius and talent and loosened the professorial reins accordingly. Two works of this period, in particular, demonstrate the significant contrast between Chopin the industrious pupil and Chopin the burgeoning creator.

The Sonata in C minor, dedicated to Elsner, is Chopin's first attempt at a major work: a large-scale, four-movement structure of self-conscious drama and unnatural gravity. Traditionally written off by biographers and other commentators, it has its stout defenders too, and no one seriously interested in Chopin's development should pass it by. The very opening bars are full of promise and foreboding, even if much of the promise remains unfulfilled. Though the work lacks anything that might instantly identify it as Chopin's and shows little of the organic development characteristic of his best music, it has nevertheless a number of features that point to a distinctly original cast of mind: the recapitulation of the opening movement, for instance, begins a whole tone below the tonic (not in C but in B flat minor, an astonishing stroke), and the use of quintuple metre in the central Larghetto is equally arresting. (In later years Chopin effectively disowned the Sonata and refused to edit it for publication.)

Far more interesting is the *Rondo à la mazur*, in which he forgets about academic orthodoxy and follows his instincts, with intriguing results. Here for the first time is a work in which the personality of Chopin himself emerges in an unmistakably individual and original manner. Those who anticipated another rondo like op. 1 must have been mildly startled, not least by Chopin's unconventional recourse to the music of the Polish peasantry, something that later listeners would come to expect of him. Coupled with his obvious delight in the very rawness of his material, with its catchy rhythms and unusual harmonies, is a wholly Chopinesque restraint in his treatment of it. He resists the temptation to use his exotic subject matter as a springboard for facile display, inviting the listener, instead, to savour the substance and character of the music itself. More, perhaps, than in any other branch of his output, Chopin regarded the form and styles of the mazurka with an abiding respect, which bordered at times on the religious. There was no form to which he turned so often, nor any period of his life in which he neglected it. In his mazurkas, as nowhere else, we come as close as possible to his musical autobiography. The *Rondo à la mazur* may not be a masterpiece, but in its timing as in its tone, it stands, in contrast to the C minor Sonata, as a kind of declaration of independence at the beginning of Chopin's formal apprenticeship.

In many ways, Chopin's years as a student in Warsaw were the happiest of his life. Secure in the loving embrace of his family and feted by the local aristocracy, he enjoyed the unstinting admiration of his peers and teachers, he felt the indescribable exhilaration of his growing musical powers, and he discovered with a quite new level of intensity the joys of friendship.

Following the composition of the *Rondo à la mazur*, his musical personality matured with extraordinary rapidity. As both pianist and composer he was developing a style uniquely his own, a style, what's more, that was uniquely, and unprecedentedly, pianistic. There seemed to be an almost mystical connection between Chopin's creative imagination and his physical contact with the keyboard. Even at the height of his powers, many years later, he was effectively dependent on the presence of a piano for his musical ideas to prosper. And this symbiotic union is preserved in the character of his works. As many pianists can testify, there is a tactile element in Chopin's music that is inseparable from the fullest experience of his works. To this extent the mere listener, the passive member of the performing equation, is finally denied the keys to Chopin's inner sanctum. Nor is the pianist necessarily guaranteed entry. To a degree perhaps unique in musical history, Chopin's music is ultimately inseparable from the physical gestures required to release it in all its myriad variety. Few pianists reared in the German tradition, for instance, have achieved anything like supremacy as Chopin players, just as they have seldom excelled (Walter Gieseking being the exception that breaks all rules) in the work of the French Impressionists, whose debt to Chopin is incalculable. This isn't music for stiff wrists and typewriter fingers, it's a kind of choreography for the hand and the arm which at the time was something entirely new, and there we encounter another Chopinesque paradox: from the beginning, his music was dominated by the dance – mazurkas, waltzes, polonaises, écossaises – yet never once in his voluminous correspondence does he so much as mention the ballet, nor as far as we know was he ever tempted to write for it. (The popular *Les Sylphides* is the fruit of other, later hands.) The tactile element in Chopin's music is evidence enough that he was never happier or more at one with himself and the world than when he was at the piano. The melancholy, even tragic strain in much of his music has often been stressed by writers and pianists alike at the expense of the joy, the sense of fun and the sociability that are also to be found there. Neither in his letters nor in the reminiscences of those who knew him does the teenage Chopin emerge as a brooding or introverted, much less as a tormented, soul. Nor do we find such a picture in his music. With few exceptions, the music of his prentice years is predominantly lightweight, even frivolous. The profusion of notes per page testifies to the exuberance of a youth for whom technical difficulties at the keyboard were essentially unknown. From his earliest boyhood, Chopin had been surrounded by conviviality, both in and out of the home. He was a gifted caricaturist and his impersonations earned him an early reputation as an entertainer. Much of his music followed suit. It is music to be heard, to be enjoyed and, most emphatically, to be applauded. One can almost hear the delight and support of his friends as they gathered round the keyboard. And it was in Warsaw, as a student, that he formed the friendships which proved in many ways the closest and most durable of his life. As in manhood, so in his youth, Chopin was not always the easiest of friends, as when he addressed Jan Bialoblocki thus in 1827:

> You are not worthy, you scoundrel! Forgive me for being compelled to use in my indignation a title so justly belonging to you – you are not worthy that I should extend you a hand with a pen in it! This is your gratitude for the bloody sweat of the brow of my excellence, for the fatigue and toil I have endured in buying Mickiewicz, or those tickets? Is this your response to my New Year wishes? Yes, pause; and confess that I am right in saying you are not worthy that I should extend my hand to you!

Behind the sometimes laboured humour and the odd outbreak of petulance lay the discomforts, privations and anxieties of a frail and vulnerable constitution, not always eased by the forms of treatment then in fashion. To Bialoblocki again, on 12 February 1826:

> My head is tied up in a nightcap because it's been aching, I don't know why, for the last four days. They have put leeches on my throat because the glands have swelled, and Roehmer says it's a catarrhal infection. It's true that from Saturday to Thursday I was out every evening till two in the morning, but I'm sure it's not that.

And later:

> I go to bed each night at nine; all teas, soirées and balls are forbidden me; I drink an emetic water on Malcz's [the family doctor's] orders, and feed myself only on oatmeal, like a horse. And the air here is not so good for me as at Reinertz; they say I may have to return there next year. Personally, I think Paris would be better for me!

Nor was Chopin alone in his infirmity. In January he reports:

> Mama is not well. She has been in bed for four days; she suffers a great deal from rheumatism. She is a little better now, and we hope that God will grant her a complete recovery.

And in March, again to Bialoblocki (now himself in poor health; he was to die only a few years later):

> Carnival time came to a sad end. Old Benik is dead; and you can guess what that has meant for Papa! His daughter Klementyna has also died, before she had lived with her husband for nine months. In a word, the most miserable things have happened to sadden us. And we have illness in our own house. Emilia has been in bed for the last month. She started to cough and spit blood, and Mamma became frightened. Malcz ordered blood-letting. She was bled once – twice; then countless leeches, blisters, synapisms, herbal remedies, all sorts of nonsense. During the whole time she ate nothing; she got so thin that you would not have known her, and only now is she beginning to recover.

But it was not to last. On 10 April 1827 Chopin's youngest and in many ways his closest sister died after a long battle with tuberculosis. The epitaph carved in her headstone is a poignant reminder of life's fragility:

> *Emilia Chopin,*
> *passed away in the fourteenth spring of her life,*
> *like a flower blossoming*
> *with the hope of a beautiful fruit.*
> *April 10, 1827*

It was during this period that Chopin wrote his darkest work to date, the brooding, intense and precociously self-disciplined Nocturne in E minor, perhaps the most emotionally compelling piece to arise from his middle teens, far surpassing in its immediacy the more formalistic Funeral March of the previous year (unconnected, as far as we know, with the death of any particular individual). Almost exactly one month before Emilia Chopin's tragic end, the world of music had sustained the loss of its greatest figure with the death of Beethoven, in Vienna, at the age of fifty-six. Chopin's reaction is not recorded, but the significance of this event can only have been dulled for him by the agonizing spectacle of his sister's decline.

The loss of her youngest daughter dealt a blow to Chopin's mother from which she never fully recovered. From that day to her own death thirty-four years later, having by then outlived two of her four children, she dressed always in mourning. And a major trauma was soon followed by a lesser one. In the summer, while Frédéric was on one of his prolonged excursions in the country, the Chopins exchanged their rented rooms in the Kazimierowski Palace (nothing like so grand as its name suggests) for an apartment in the Krasinski Palace across the street. Their financial circumstances no longer required them to take in lodgers, and the new apartment was not so tainted with memories of Emilia's illness and death. It combined comfort with quiet and convenience, and afforded significantly greater privacy. It had the incidental virtue, too, at least from their parents' vantage point, of putting a discreet distance between Isabella and Ludwika (fast maturing into womanhood) and the increasingly attentive young men who had lately shared their lodgings. Frédéric himself, of course, was likewise maturing, and enjoyed indulging his naturally gregarious temperament outside the family home (and often into the small hours of the morning, to the evident detriment of his health, although, as we have seen, he himself rejected this diagnosis). As he reported to a friend: 'For the last week I've written absolutely nothing. I'm simply running around from one place to another. This evening I'm going to Mme Wincengerode's soirée, and after that to another at Mlle Kicka's. . . . I shall be at dinner tomorrow with Mme Pruszak, as I was last Sunday.' Wherever he went, he was asked to improvise at the piano. Invariably he obliged, often for hours at a time. No one ever suggested that he had outstayed his welcome.

While he applied himself diligently to his studies with Elsner, he began increasingly to feel the frustrations, as he had long enjoyed the pleasures, of being a big fish in a little pond. His growing sense of isolation was briefly eased, and subsequently intensified, during a visit to Warsaw in 1828 by the most famous of his living mentors (ironically, the reputation of Schubert, who died in November of that year, had barely spread beyond the boundaries of his native Vienna). Johann Nepomuk Hummel, lionized throughout Europe, was thirty-two years Chopin's senior, but the two conceived an instant liking for each other, and Hummel's encouragement had a decisive effect on Chopin's immediate ambitions. Still unknown outside Poland but emboldened by the enthusiasm of the world's most eminent pianist, the nineteen-year-old composer sent off two of his most recent works to publishers in Vienna and Leipzig. One was the derivative, academic and conspicuously flawed C minor Sonata, the other was the most brilliant, and the most strikingly individual thing he'd yet achieved: a set of variations for piano and orchestra on the aria 'Là ci darem la mano' from Act I of Mozart's *Don Giovanni*. It was his first orchestral work, and as such it was negligible: the piece can be played as a piano solo (indeed Chopin often played it so) with a minimal loss of effect. Its musical ideas, on the other hand and the cut-glass virtuosity of the piano writing, occasioned Schumann's celebrated exhortation 'Hats off, gentlemen, a genius!' and it was this work more than any other that was to serve as Chopin's 'open Sesame' in Europe. Following Hummel's departure, he resumed his studies with Elsner, concentrating on his first (and barring three works for piano and cello, his last) piece of chamber music, the Trio in G minor, which, like the earlier Sonata, reveals more of the student than of the budding genius. Having achieved something really original in the Mozart Variations, he turned his attentions once more to orchestral work with the proudly nationalistic *Krakowiak* Rondo and the Fantasia on Polish Airs.

Returning to Warsaw in September after a summer in the country, he was jolted out of an increasingly listless mood by a surprise that eclipsed all thoughts of frustration: an invitation by one of his father's colleagues, Professor Jarocki, to accompany him on a journey to Berlin, where he was attending an international scientific congress, with all expenses paid. It was Chopin's first opportunity to visit a major European capital, and he leapt at the chance with an almost uncontainable enthusiasm. Berlin, then as now, was one of the great musical centres of the world.

On Wednesday, 10 September 1828, Jarocki and his young companion climbed into their stage coach, whose various occupants between Warsaw and Berlin seem to have attracted Chopin's attention to the virtual exclusion of all the towns and countryside through which they passed.

> The journey wasn't so bad as it looked at first. Although one is almost ground to a powder in these ill-sprung Prussian stage-coaches, things turned out quite well for me and I'm really in excellent health. The party in our coach consisted of a German lawyer from Poznan, remarkable for his heavy German humour, and a fat, greasy Prussian farmer who has travelled a great deal and has picked up his education in stage-coaches. That was all the company we had until the last stop before Frankfurt, where we were joined by a Teutonic 'Corinna' [Mme de Staël's heroine] full of 'achs', 'jas' and 'neins': a real romantic doll! But it was all very entertaining, especially since she kept nagging away at her neighbour (the lawyer) for the entire journey.

And this is all Chopin has to report after five days of travelling. On the subject of Berlin itself he was more forthcoming.

> 16 September: My general impression of Berlin is that it's too widely built: that double the amount of population could fit into it easily. The environs of the city aren't particularly beautiful, but impress one

through their neatness, cleanliness, selection of things; that is, by a certain circumspectness that catches the eye at every touch and turn. And by the way, Marylski hasn't a farthing's worth of taste if he says the Berlin women are beautiful. They all have the same empty jaws, or to put it otherwise, the same toothless mouths. They dress well, that's true; but it's pitiful to see these gorgeous rumpled muslins wasted on such kidskin dolls!

On the day of our arrival Jarocki took me at once to Lichtenstein's where I saw Humboldt. Lichtenstein promised to introduce me to the principal masters of my art; he is sorry that we didn't arrive a day earlier, as that very morning his daughter played with the orchestra. Not much loss, I thought privately. Was I right? I don't know, because I've neither seen nor heard her. . . . Until now I've seen nothing but the zoological congress; but I already know a good deal of the town, as for two days I have poked about and gaped at the handsomest streets and bridges. . . . Truth to tell, I'd rather spend the morning at Schlesinger's music shop than wander about the 13 rooms of the zoological congress. They're very fine, of course, but Schlesinger's would obviously be far more use to me. Still, you can't have too much of a good thing, so I'll go to both.

As for the eminent scientists, Chopin granted Humboldt a certain 'competence' while dismissing most of his colleagues as figures of fun ('a bunch of scientific monkeys') and memorializing them in a series of caricatures. Musically, however, Berlin was all he'd hoped. Or almost. Six days after his arrival he was able to report to his family,

From Tuesday onwards there has been something new at the theatre every day, as though put on especially for me. Best of all, I have already heard one oratorio at the Sing-Akadamie and also, with great satisfaction, *Cortez*, Cimarosa's *Secret Marriage* and Onslow's *Colporteur*. However Handel's oratorio *St Cecilia* came nearest to the ideal which I had formed of great music. . . . I had an excellent seat and saw everything and even had a good look at the Crown Prince. I saw Spontini, Zelter and Mendelssohn but spoke to none of them as I did not dare put myself forward. The day before yesterday we visited the library. It's quite enormous but has very little in the way of music.

Chopin's apparent indifference to anything other than music has occasioned a great deal of adverse criticism, but there may well have been a quite rational and practical explanation. Genius, musical or otherwise, is not necessarily accompanied by a wide-ranging general intelligence. In Chopin's case, however, there is no reason to suppose that it wasn't. Throughout his adult life he enjoyed the lasting admiration and friendship of writers, painters, poets, politicians, bankers, publishers, philosophers, men and women of exceptional distinction, many among the foremost figures of nineteenth-century culture. If he appeared to confine his interests to the one field in which he possessed supreme gifts, it may be to some extent that he was simply rationing his energies. While he was by no means an invalid for the better part of his life, he was always of a delicate disposition, and the death of his sister may well have struck him as a sinister omen for his own life. Even at his healthiest, he lacked physical strength and tired easily. If he failed to cultivate the range of interests that galvanized so many of his contemporaries, if he stood largely apart from the Romantic obsessions of his time, most of them characterized by emotional extravagance, it may have been as much for want of energy as from lack of curiosity.

At the same time, energy is as much a matter of intellectual and emotional engagement as of physical stamina, and certainly from his early teens onwards Chopin was given to periods of profound mental lethargy, sometimes accompanied by the conscious experience of melancholy. When he described himself to Jan Bialoblocki as 'so fat and lazy that I don't want to do anything – anything at all', he was wide of the mark only in a physical sense (he was never remotely fat). As with a number of other virtuosos before and since, his extraordinary abilities at the keyboard apparently owed more to fate than to personal industry. 'The mechanics of piano-playing,' wrote his father, 'occupied little of your time; your mind was always busier than your fingers. If others have spent whole days working at the keyboard, you rarely spent as much as an hour playing other men's music.' That he was interested in other men's music is beyond doubt, but as evidenced on his trip to Berlin it was not generally piano music. Bach and Mozart he played a lot, Beethoven rather less so; and although he knew and admired the music of Hummel, Moscheles and Field, he reserved his greatest enthusiasms for the opera, and even here, the works of Rossini, Bellini, Spontini and Meyerbeer played a greater part in his day-to-day life than the operas of Mozart; of symphonies he mentions hardly one in the correspondence of a lifetime; chamber music, too, is seldom mentioned.

To a certain extent, until his twentieth year his horizons were circumscribed by the horizons of Warsaw itself, to which he returned on 12 September with mixed feelings. If Berlin had failed to satisfy his highest hopes of it, he had nevertheless glimpsed in it a world whose sophistication and great traditions were incomparably more developed than anything to be found in Poland. Having dipped his toe in the mainstream of European musical culture, he was more than ever eager to explore it at greater depth. From now until the end of his formal apprenticeship, his thoughts were increasingly focused on a life of travel. The key to such liberty lay not in composition but in the career of a touring virtuoso. To that end, he began to apply himself with renewed energy to the kind of showpiece for piano and orchestra that he had explored with such success in the Mozart Variations and that were the stock in trade of the early concert pianists, from giants like Mozart, Beethoven and Weber to such fashionable small fry as Herz,★ Hünten, Pixis and Kalkbrenner, virtually all of whom were also composers.

At the dawning of 1829 Chopin looked forward to his nineteenth birthday with mixed feelings. Until July and his graduation from the Conservatory, he would effectively be anchored to Warsaw. And where his work was concerned, he fell prey to increasing distraction. The gulf between his inner creative impulses and the requirements of Academia was perceptibly widening, and the pleasures of society (not least of female society) were making it progressively harder to concentrate on the 'practical exercises' laid down by the Conservatory. In the months ahead he was to fall seriously in love for the first time, and succumb to the spell of the greatest musical sorcerer of the day.

Celebrity and Secret Love
1829–1831

It may well be true that Paganini was the greatest violinist who has ever lived. Certainly Liszt, Berlioz, Rossini, Schubert and Schumann thought so, and his effect on audiences was mesmeric. He was one of those rare figures who can electrify the atmosphere in a room by his very presence, yet he cultivated his image almost as assiduously as his music. With his every appearance, he fanned the flames of fame and notoriety alike. Rumours about him, most of them sinister, spread like a virus, and he did nothing to deny them. As he himself recalled of a concert in Vienna,

> One individual, of sallow complexion, melancholy air and a bright eye, affirmed that he saw nothing whatever surprising in my perform- ance for he had distinctly seen, while I was playing, the devil at my elbow, directing my arm and guiding my bow. My resemblance to him was proof of my origin. He was clothed in red, had horns on his head, and carried his tail between his legs. After so minute a description, it was impossible for anyone to doubt the fact. Hence many concluded that they had at last discovered the true secret of what they term my wonderful feats.

On two composers in particular Paganini's influence was decisive, and neither was a violinist. One was Liszt; the other was Chopin. Both resolved that they would do for the piano what Paganini had done for the violin; that they would reveal its very soul, discovering in it hitherto untapped resources and achieving heights of virtuosity never before dreamt of. That two men with the same aim, at the same time, should have accomplished it in such divergent ways is one of the most fascinat- ing delights in musical history, and constitutes the most important chapter in the long and colourful story of the piano.

Paganini visited Warsaw in May 1829 and stayed until mid-July, steal- ing much of the thunder from the unpopular Tsar, who had recently

arrived in the city for his coronation as King of Poland. It was at this
time that the nineteen-year-old Chopin began work on his epoch-
making études, the first keyboard studies since Bach to combine a didactic purpose with the highest level of art. In their particular blend of
method and inspiration they remain unsurpassed and, in the opinion of
many, unequalled, certainly in the piano repertoire. No one seriously
questions the connection between the inception of these small miracles
and Paganini's visit, yet Chopin himself left no written testimony as to
the quality and effect of the Italian wizard's performance, nor is there
any evidence that the two were ever even introduced. Significantly,
Chopin's only overt tribute to Paganini is a subtle and delicate set of
variations on 'The Carnival of Venice', a popular tune, which Paganini
used as the basis for some dazzling variations of his own. Like Schubert
in Vienna, Chopin was obviously as much impressed by the poetry and
lyricism of Paganini's playing as by his diabolical virtuosity.

Apart from Paganini's visit, the most significant event of Chopin's
summer was his graduation from the Conservatory. There was no doubt
in Elsner's mind that his *laissez-faire* policy had paid off. 'Chopin,
Fryderyk,' he wrote in the register, 'Third year student; outstanding
abilities; musical genius.' And elsewhere: 'Chopin has inaugurated a new
era in piano music through his astonishing playing as well as through
his extraordinarily original compositions.' In its turn, his graduation
inaugurated a new era in Chopin's life. His childhood was behind him;
his years of dependency must, perforce, be drawing to an end; it was
a time to plan.

Whatever the charms of Warsaw and the company of family and
friends, it was now clear to Chopin, as to everyone else, that his immediate future lay elsewhere. While not quite the cultural backwater suggested by some writers, Warsaw in 1829 could hardly compare with
London or Paris, Berlin or Vienna, when it came to opportunities or
influential contacts. Chopin was all too well aware that, however grati-
fying they were, his successes in Warsaw were those of a big fish in a
little pond. If he was to make his mark on the world he must go out
into it. It was both a natural and a wise decision, yet more than once he
showed a curious reluctance to act on it. Despite his already prodigious
accomplishments he retained in some measure the attitude of the appren-
tice. Was he really ready to take on the challenges of a world that
had only just bade farewell to Beethoven and Schubert? Would Elsner
approve? Neither for the first nor the last time, he hung precariously
poised between an intuitive recognition of his own genius and a nagging
self-doubt, which in some senses was to prove his greatest enemy – the

father of his reserve and the mother of his caution. At this formative stage of his life, he accepted his limitations better than he knew them. His father, on the other hand, too much a realist to tarry long in the grey areas of human psychology, addressed himself, as ever, to practicalities. Writing to the imposingly entitled Minister for Public Instruction, he appealed for government assistance, setting forth his case with characteristic straightforwardness, leavened with the requisite degree of bootlicking:

> I have a son whose innate musical gifts call out for him to be educated in this art. His late Imperial Majesty Tsar Alexander, of blessed memory, graciously deigned to present him with a precious ring as a mark of his satisfaction when my son had the honour to be heard by the Monarch, His Imperial Majesty. His Imperial Highness the Grand Duke, Supreme Commander of the Army, has often been most graciously pleased to allow him to give proofs of his growing talent in His Most Serene presence. And lastly, many of the highest personages and musical connoisseurs can support the view that my son could be a credit to his country in his chosen profession if he were given the opportunity to pursue the necessary studies to their conclusion. He has completed his preliminary studies; all that he now needs is to visit foreign countries, especially Germany, Italy and France, so as to form himself upon the best models. For the purposes of such a journey, which might last for three years, funds are required which my modest resources, based solely upon my earnings as a teacher, are insufficient to provide.

The Treasury, despite the sympathetic intercession of the Minister, was unmoved, stating flatly that: 'Public funds cannot be wasted for the support of this class of artists.'

Nevertheless, after much soul-searching and calculation, the family were agreed that Frédéric must venture forth, with or without outside assistance. He therefore grasped the nettle, and set out with four friends on a warm summer evening, arriving in Vienna on the last day of July. Their chosen mode of transport stands in amusing contrast to Chopin's later way of life.

> After dinner on Sunday, we engaged a peasant's cart of the 4-horse Cracow type and started off in fine style. After leaving the city and the beautiful environs of Cracow, we told our driver to go straight to Ojcow where we expected to find Pan Indyk, the man who usually puts everyone up for the night. As ill luck would have it, Indyk lives

a whole mile from Ojcow, and our driver, not knowing the way, drove straight into the Pradnik, a little river, or rather a clear stream, and no other way could be found, as there were rocks to the left of us and rocks to the right. About nine in the evening, when we were wandering about and not knowing what to do, we met two strangers, who took pity on us and undertook to guide us to Indyk. We had to go on foot for a good two-and-a-half miles, in the dew, among a mass of rocks and sharp stones, and to keep crossing the stream on round logs; and all this in the dead of night. At last, after many efforts, bumps and grumbles, we crawled out at Pan Indyk's house.

It was an inauspicious beginning to a highly successful journey.

From the time of his public début at the age of eight, Chopin had been acutely conscious of his appearance (then, of course, it was his 'little English collar'). One of his first priorities on arrival in Vienna was the engagement of a hairdresser who would attend him on a daily basis. It was here, too, that he first made a point of the white gloves which were soon to become his unofficial trademark.

In 1830, Vienna was notably richer than it is today in reminders of its distant past. In many ways it still bore the trappings of a medieval garrison-city, complete with outer walls and surrounding moat. Vienna's skyline was dominated by architectural appeals to the Almighty, just as its more recent palaces and squares proclaimed the spoils of more earthly might. More imposing to Chopin, however, were the reminders of its late musical masters: the famous Kärnthnerthor Theatre, scene of countless musical triumphs, including the première of Beethoven's Ninth Symphony a mere five years earlier; the homes and graves of Beethoven, Schubert, Haydn and Mozart.

Armed with a letter of introduction from Elsner, Chopin sought out the influential publisher Tobias Haslinger, who had earlier responded with stony silence when Chopin had sent him the scores of the 'Là ci darem' and 'Swiss Boy' Variations and the academically minded but unexciting Sonata in C minor, but on meeting and hearing the young composer, Haslinger now welcomed him with open arms – or at any rate, with the promise of open arms. This was Chopin's introduction to the element of barter in building a career. Haslinger agreed to publish the Mozart Variations on the condition that Chopin perform them in public without delay, and – a still more startling suggestion – that he should do so without a fee. Characteristically, the composer demurred. He had not come prepared to make a large-scale début, and in any case he vastly preferred the intimacy of the drawing-room to the glare of the arena (no great pianist ever gave fewer public concerts, barely thirty in a lifetime). The drawing-room not being bound by the strictures of the confessional, however, word had already got around that Vienna was harbouring a young pianist of astonishing accomplishment and a unique originality. Within a week of his arrival Chopin was already becoming a legend. He relented to public pressure and on 11 August, under the auspices of Count Gallenberg, he appeared for the first time before a public who had heard every great pianist of the day. Many had heard Beethoven. Some could even remember Mozart. One may imagine, then, the feelings of the slender, graceful youth as he made his way to the magnificent Graf piano, brought in especially for the occasion. His account of the concert in a letter to his family sheds interesting light on the musical conventions of the day:

Yesterday, Tuesday, at seven o'clock in the evening I made my bow on the stage of the Royal and Imperial Opera House! The sort of performance that took place yesterday in this theatre is called here a 'Musical Academy'. Since I got nothing out of it, and didn't try to get anything, Count Gallenberg put it on quickly and arranged the programme thus:

A Beethoven Overture
My Variations
Song by Mlle Veltheim
My Rondo

then another song after which the evening ended with a short ballet. The orchestral accompaniment went so badly at rehearsal that I substituted a Free Fantasia for the Rondo. As soon as I appeared on the stage they started clapping; and the applause was so great after each variation that I couldn't hear the orchestral *tuttis* [Chopin being on the stage, the orchestra down in the pit]. At the end they applauded so loudly that I had to come back twice and bow. Although my Free Fantasia didn't turn out particularly well they clapped still louder and I had to take yet another bow. I came out the more willingly since the appreciation of these Germans is worth something. . . . The journalists have taken me to their hearts; perhaps they will now give me a few pin-pricks, but that is necessary so as not to overdo the praise. . . . Celinski will tell you how little was said against me. Hube heard the worst: 'It is a pity the young man looks so unimpressive,' declared one of the ladies. Well if that's the only fault they could find with me then I've nothing to worry about.

Unlike the marathon programmes still common in Vienna, Chopin's début was unusually short and served, in effect, as a kind of curtain-raiser to the ballet, *A Masked Ball*, which was evidently the main draw of the evening. Interestingly, he didn't play from memory but secured the services of a page turner, whose flashy dress and brightly rouged cheeks contrasted strangely with the pale countenance and sartorial dignity of the soloist.

Once having agreed to Haslinger's insistence on the op. 2 Variations, Chopin had hoped to play as well the less original but more accessible *Krakowiak* Rondo. In the event, the idea had to be scrapped, and for typically Chopinesque reasons. Rehearsals proved impossible owing to the inadequately written orchestral parts, and Chopin improvised instead on themes from a currently popular opera by Boieldieu and, closer to his heart, the Polish wedding-song 'Chmiel', 'which electrified the public, unaccustomed as it is to this kind of melody. My spies on the floor of the house declare that the people were dancing up and down in their seats.' Of his performance with the orchestra, he reports that 'the general opinion is that I play too quietly, or rather too delicately . . . there always has to be some kind of "but" of course, and I'd prefer it to be that rather than have it said that I play too loudly.' He then goes on to express concern lest 'Mr Elsner be displeased' at his having performed in public without adequate preparation, and adds, defensively, 'but they really insisted so much that I couldn't refuse'.

Neither orchestra nor audience seem to have been much put out by the dropping of the *Krakowiak* Rondo. The concert was a huge success and resulted in the instantaneous demand for another. As Chopin wrote home to his family, 'I don't know how it is, but the Germans [*sic*] are amazed at me – and I am amazed at them for finding anything to be amazed about!' False modesty? Perhaps. Or genuine humility, from a young man standing almost literally in the shadow of Haydn, Mozart and Beethoven.

With his usual reluctance, Chopin yielded to public pressure and on this second occasion, which followed a mere seven days later, the *Krakowiak* was performed and loudly applauded. The piano on this occasion was lent to Chopin by Count Lichtenstein, who had been one of Beethoven's patrons. Like others, he had been struck by the small tone at Chopin's first concert but had attributed it as much to the instrument as to the performer. Chopin was honoured by the gesture but knew himself too well to accept the diagnosis. As he wrote unconcernedly at the time: 'It's the way I play – which once again the ladies found most attractive.' There are worse fates. The Viennese press was polite and enthusiastic, if some way short of rapturous, and as usual when Chopin gave public concerts his playing was criticized for its lack of projection and an excess of (albeit miraculous) 'delicacy'. To Chopin's irritation, much surprise was expressed that such a refined and accomplished musician should have emanated from so provincial and 'primitive' a place as Warsaw. As always he demonstrated the utmost loyalty to Elsner and his other teachers, claiming that the rankest dunce couldn't fail to benefit from such methodical and enlightened instruction. The Viennese, in their turn, were as enchanted with the young Pole's modesty as they were impressed by his genius (not to mention an impeccably aristocratic demeanour, which they were at a loss to explain). When he left them, on the morning after his second concert, he was buoyed by his reception and confident that the connections he had made, including Haslinger, Dr Malfatti (the emperor's private physician and a friend of Beethoven's), Count Gallenberg and the sweet-natured Czerny,* would assure his continuing success in the Austrian capital. On that score, at least, he was to be sadly disillusioned.

From Vienna, like Mozart forty years earlier, Chopin made his way to Prague, then as now among the most musical cities in Europe. Here again he manifested his priceless gift for friendship, and particularly valued the interest and affection of the German August Klengel, a much respected pianist, organist and composer, some thirty years his senior, who regaled his new acquaintance for two hours with canons and fugues of his own composition, inspired by Bach's *The Well-tempered Clavier*. When Chopin himself was then invited to play, he politely declined. Ready as always to learn from others, he spent three days in Klengel's company, and of all his pianistic acquaintances thus far, he wrote: 'I value him the most – far above poor old Czerny (but hush!).' Elsewhere he nevertheless described Czerny as a 'close friend', while noting that there was 'more warmth in the man than in his compositions'.

From Prague, Chopin travelled by special coach to Teplitz, where he lost no time in seeking out the small but distinguished Polish community. Through one of these he secured an invitation to dine at the home of the Prince and Princess Clary, 'an important, almost sovereign family, with huge estates, who own the town of Teplitz itself'. After doing the rounds as a keen-eyed sightseer he prepared to depart from his original itinerary.

In the evening, instead of going to the theatre, I got dressed, pulled on the white gloves I had worn at my last concert in Vienna, and at half past eight went off with Lempicki to the princely house.

In we went – a small but cultivated assembly: a kind of Austrian prince, a general whose name I forget, an English sea-captain, a few young fashionables, and also, it appears, some Austrian princes and a Saxon general called Leiser, frightfully bemedalled and with a scarred face. After tea, during which I had a long talk with the Prince himself, his mother asked me if I would *deign* to take my seat at the piano. I *deigned*, requesting, for my part, that they, in turn, would *deign* to give me a theme for improvisation. At once among the fair sex, who sat around a large table, embroidering, knitting or weaving, there ran a murmur: 'a theme!' Three charming young princesses put their heads together; then one of them referred the matter to Mr Fritsche (young Prince Clary's tutor, I imagine) and he with general approval proposed a theme from Rossini's *Moses*. [Chopin obliged, and as always when he improvised left the assembled company thunderstruck.] General Leiser had a long talk with me afterwards and on hearing that I was headed for Dresden at once wrote the following letter [in French] to Baron von Friesen: *Mr Frédéric Chopin is recommended by General Leiser to Baron von Friesen, Grand Chamberlain to H.M. the King of Saxony, who is requested to assist him during his stay in Dresden and to favour him with the acquaintance of a number of our principal artists.* And underneath he added in German: *Mr Chopin is one of the most eminent pianists I have ever heard.* Such is an exact copy of General Leiser's note, written in pencil and left unsealed.

Fussed over and honoured by royalty since childhood, Chopin seems to have been quite unfazed by matters of rank and to have moved among aristocrats and the nobility with practised ease. Despite pleas from the three starry-eyed young princesses that he extend his stay in Teplitz and dine with them again the following day, Chopin, ever sensible to the feelings of those around him, was unwilling to inconvenience his companions by any further delay. And so, at five o'clock the next morning, the travellers left Teplitz for Dresden, where they arrived, tired but in high spirits, after eleven hours in a hired coach. Equipped with glowing references from Klengel and the General, Chopin at once sought out the Court Chamberlain, Baron von Friesen and 'The Most Illustrious Chevalier Morlacchi, First Conductor of the Royal Band'. As well as making musical contacts, he queued in the street for an hour and a half to see Goethe's *Faust* ('a frightening but powerful fantasy') in a production lasting just over five hours, attended the Art Gallery with great interest and took special pleasure in the Horticultural Show, as well as the city's principal gardens.

On his return to Warsaw, where he should have been welcomed like a conquering hero, he was incensed to discover that the local newspapers had either mistranslated or deliberately distorted his glowing Viennese notices. Indeed one had exactly reversed the verdict: 'Here is a young man,' it now read, 'whose desire to please the public comes before the endeavour to make good music.' Of no musician could this have been untruer than of Chopin. Nor had the Viennese been impressed by his playing alone. Following his departure there had been detailed discussion and praise of his compositions in both *Der Sammler* and the *Zeitschrift für Literatur*. For a young man of nineteen this was not bad going.

Warsaw's musical life was no match for Vienna's but the fare on offer gave a truer reflection of Europe as a whole. Of the prominent names of the day, most, with the exception of the Classical giants (Mozart, Haydn, Beethoven) and such operatic front-runners as Rossini, Bellini, Donizetti and Meyerbeer, have long since slipped into the shadows: Spohr, Moscheles, Spontini, Ries, Gyrowetz, Kalkbrenner, Field, even Hummel. It was in Warsaw, however, not Vienna, that Chopin first heard Beethoven's 'Archduke' Trio. So much has been made of his supposed aversion to Beethoven that his reaction on this occasion is worth noting. 'I have never heard anything so great,' he wrote. 'In it Beethoven snaps his fingers at the whole world. There were other things which came after it but they did not suffice to efface the enormous impression which this Trio made on me, particularly as it was well performed.' Less powerful, perhaps, but no less genuine was his admiration for the A flat Sonata, op. 26, which he often played and taught and which played a formative role in the creation of his own Sonata in B flat minor. Among other works that show a distinctly Beethovenian influence are the two C minor Études (op. 10, no. 12, the so-called 'Revolutionary', and op. 25, no. 12) and the Fantasie-Impromptu, which shows an analytically demonstrable kinship with the 'Moonlight' Sonata, which Chopin may have regarded as too close for comfort.†

In the absence of appropriate celebration at home, Chopin's thoughts kept returning to Vienna and to the still greater musical world beyond. From Prince Radziwill and his wife he had a standing invitation to visit Berlin as their guest. He had promised a return to Vienna, and there was talk of visiting Italy, then still a Mecca to serious students of music. It was abundantly clear that his greatest opportunities would continue

† The Schenkerian analyst Dr Ernst Oster has suggested that it was precisely because of this that Chopin suppressed the publication of the piece in his lifetime.

to lie outside Poland, and there can be no doubt that he found Warsaw's provincialism increasingly irksome. Yet rather than act on his recent successes, he held back, mired in a characteristic trough of indecision whose immediate roots are first alluded to in a letter to his friend Titus dated 3 October 1829. Referring to a comely young woman in Vienna, he goes on to say that 'while I think I told you she is young and pretty and plays well, it is perhaps my misfortune that I have already found my ideal, whom I have served faithfully, though without saying a word to her, for six months; whom I dream of, in whose memory [sic] the Adagio of my concerto has been written, and who this morning inspired me to write the little waltz I am sending you [the D flat, op. 70, no. 3].' And yet, 'you wouldn't believe how depressing Warsaw is for me just now. If it weren't for my family's devotion I couldn't put up with it. How awful it is to have no one to go to in the mornings, no one with whom to share one's joys and sorrows (you know what I mean).' And he adds, significantly, 'I now tell my piano things which I once used to tell you.' Among the confidences which he entrusted to the keyboard at this time, in addition to op. 70 waltzes, are the three of op. 69, most of the F minor Concerto, and many of the trail-blazing études, op. 10.

The unknowing object of these outpourings was a young singer, Chopin's exact contemporary and a student at the Warsaw Conservatory, whose charms ensured that she was always surrounded by male admirers, and not only young ones. Constantia Gladkowska, the daughter of a theatrical producer and local dignitary, had the dark good looks and melancholy air that personified Romantic notions of feminine beauty: sensitive, sensuous, vulnerable, she had a lovely voice and a grace, both physical and musical, which went straight to the young Chopin's heart. It was his first intense experience of sexual infatuation, and on the evidence it seems safe to assume that he was as much in love with the condition as with the girl. Of Constantia herself we know very little, although Chopin himself has bequeathed us some picture of her artistry. That his musical judgment, like Mozart's, was unaffected by his emotional attachments seems self-evident. Of her operatic début in August 1830 he wrote to Titus,

Gladkowska leaves little to be desired. She is better on stage than in the concert-hall. I need say nothing of her acting in tragedy which is first-class; as for her singing, if it were not occasionally for those high F sharps and Gs, we need look for nothing better in her class. You would be enchanted with her phrasing, and her *nuances* are splendid; and although her voice trembled at the beginning when she came on, she later sang with great confidence. . . . We are all agreed that we shall not have another like Gladkowska for clarity and intonation and that superior expressiveness which she displays on the stage.

A long article in a German paper of the time confirms this impression, but although she enjoyed considerable success in Warsaw, her career seems never to have taken her beyond the Polish border. After Chopin left the country in 1831, she married a wealthy man, unexpectedly and rather suddenly lost her sight and lived a long life of ever-increasing bitterness, surviving Chopin by 40 years. Of her relationship to Chopin, we know little more than what can be gleaned from his letters. Months after confessing his (already six-month-old) obsession to Titus, he remained tongue-tied in her presence and thus his friend received, by proxy as it were, the love-letters that by rights should have been addressed to her.

Oh my dear beloved Titus! There is nothing in life I desire more at this moment than to see you. You said that you would like to have my portrait: if I could steal one from Princess Eliza I would send it to you – she sketched me twice, and they say that it's a good likeness. . . . As long as I live I shall never give you up.

And later:

Never, ever, have I felt your absence so much as at this moment! A single glance from you after each of my concerts would have been more to me than all the praises from journalists or people like Elsner, Kurpinski, Soliva and so on. . . . I will send you my portrait, as soon as I possibly can; you want and shall have it, but nobody else. Well, I *might* give it to one other person, but not before you, who are ever dearest to me. Now, as always, I carry your letters around with me (I keep them like a lover's ribbon). In May, when I go for a walk outside the town, thinking of my approaching journey, what a joy it will be to take out your letters and learn again, beyond doubt, that you love me; or at least I can look at the hand and writing of one to whom I am absolutely and utterly devoted.

If Warsaw was irksome to Chopin, his chronic indecision was growing intolerable to his father. Now seriously concerned about his still dependent son's stability, Nicholas insisted on a change of scene. Consequently, on 20 October, Chopin removed himself from Warsaw for a week with the Radziwills at their country estate near Poznan. As a potential patron, the Prince proved a disappointment, particularly to Chopin's father, who had entertained high hopes of him. He provided, however, some interesting distraction in the person of his two charming daughters. In the company of two impressionable princesses, Chopin seems to have forgotten all about his distant beloved. His accounts of the visit have none of that narcissistic melancholia which is the hallmark of the infatuated, unrequited lover. On the contrary. They exude health, good cheer and the careless energy of youth.

> I was hard put to it to find reasons for declining to stay longer. If it had been left to my own choice I could have stayed there until they kicked me out, but my private affairs, especially my concerto, forced me to quit that Paradise! It contained two Eves, the young princesses, extraordinarily charming and kind, musical and sensitive creatures.

As a token of his gratitude and friendship, Chopin marked the visit with a polonaise for the cello-playing composer-Prince to perform with his daughter Wanda, who was, to judge from the music, an accomplished technician, if nothing else. Chopin was supposed to be giving her lessons, but found himself preoccupied with extra-musical matters. And why not? She was 'young (seventeen), pretty, and it was a real joy to place her little fingers on the keys'. Chopin was quite prepared to stay on at the Radziwills' indefinitely, but however much he may have wished it otherwise, there was business to attend to in Warsaw.

As the autumn progressed, Chopin continued to stand still. He grew listless. Rather than immersing himself in composition or in learning new repertoire, he drifted. Letters that could profitably have been sent to the musical movers and shakers of Europe remained unwritten. Nor did Chopin seriously attempt to involve himself in the musical life of Warsaw. He wanted to escape yet did nothing. He wandered the streets, becoming an increasingly familiar figure in the city's many coffee houses. There he would sit for hours with friends, enjoying the pleasure of their company but seldom adding to their conversation, which bristled with careless talk of revolution, a carelessness that eventually cost them dear. More as a means of distraction than through any artistic compulsion he began work on a piano concerto, far and away the largest and most demanding form he had tackled to date. He was soon to receive public encouragement.

Whatever the misrepresentations of the Polish press, news of his Viennese triumphs had spread by word of mouth, and there was mounting pressure on him to declare himself openly as an artist, and a specifically Polish artist at that. There was undoubtedly a certain natural chauvinism at work, neatly summed up by an article in the *Warsaw Courier* that December:

Does Mr Chopin's talent not belong to his own country? Does he believe that Poland is incapable of appreciating him? Mr Chopin's works unquestionably bear the stamp of genius; among them is said to be a Concerto in F minor, and we hope that he will delay no longer in confirming our conviction that Poland, too, can produce distinguished talent.

In terms of any immediate result they hoped, predictably, in vain. Chopin delayed the requested confirmation for another two and a half months. For a start, he would permit nothing to interfere with his enjoyment of Christmas, always the high point of the Polish year and enriched by many ancient and colourful traditions including a wealth of carols, one of which, 'Lulajze Jezuniu' (a lullaby for Jesus), he made world-famous in the middle section of his Scherzo no. 1 in B minor.

Christmas Day itself began with a fast, broken only by the rising of the first star (or at six o'clock if the sky was overcast), in celebration of the star of Bethlehem. The head of the family would then distribute wafers blessed earlier by a priest, and with much kissing and embracing the assembled company would repair to the dining room, where, in another symbolic gesture, the household's finest tablecloth would be spread over a scattering of hay, commemorating both the manger and the reaping of the season's final harvest. And then came the food, thirteen courses of it, each prescribed by long tradition. Nor were the livestock excluded from the celebrations: a trip to the stables with extra fodder was incumbent upon every farmer or carriage-owning host. And after the meal came the opening of presents and a cornucopia of songs, which nourished Chopin's memory to the end of his days.

Christmas passed, and by the end of January he had basically completed his concerto. He was, however, characteristically doubtful of its quality and therefore arranged a number of try-outs. Despite the almost unqualified raptures of his friends, family and colleagues, he remained dissatisfied and spent most of February revising the work. By mid-March he was ready. On the evening of Wednesday, 17 March, before an audience of 900, Chopin made his way to the piano on the stage of Warsaw's National Theatre, nervous as always but looking the very picture of authoritative composure, and made his long deferred Polish début as a fully fledged concert virtuoso.

The programme that marked the unveiling of the F minor Concerto may seem bizarre today, but it was wholly characteristic of its time. After an overture by Elsner, Chopin played the opening movement of his new concerto and then yielded the platform to a horn player who entertained the audience with a Divertissement by a certain M. Görner. Only then did Chopin return to play the concerto's Adagio and Rondo. This was now followed by the overture to an opera by Kurpinski* and some vocal Variations by the then celebrated Ferdinand Paër, after which Chopin returned to play his Grand Fantasia on Polish Airs. Such was the success of the evening that a second concert was given five days later, with a revised programme and to a full house. What most enraptured the audience on this occasion were his improvisations on two popular Polish songs, in which, somewhat against his natural inclination, he brought all the skills of the born showman to his deliberate manipulation of the crowd. 'To tell the truth,' he later wrote, 'that's not how I felt like doing things, but I knew that's what they wanted more than anything else.' And the critical acclaim was all he could have hoped for. The reporter from the *Pamietnik dla Plci Pieknej* (Album for the Fair Sex) hailed him as a genius for his composition and performance alike; for the critic of the *Warsaw Gazette* 'every stroke of the keys was an expression of the heart'; the *Dekameron Polski* dubbed him 'a new Mozart'; while *Daily National Standard* went five better by ranking him with Bach, Handel, Gluck, Cherubini and Beethoven as well. Such was his success that another concert was arranged to take place five days later. This too unleashed a torrent of superlatives. Yet despite the professional triumphs, Chopin himself was disappointed. As he reported to Titus,

> The first concert, although it was sold out and there was not a box or seat to be had three days beforehand, didn't make the impression on the public which I thought it would. The first Allegro of my concerto, which relatively few could grasp, called forth applause, but it seems to me that people felt they had to show interest ('Ah, something new!') and pretend to be connoisseurs. The Adagio and Rondo produced the greatest effect and exclamations of admiration could be heard, but the pot-pourri on Polish Airs didn't in my opinion fully achieve its aim. They applauded because they felt they must show at the end that they hadn't been bored.
>
> I'm frankly surprised that the Adagio made such a general impression: wherever I go they speak of nothing else. It seems that everyone was quite entranced. Mlle de Moriolles sent me a laurel wreath and somebody else has sent me a poem. Orlowski has written mazurkas and waltzes on themes from my concerto, and Sennewald has asked for my portrait [to have it engraved and sold], but I could not allow that – it would be going too far: I have no wish to see myself used for wrapping up butter, which is what happened to

Chopin's birthplace at Zelazowa Wola. The house is now a museum.
(*Hulton Deutsch*)

Joseph Elsner, Chopin's first real
musical mentor, painted *c.* 1808.
(*Chopin Society*)

Chopin at nineteen. The strongly
aquiline nose evident in many other
portraits has here been discreetly
modified. (*Chopin Society*)

Constantia Gladkowska, Chopin's
first love, painted well after Chopin's
departure from Warsaw and hinting at
the sadness and disillusionment that
were to blight most of her adult life.
(*Chopin Society*)

A self-portrait by Maria Wodzinska.
If this is accurate, she was an anatomical
marvel. (*Chopin Society*)

Above The house at Nohant where
George Sand was born, and to which
she returned in 1837. (*Mansell Collection*)

Right Sand in male dress, as affected by
her at the time of her first meeting with
Chopin. (*Mary Evans Picture Library*)

Sand, as enigmatic as the *Mona Lisa*. (*Mansell Collection*)

A portrait by George Sand, said by Chopin to be the most accurate likeness of
him ever done, though he can never have seen himself in full profile.
(*Mansell Collection*)

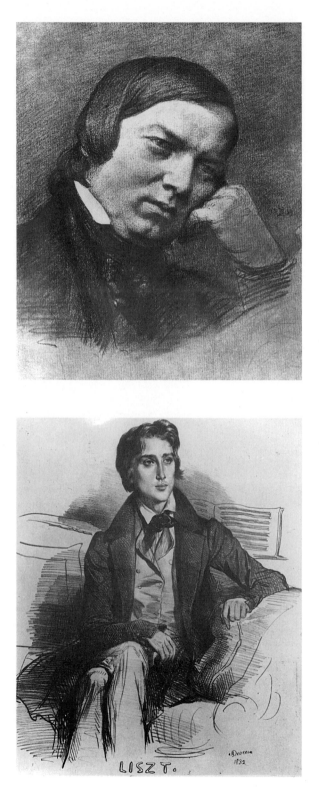

Robert Schumann, a pensive portrait capturing little of the exuberance with which he first hailed Chopin's genius. (*Hulton Deutsch*)

Franz Liszt at twenty-one, a portrait more redolent of doubt than of the flamboyance that characterized his public life. (*Hulton Deutsch*)

Hector Berlioz in 1845, still a
revolutionary eagle at forty-two.
(*Mansell Collection*)

Felix Mendelssohn-Bartholdy,
here bearing a curious
resemblance to Chopin.
(*Mansell Collection*)

Countess Delfina Potocka,
uncharacteristically turning
her back on the portraitist.
(*Mary Evans Picture Library*)

Delacroix by Delacroix.
(*Mansell Collection*)

Lelewel's portrait. They want me to give another concert but I have no desire to do so. You cannot imagine what a torture the three days before a public appearance are to me.

Nerves before a performance are generally taken for granted. For some they are no more than a temporary discomfort, which vanishes soon after the performance itself has begun. For others, including many of the greatest and most famous performers in the world, they can be almost disabling. Less well recognized is the depression that often follows the most sensational of triumphs, which can be severe and lasting, as it appears to have been with Chopin now. Three weeks after entering the history books at the National Theatre, he wrote to Titus: 'What a sense of relief I feel in the midst of my unbearable melancholy when I receive a letter from you; I needed one especially today, for I have never been so depressed. I wish I could throw off the thoughts which poison my happiness. And yet,' he adds, with a revealing shaft of self-perception, 'I take a kind of pleasure in indulging them.' This confession is of fundamental importance in the story of his music.

Whatever the torments entailed in the giving of them or the anti-climactic slumps experienced in their wake, the two concerts had galvanized Chopin back into action. The lassitude of the previous months gave way to a determined attempt at a second concerto. By mid-May he had completed the substantial first movement and was close to finishing the Adagio, of which he wrote, with a programmatic allusion unique in his correspondence:

This is not designed to create a powerful effect; it's rather a Romance, calm and melancholy, giving the impression of someone looking gently towards a spot which calls to mind a thousand happy memories. It's a kind of reverie in the moonlight on a beautiful spring evening. The accompaniment is muted: that is, the violins are stifled by a sort of comb which fits over the strings and gives them a nasal and silvery tone – perhaps it's not a good idea, but why be ashamed of writing badly, against one's better knowledge, since only the result in actual performance will reveal the mistake? In all this you will recognize my inclination to do things wrongly in spite of myself. Yes, it is so; in spite of myself some idea comes into my head and I take pleasure in indulging it. The Rondo [finale] isn't yet finished: I must be in the right mood for that. But I'm in no hurry.

Chopin was never a man to grab the main chance. He had little of the politician in him. From a purely practical, strategic point of view, there was every reason why he *should* hurry. In June, the Tsar was scheduled to visit Warsaw for the state opening of the Polish Diet. As with his late brother's visit for the same purpose five years earlier, the city would be alive with gala events, social, political and musical. If Chopin could impress Nicholas as much as he had impressed Alexander, it might have long-term benefits for his still embryonic career, possibly resulting in a reversal of the decision to deny him a government stipend.

As it turned out, the Tsar arrived earlier than announced, on 20 May, and there was no question of the concerto being finished before his departure. In any case, a twenty-year-old composer was nothing like as noteworthy as a fifteen-year-old virtuoso on the Aeolomelodikon, and Nicholas showed not the slightest interest in either Chopin or his accomplishments. Under the circumstances, it was perhaps just as well. Initially bruised by his evident exclusion from the celebrations, Chopin quickly arrived at a convincing if sinister hypothesis. The chickens of those careless revolutionary chats were coming home to roost. For many weeks the coffee houses of Warsaw had been under surveillance by the Tsar's police. Chopin's taciturnity in the presence of his friends now paid off. No revolutionary sentiments had ever been heard to escape his lips. Yet he was a known associate of men considered by the Russians to be dangerous. If his only punishment was to be snubbed by the Tsar he could count himself lucky. But time was not on his side. The longer he remained in Warsaw, the more he would put himself, and his family, at risk. In the absence of suitable plans for a period abroad, he seized an opportunity to visit Titus on his farm in the country. Scarcely had he unpacked his bags, however, before he learnt that Constantia Gladkowska was soon, and at unusually short notice, to make her operatic début in the title role of Paër's *Agnese*. Leaving a bemused Titus behind him, he bade his host a fervent farewell and returned post-haste to Warsaw. The performance was a great success and emboldened the timid lover to approach the singer, inviting her to appear at his next concert in Warsaw, though as yet neither date nor programme had been settled. Deeply flattered by the honour, she accepted with alacrity and gratitude. Having thus expended his conversational ploys, Chopin once again withdrew from Warsaw, joining his family on the Skarbek estate at Zelazowa Wola and thereby compounding his unwitting snub of the abandoned Titus, with whose hospitality he had dispensed in such whimsical fashion. Titus himself, clearly annoyed, had retaliated by refusing to answer two of Chopin's letters, each written with insouciant innocence of any offence he might have given.

Warsaw, 21 August 1830

Disgusting Hypocrite!

After returning here happily with the Baron [?] I wrote to you at once; but as my parents were at Zelazowa Wola, it was perfectly natural that I didn't stay long in Warsaw. . . . I feel homesick for your fields; I can't forget that birch tree under the windows. . . . My chief interest in Warsaw has been Paër's *Agnese* [as though Titus didn't know that this was the sole reason for his unexpected departure]. Gladkowska leaves little to be desired . . . Matuszynski is my only friend to have remained true to me and who isn't a false hypocrite, scoundrel and rogue like . . . I leave it for you to guess who!

Chopin's concerts at the National Theatre in March had made him a national celebrity, and consequently a subject for national gossip. Sudden fame invariably results in a diminution of privacy and in the misappropriation of one's name. In the immediate aftermath of his concerts Chopin found himself, through no fault of his own, being used as a pawn in a bitter dispute between the adherents of an essentially Germanic tradition, as espoused by Elsner, and the stridently pro-Italian faction unofficially marshalled under the flag of Kurpinski, who had conducted both of Chopin's concerts in March. The thought of being treated as public property was abhorrent to Chopin. 'I don't want to read anything more that people write about me, or to hear anything they have to say,' he wrote to Titus. While he must have felt gratified at his general reception, he dismissed much of it, especially the facile comparisons with Mozart, as the sheerest nonsense. Now being exposed to the glare of publicity, he was more than ever reticent about revealing to Constantia his true feelings for her, and determined to remove himself from the spotlight of public curiosity as soon as it was practicable. To Titus again:

I don't intend to stay in Warsaw any longer than I must, and if you suspect it's because of a love affair, as many people in Warsaw do, you can put such thoughts out of your head and believe me when I tell you that where my self-interest is concerned I can be above all such things. Even if I *were* in love, I could be strong enough to hide an idle passion which could come to nothing anyway.

A strange protest, considering his earlier unburdenings; and he ambiguously returns to the subject later in the same letter:

Let us consider that moment when I shall see you abroad; perhaps I shan't be able to control myself and I shall blurt out what I never cease to dream of, what is constantly before my eyes, what rings at every moment in my ears and gives me the greatest joy in the world, and at the same time the greatest misery. *But don't go and think I am in love – that is something which I am reserving for later on.*

Can Chopin really have believed that falling in love is something that can conveniently be put on hold, to be 'reserved' for the most propitious moment? Was it not, in fact, already too late to deploy such controls? And of what love is he speaking? His love for Constantia, whom he continues to identify as his 'ideal'? If so, why does he speak of 'an idle passion which could come to nothing'? Why idle? Why doomed to barenness? Or is he speaking here of Titus?

His letters to Titus are unique in Chopin's correspondence for the fervour and abandon with which he expresses his love. Many have seen this as evidence of his latent (or perhaps not so latent) homosexuality, although none has cited any evidence for a physical dimension in their relationship. Others have been at pains to point out that the apparently extravagant verbal gestures repeatedly employed by Chopin when addressing Titus are no more than the common change of nineteenth-century Polish manners and that it is naïve to seek for any sexual significance behind them. If this is so, however, why do we look in vain for any comparable ingredients in Chopin's letters to his other friends or in much other Polish correspondence of the time? Why is there no suggestion of any verbal reciprocity on the part of Titus? To none of his other friends, past, present or future, does Chopin declare 'I keep your letters like a lover's ribbon', or repeatedly assert 'I love you to madness', 'My dearest life, my soul, give me your lips', or write like this:

> I must go now and wash. So don't embrace me now, as I haven't yet washed myself. You? If I anointed myself with fragrant oils of the East, you wouldn't embrace me, unless I forced you to by magnetic means. But there are forces in Nature, and tonight you will dream that you are embracing me. I have to pay you back for the dreams that you caused me last night!

It would seem from this that any homosexual yearnings on Chopin's part were not reciprocated by his older friend, yet Chopin clearly felt no risk in so expressing himself. If he had been truly 'in love' with Titus, his boomerang visit to the latter's farm (its brevity occasioned, as we have seen, by fresh news of his 'ideal'), could easily have been resumed. Yet Chopin chose instead to join his parents, and thereafter remained by choice in Warsaw, mired, apparently, in a sea of indecision as he contemplated his imminent escape. In mid-September he wrote again to his beloved friend:

When I reflect, I feel so sorry for myself that I often become completely distracted. When I am preoccupied in this way, I might be run over by horses, and I would not know it. The other day I almost suffered such an accident in the street. On Sunday, struck by an unexpected glance from someone in church [Constantia?] – it happened to come at some moment of pleasant numbness – I ran out at once; for a quarter of an hour I did not know what was happening to me, and, running into Dr Parys, I did not know how to explain my confusion to him. I finally pretended that a dog had run up against my feet and that I had stepped on it. Sometimes I act so like a madman that it frightens me.

Before he could leave Poland with a clear conscience he still had his second Concerto to finish, whose rondo finale had been sketched even before the arrival of the Tsar in May. Day after day he delayed, announcing his departure and then postponing it. But the fault, he pointed out, was not entirely his own.

For the last few weeks my father has not wanted me to leave, on account of the disturbances which have broken out all over Germany. Apart from the Rhineland provinces and Saxony (where they already have a new king), Brunswick, Cassel, Darmstadt etc., we heard that in Vienna also a few thousand people have started a rebellion – something to do with flour. . . . In the Tyrol too there has been a row. Italy is at boiling point and one may expect to hear about trouble there at any moment. . . . I've done nothing yet about my passport, but everyone declares that I shall get one for Austria and Prussia – not a hope for Italy or France.

Before settling the matter of his travel documents, he had good news to report at last to Titus:

My second concerto is finished. And yet I feel like a novice, just as I felt before I knew anything of the keyboard. It is far too original and I shall end up by not being able to learn it myself. . . . As it is, I don't suppose it will have any remarkable success. The Rondo is effective and the first movement Allegro is impressive. Oh, this cursed self-admiration! But it is you, the egoist, who are to blame, if anyone, for this conceit of mine: one picks up one's manners from one's friends. There is, however, one thing in which I do not imitate you: the making of swift decisions. Nevertheless I have made up my mind, quietly and without a word to a soul, to clear out a week from Saturday, without so much as a by-your-leave, in spite of all weepings and wailings and implorings on bended knee. And so, with my music in my knapsack, my ribbon next to my heart and my soul slung over my shoulder, I shall jump into the stage-coach. Tears as large as peas will flow throughout the town.

Saturday, and the next Saturday, came and went and still Chopin remained. But now, at least, he could show good reason.

I badly needed your letter to allow me to get on quietly with what I have to do. You can't imagine how this cursed but inevitable killing of time wearies me. After the orchestral rehearsal of my second concerto it was decided that it should be given a public performance, and so I shall appear in it next Monday. Although in one way I'm not too pleased about it, on the other I'm curious to see what general effect it will make. I believe the Rondo is bound to impress everyone. . . . If only I didn't have to have those wretched clarinets and bassoons in between concerto-movements I could produce what one might call a very nice evening. . . . *Not later than a week after my concert, Warsaw will have seen the last of me!* My trunk is bought, my outfit is ready, my scores corrected, my handkerchiefs stitched and my trousers tailored. It only remains to say good-bye – the worst of all.

And one week later, he reported:

Yesterday's concert went off very well. I wasn't the least bit nervous and I played as I do when I'm alone. . . . This time I understood what I was doing, the orchestra understood what it was doing, and the audience realized it too. This time, as soon as they heard the first bars of the Mazurka in the Finale [of the Fantasia on Polish Airs] they burst into applause, and at the end – the usual silly business – I was called back four times.

He goes on to say that while they obviously enjoyed his playing, they enjoyed still more the singing, and appearance, of Mlle Wolkow, information which he imparts ('she looks marvellous on the stage') without the slightest sign of pique. As with a surprising number of geniuses fully at home with their gifts, Chopin showed from the beginning a genuine modesty, usually (though not always) accompanied by an equally genuine simplicity and generosity of spirit.

Three weeks after the long-deferred concert, Chopin was ready to depart. Much has been made of the ostensible premonition he had shared with Titus some weeks earlier: 'I believe,' he had written, 'that when I leave it will be to forget home altogether; I feel that I am leaving home only to die. How awful to die far away from where one has lived!' And then he switched tense, from conditional present to absolute future: 'How frightful it will be for me to see some cold-hearted doctor or servant by my deathbed instead of my family.' There is an eerie quality in the certainty with which he seems to anticipate not only his death abroad but a premature death (how else are we to interpret the reference to his family?). Those writers for whom the tone of these remarks is a predictable by-product of youthful melodrama do Chopin an injustice. In any age, it is a natural phase of youth to be concerned with death. In an era riddled with epidemics, revolutions and widespread infant mortality it would be unnatural not to be. Nor is there anything paranormal in Chopin's intimations of exile. With Europe in general (and Poland in particular) poised on the brink of revolution, it was a risk for any traveller whose homeland was under threat.

As the time for his departure drew close, Chopin said a great many farewells, but perhaps none caused him more nervous apprehension than his leave-taking of Constantia, to whom, at the eleventh hour, he had at last declared himself, though probably with the greatest reserve. She was both touched and flattered, and more than a little surprised. What passed between them is not known in any detail, but they got as far as exchanging rings and it was arranged that Chopin would write to her, with Matuszynski acting as go-between.

On the eve of his departure, a party was held, with much dancing and singing lasting well into the night, before the entire assembly accompanied Chopin on the walk back to his home. The next morning, as he made his final preparations, Ludwika put the finishing touches to her copies of his études, and in the afternoon, with the family gathered at the coaching station, the 'tears the size of peas', which he had forecast, were duly shed. For the first time in his twenty years, Chopin was heading out into the world alone. Steeling himself for the moment he had dreaded for so long, but not without a certain excitement, he clambered aboard the stage coach and was gone, heading southwards through Kalisz, where he would be joined by Titus, and thence on, via Breslau, to Vienna. Not long after passing the Warsaw city limits, the coach was waylaid by a band of men, none of whom the driver was able to identify. Peering anxiously out of the window, Chopin recognized their leader at once and several of the men behind him. At a signal from their captain, they drew in their breath as one and began to sing. The music

– a farewell cantata – was unfamiliar, having been composed and rehearsed by Elsner especially for this occasion. For decades to come it was asserted by one biographer after another that Chopin was also presented at this time with a silver goblet full of Polish earth, which would one day be sprinkled over his grave. No evidence exists to substantiate the story, and in any case it suggests, improbably, a collective presentiment that he was never to return. It was true, but on 2 November 1830 neither he nor his friends could have known it.

Interlude: Chopin and the Orchestra

His six compositions with orchestra, all but one of them written before his twenty-first birthday, have earned Chopin more abuse than any other area of his output. Of these works, only the two concertos have found their way into the mainstream repertory, but the others, while laying no great claim to profundity, are worthy of more frequent revival than they have received. The traditional criticism of all six has by now achieved the status of a cliché, recited like a mantra by hordes of commentators, most of whom have never studied the works in any detail. This is not to suggest, however, that the criticisms are not substantial. Broadly speaking, they divide into two categories: those levelled at the role of the orchestra in the overall conception of the works, and those concerning the quality of the orchestration itself.

In the first case, Chopin is accused, not without some justice, of treating the orchestra as a more or less dispensable handmaiden; a charge substantiated by his own practice of performing most of the works in question, including the two large-scale concertos, as piano solos. In the case of the popular Andante Spianato and Grand Polonaise, such treatment is now the rule rather than the exception. By the standards of Mozart and Beethoven, whose essentially symphonic conception of the concerto ranks with the most important innovations in musical history, Chopin's orchestral works are undeniably inferior. But Mozart and Beethoven, as already noted, were not his models here. Indeed their concertos were scarcely known in the Warsaw of Chopin's youth. Just as Mozart in *his* youth drew most heavily not on the great composers who immediately preceded him (Bach, Handel, Vivaldi, Telemann, etc.) but on fashionable composers of his own time like Jomelli, Wagenseil and J. C. Bach, so Chopin looked to the example of Hummel, Field, Spohr, Gyrowetz, Moscheles and Ries. In that context Chopin does not look so bad. He was writing in the fashion of the day and specifically for the audiences of the day.

As to the quality of Chopin's orchestration, there is no denying that his heart was never in it. His music was for the piano, his style was conceived entirely in pianistic terms, and for all the range and delicacy of his pianistic palette and his love of the human voice, the orchestra never really interested him. In this he was the polar opposite of his future friend Hector Berlioz. Small wonder that Berlioz later wrote of Chopin's scoring: 'When they [the orchestral instruments] play *tutti*, they cannot be heard, and one is tempted to say to them: why don't you play for heaven's sake! And when they accompany the piano, they only interfere with it, so that the listener wants to cry out to them: be quiet, you bunglers, you are in the way!' That Chopin's neglect of orchestral refinement was more a matter of indifference than of native ability is revealed in the operatic middle-section of the Larghetto in the F minor Concerto, where the accompaniment (tremolo string chords with ominous double-bass pizzicati) is as deft a piece of instrumentation as one could hope to hear. The haunting opening of the *Krakowiak*, with its spare octaves in the piano melody set against a simple, string accompaniment, is likewise tantalizing, looking forward to Rachmaninov's more famous use of the same technique at the opening of his Third Piano Concerto. Had Chopin lived another twenty years, he might well have returned to the orchestra with a new wisdom and maturity.

There is, of course, more to concertos than orchestration and, despite the demonstrable influence of other composers, Hummel perhaps foremost among them, Chopin's concertos find him emerging from his prentice years with a confidence and style already uniquely his own. In contrast to such earlier works as the *Rondo à la mazur* and Fantasia on Polish Airs, variation is now very much more than mere decoration, arising, as in the works of Bach and Mozart, out of the very essence of the musical ideas they serve to enhance. These are no longer well-behaved, self-consciously 'interesting' pieces, nor are they primarily exercises in virtuoso display, although their difficulties are great, not least because to be effective they must sound effortless. To borrow a favourite phrase of Mozart's, they must seem to the listener 'to flow like oil'. As experienced pianists can attest, the most obviously dazzling display pieces are often quite straightforward (this is true of large swathes of Liszt), whereas the most intractable passages of many masterworks, from Schubert to Ravel, may appear outwardly quite simple.

If harmonic tension and tonal structure are of paramount importance to your enjoyment of large-scale musical 'arguments', then Chopin's concertos are bound to disappoint. For a start, argument was not his style. Neither in his conversation nor in his music was he a debater. What moved him most in Bach and Mozart was not structure, nor symphonic synthesis, but melodic invention, textural refinement, translucency of colour, a sense of proportion and a profound emotionalism, which was a stranger to exaggeration. There is no denying that his tonal procedures in the concertos are sometimes enigmatic, to say the least. Sir Donald Tovey described the key scheme in the first movement of the E minor Concerto as 'suicidal', his point being that there hardly is one: the second main theme appears in the tonic major both in the orchestral ritornello and in the first solo section, thereby sacrificing tonal tension as a generative agent and using what key contrast there is to primarily colouristic effect, beautiful in itself but psychologically and dramatically emasculated. The casting of the same theme in the relative major G, on its recapitulation is a curious reversal of standard practice, but less 'suicidal' by far than the casting of the second movement in the same key again.

Chopin's concertos have so often been criticized for what they are not that one may feel self-conscious about enjoying them for what they are: virtuoso show-pieces of unprecedented pianistic resource, replete with exquisite shafts of melody and harmonic colouring and over-flowing with emotional nuances from the subtle and poignant to the thrilling and fiery. Musical experience is necessarily subjective, but beneath the bravura rhetorical flourishes there is a sincerity in this music that speaks directly to the heart. This is a quality, of course, that, happily, lies beyond the reach of objective analysis. The idea that Chopin, a musical genius of exceptional intelligence if not of specifically intellectual inclinations, was somehow unable to construct a convincing large-scale sonata movement according to Classical models is at best patronizing. Chopin could see the structural 'flaws' in his music quite as well as the standard well-educated academic of our own or any other time, and his compositional skill exceeded that of most. Had he seen fit, he could easily have adjusted the music to suit the preferences of his critics. The point is that he did not see fit. He subscribed to different priorities and aspired to different ends. To fault him for pursuing them is like criticizing a butterfly for its inability to swim.

For very many years – well into the twentieth century, in fact – the two concertos were usually performed in re-orchestrations by Klindworth, Tausig, Burmeister, Cortot and the like, whose ultimate failure to solve the 'problems' of Chopin's scoring reveal the curiously symbiotic relationship between the orchestration and the style of piano-writing it was designed to accompany and, more to the point perhaps, to illuminate. Chopin's use of the orchestra is in hardly any sense symphonic; it derives straight from his uniquely pianistic soundworld, serving rather as a frame and lightscape for keyboard textures and figuration that are so fully realized that they require no more. Alter the frame and you must alter the picture. Klindworth, indeed, attempted to do just that, tampering with Chopin's piano-writing to the detriment of all concerned. Other well-wishers who struggled to 'correct' the wayward Pole include Granados, Balakirev and Rimsky-Korsakov.

Even his sternest critics have generally conceded that the real heart of Chopin's concertos is to be found in their slow movements. And here, freed from some of the deeply ingrained preconceptions that have prevented their surrender to the outer movements, his detractors have readily acknowledged that Chopin is very nearly at his best. Berlioz went so far as to applaud the orchestration in the Larghetto of the F minor, and well he might. Accompanied nocturnes these may be, but in the face of such freshness, such unguarded lyricism, such elegance and poignancy, who is to complain? In both Finales, Chopin draws on Polish folk traditions, that to the E minor Concerto being a second foray into the world of the *Krakowiak* (but just listen to the distance travelled since op. 14!), while the F minor pays tribute to his favourite of all dances, the mazurka.

— 4 —

Patriots, Pleasures, Pain and Profits
1830–1832

Four weeks after Chopin left Poland, students from the Cadet School (where his father had once taught) invaded the Belvedere Palace in an attempt to assassinate the Grand Duke Constantine and overthrow the government. Elsewhere on the same night, another group attacked the Russian cavalry barracks in the Lazienki Park. Neither was successful, but the gesture was enough. The anti-Russian insurrection had begun. Chopin knew nothing of this, but he was well-acquainted with many of those involved and sympathized with their cause. When he learned of their action, in early December, he can only have been relieved that he himself had not been there at the time. There would have been no question of his joining them, of course. Physical valour was never his strong suit, and in any case he regarded their action as ill-advised and highly dangerous. If even Kosciuszko and his forces had failed against the Russians, what chance had a band of idealistic students? As their well-observed associate, however, he would almost certainly have been arrested, which would have put his family at risk. After long and intense deliberation, it was decided that Titus should return at once to Warsaw to join the revolution while Chopin should remain behind and fulfil the purposes of his journey – a decision heartily welcomed by his family. But as Chopin was all too well aware, the Polish upheavals were hardly unique. Europe generally was in a state of turmoil. Paris was still recovering from the July Revolution of 1830, in which Charles X, last of the French Bourbons, had been driven into exile, to be replaced by the 'bourgeois king' Louis-Philippe of Orleans; the newly independent state of Belgium was just emerging from the embers of revolution in the Netherlands; mass demonstrations in Switzerland had shaken the government there to its foundations; while Germany, Italy, Spain and Portugal had all been subject to revolutionary disturbances of one kind or another. Not even England was entirely immune to the wave of social unrest that was sweeping the Continent, though here, at least, it fell short of armed insurrection.

In any case, leaving Vienna was easier said than done. The Russian authorities, on whom Chopin was necessarily reliant, refused him permission to go to Paris and impounded his passport, which they subsequently claimed to have lost. 'And not only will they not trouble to look for it,' he wrote, 'they say that I must make fresh application for a new one. We Poles have to put up with a lot of queer things these days. You know how indecisive I can be, yet here I am all ready to go, and cannot move!' A further impediment was the unexpected requirement of a health certificate. 'The people here are terribly frightened of cholera,' he explained, 'and you really can't help laughing. They're selling printed prayers against the cholera, they won't eat fruit; and most of them are fleeing from the town.' If indeed Chopin *was* laughing, which seems doubtful, it can hardly have been from mirth. The epidemic, which had started in India, had now spread through Russia and Poland into Austria. Hard on the heels of Chopin's departure for Munich at the end of July, it swept through Vienna itself, sending a wave of some 60,000 terrified refugees ahead of it in a single month and leaving innumerable casualties in its wake. Businesses tumbled like ninepins, the houses of the afflicted were burnt to the ground, and while members of the court huddled behind the boarded windows of the Schönbrunn Palace, the streets were rank with the smell of smoke and putrefying flesh. In the prevailing panic many sufferers were buried alive.

In neighbouring Bavaria, soon itself to be invaded by the virus, Chopin's thoughts were firmly centred on the future. Having arrived in Munich, by way of Linz and Salzburg, where he visited Mozart's birthplace, he was again marooned by lack of funds. The money he had requested of his father had failed to materialize, and he was obliged to remain in Munich for a month. During this time he made the acquaintance of the city's leading musical lights and struck up a friendship with Mendelssohn, who, like himself, was passing through. On 28 August he gave a concert at which he again played the E minor Concerto as well as the Fantasia on Polish Airs. Only one critic attended, but Chopin was praised for his 'outstanding virtuosity' and his 'cultivated style', and reportedly 'aroused applause from all quarters'.

Still better news was the belated arrival of his father's money. In good health and high spirits, he set off at last for Stuttgart. Here, alone and with no very clear sense of purpose, he fell with startling rapidity into one of those troughs of depression that were to become a regular feature of his adult life (the cyclical alternation of euphoria and despair is a characteristic of many creative artists and is mirrored, as we shall see, in the overall pattern of Chopin's compositions). In any case, a streak of morbidity was common to most artists of the Romantic era and the twenty-year-old Chopin did little to dispel it. In later years his innate sense of humour often kept him from the worst excesses of self-pity but in Stuttgart, now, he offered no resistance. Contemplating his cheerless room, he succumbed entirely.

Stuttgart. How strange! This bed on which I shall lie has been slept on by more than one dying man, but today it does not repel me! Who knows what corpses have lain on it and for how long? But is a corpse any worse than I? A corpse too knows nothing of its father, mother or sisters or Titus. Nor has a corpse a sweetheart. A corpse, too, is pale, like me. A corpse is cold, just as I am cold and indifferent to everything. A corpse has ceased to live, and I too have had enough of life. Enough? . . . Why do we live on through this wretched life which only devours us and serves to turn us into corpses? The clocks in the Stuttgart belfries strike the midnight hour. Oh how many people have become corpses at this moment! Mothers have been torn from their children, children from their mothers – how many plans have come to nothing, how much sorrow has sprung from these depths, and how much relief! . . . Virtue and vice have come in the end to the same thing! It seems that to die is man's finest action – and what might be his worst? To be born, since that is the exact opposite of his best deed. It is therefore right of me to be angry that I was ever born into this world! Why was I not prevented from remaining in a world where I am utterly useless? What good can my existence bring to anyone? . . . But wait, wait! What's this? Tears? How long it is since they flowed! How is this, seeing that an arid melancholy has held me for so long in its grip? How good it feels – and sorrowful. Sad but kindly tears! What a strange emotion! Sad but blessed. It is not good for one to be sad, and yet how pleasant it is – a strange state. . . . Alone! Alone! All alone! Oh my misery is indescribable! My heart can scarcely bear it! [and this is a shortened extract]

Primed by the final fling of adolescent self-indulgence, he was pushed to the very brink of sanity by news that reached him by chance some days later.

After nine months of increasingly bitter resistance Warsaw had fallen to the Russian army under the ruthless command of General Pash-kievitch,* a natural despot who delighted in his reputation for barbarous cruelty. Few would have guessed that the rebellion could have lasted so long. The Poles were hopelessly outnumbered, and they fought alone. At the start of the revolt, Prince Czartoryski had used his considerable diplomatic skills to negotiate a peaceful solution, but the rank and file were in no mood for compromise. Nor was there hope of assistance from abroad, for Czartoryski's appeals to France, England and Austria were in vain. The rebels themselves were in disarray – within the first seven months, the revolutionary leadership had changed three times. Yet for almost a year they had resisted both the intransigence of the Tsar ('I am King of Poland. At the first shot fired by the Poles I shall annihilate them.') and the might of his forces: 150,000 Russian soldiers as against 80,000 Poles. When Warsaw finally fell, it was under relentless bombardment by some 300 cannon. Inevitably, many suffered, both during the siege and after it. There was the usual retributive imprisonment, torture and transportation. Prussian and Siberian labour camps were swelled by a new infusion of vanquished Poles, and daily life in Warsaw was subject to many privations, but Chopin's family and his beloved Constantia remained alive and physically unharmed, and their dwellings, too, were unscathed. Chopin, however, knew nothing of this. He knew only that Poland, the cradle of his youth and the object of his pride, had lost. It was an outcome not less terrible for being predictable, and it can fairly be said to have changed his life and his music, forever. In time he would draw lasting sustenance from it. For the moment it nearly unhinged him. Newly alone in a country that itself had never dealt kindly with Poles, he surrendered to a paroxysm of rage, grief and desperation.

> Stuttgart. I wrote the above lines not knowing that the enemy has reached my home! The suburbs are stormed – burnt down! Johnny! Where are you? Wilhelm has surely perished on the ramparts. I see Marcel a prisoner! Sowinski, good lad, is in the hands of those scoundrels! Oh, God, art Thou? Thou art, but Thou avengest not! Hast Thou not seen enough of the Muscovite crimes – or – or – or art Thou Thyself a Muscovite? My poor, kind father! Perhaps you are hungry and cannot buy bread for mother. My sisters! Have they fallen victims to the unleashed fury of the Muscovite scum?! . . . Oh why could I not have slain even a single Muscovite! Oh Titus! Titus! . . . Oh, God! God! Make the earth to tremble and let this generation be engulfed! May the most frightful torments seize the French for not coming to our aid!

Never again, not even in his journal, would Chopin so wholly capitulate to unreasoning emotion. From that moment, so frightening in its loss of the control which he prized so highly, was born a reserve that never left him. Never again would he unburden himself as he used to do with Titus. In his future relations with women, as with his male friends, he would keep his cards close to his chest. And although he chose to live abroad, he was never so comfortable as in the company of Poles. From that night in Stuttgart, too, dates a fundamental change in his relationship to music, both his own and other people's. There is no proof that the terrifying outpourings of the so-called 'Revolutionary' Étude were born on that night, as has often been asserted, but there is equally no reason to doubt it. The mood of the music matches the mood of the journal, and there is no comparable outburst in any of the music he wrote later, not even in the most passionate of the preludes, which have often, if mistakenly, been traced to his sojourn in Majorca with George Sand many years later. Only, perhaps, in the B minor Scherzo, begun in the aftermath of the Stuttgart crisis, do we find so savage an expression of inner turmoil. From that point onwards, the most violent emotions are everywhere tempered by the controlling hand of the master craftsman. It was not for their music alone that Bach and Mozart were Chopin's favourite composers. They were, and remain, the ultimate craftsmen, to whom excess in all its forms was anathema. Nor were Chopin's misgivings about Beethoven related to technique or to the originality and daring of his genius. It was the insolent defiance and the fearless emotional range of Beethoven's music that generally unnerved him.† To a man of his fastidious cast of mind, the titanic cavortings of a Beethoven were at best unseemly. But if Chopin after Stuttgart placed an ever greater premium on control, it was in tacit acknowledgment of emotions that *needed* controlling. Gentlemanly to his fingertips, he was prone throughout his adult life to feelings of impatience, anger, ridicule and contempt; inner stirrings to which he was never wholly reconciled. Above all, however, he had a capacity for loneliness that Stuttgart intensified with a cruelty worthy of Pashkievitch himself – a capacity without which the bleak meditations of the A minor Prelude, op. 28, no. 2, or the final, unending, F minor Mazurka would not have been possible.

The fall of Warsaw effected a sea change, not only in Chopin's perceptions of himself but of the world around him. It brought his consciousness of personal identity and his now consuming sense of mission into sharper relief than ever before, and the change was soon reflected in his music. Above all, it gave him a searingly intensified awareness of Poland

---

† 'I acknowledge only one morality,' Beethoven declared on one occasion, 'and that is the morality of power.'

and the centrality of his own, deep-rooted Polishness. It made him a patriot, and it gave to his specifically Polish music, most notably his polonaises and mazurkas, a substance, a power and a nationalistic fervour which had no precedent in the history of music. When Schumann described them as 'guns smothered in flowers' he was more perceptive than he may have known. For the moment, however, the fall of Warsaw forced Chopin out of that characteristic sea of indecision in which he had drifted for some months. Marooned, as he felt, in a city, a country, whose character and traditions were alien to his temperament and background, he had to devise some plan of action which would help to underwrite his uncertain future. The first question to be settled, and the easiest to solve, was that of his immediate destination.

★   ★   ★

It was, perhaps, inevitable that Chopin's choice should have fallen on Paris, despite his characteristic disclaimer of personal responsibility. 'The wind has blown me here,' he wrote to Titus, well after his decision to remain there. The capital city of his father's homeland, Paris in the 1830s, for all its political upheavals, was widely conceded to be the cultural capital of Europe, and where European culture was concerned, of the world. There is perhaps no parallel in modern history to the galaxy of creative and critical talent that was active in Paris at the time, with the possible, and outwardly improbable, exception of Hollywood in the 1930s. For Goethe,★ it was quite simply 'a city where all the best of the realms of nature and art of the whole earth are open to daily contemplation, a world-city where the crossing of every bridge or every square recalls a great past, and where at every street corner a piece of history has been unfolded'. In the aftermath of the French Revolution, painters, writers, poets, playwrights and many of the world's most famous and brilliant musicians converged on Paris, so that it was possible to encounter at or *en route* to one salon in a single evening such luminaries as Ingres, Delacroix,★ Stendhal, Victor Hugo, Heine, Balzac, Rossini, Cherubini, Liszt, Berlioz and Mendelssohn, as well as a host of lesser celebrities, whose fame died with them. The city's cultural life, however, was only a part of its appeal to the young Chopin. 'Paris,' he wrote excitedly to Titus in December, 'is whatever you care to make of it.'

You can enjoy yourself, get bored, laugh, cry, do anything you like, and no-one takes any notice because thousands here are doing exactly the same. . . . You find here the greatest splendour, the greatest filthiness, the greatest virtue, the greatest vice. . . . They really are a queer lot here! As soon as it gets dark all you hear is street-vendors shouting out the titles of the latest pamphlets, and you can often buy three or four sheets of printed rubbish for a few sous, with titles such as 'How to Get and Keep a Lover', or 'Priests in Love', or 'Romance of the Archbishop of Paris and the Duchesse de Berry', and a thousand similar obscenities, often very wittily put together. Honestly, one can't be surprised at the way of making a few pennies that they think up. I must tell you that there is terrible poverty here and little money about. You meet with crowds of beggars with menacing looks on their faces, and you often hear threatening remarks about that imbecile Louis-Philippe. . . . The lower classes are completely exasperated and ready at any time to break out of their poverty-stricken situation, but unfortunately for them the government is extremely severe on such movements and the slightest gathering in the streets is dispersed by mounted police.

For all the ruthlessness with which they may have suppressed political movements, the police were inclined to turn a blind eye when it came to private enterprise: robberies and murders in the streets were common-place, most thieves were armed, and pedestrians who ventured out alone at night were frequently putting their lives at risk. Or at least their health: 'At every step you see posters advertising cures for venereal disease. . . . and what numbers of tender-hearted young ladies there are!' But Chopin, to his sorrow, was temporarily out of the running. 'I regret that the memory of Teresa (notwithstanding the efforts of Benedict who considers my misfortune a mere trifle) has not allowed me to taste the forbidden fruit [Chopin here apparently refers to a bout of venereal disease, though the identities of Teresa and Benedict, like the form of the disease itself, if any, remain unknown]. I have got to know quite a few lady vocalists – and such ladies here would very willingly "join in duets".'

The life of Paris, high and low, like the beauty of the city itself, continued to bewitch him. Here, perhaps more even than in Warsaw, he felt wholly at ease with the society about him, and the prospect of remaining there for the indefinite future elated him. But it came with a price, for to stay on in the city he would have to secure a residence permit. This in itself posed no serious problem, but the possession of such a document would bring him into direct conflict with the Russian authorities in Poland and thus effectively condemn him to a life of exile.

Even to one of Chopin's indecisive nature, however, the choice seemed inevitable. Whatever love he had for homeland, family and friends, there was no future for him in Warsaw. The decision almost made itself. Fortunately he was prepared. In Vienna, Dr Malfatti had given him a letter of introduction to Ferdinand Paër, director of music at the court of Louis-Philippe and a man well acquainted with those in authority. Taking only slight liberties with the truth, as befitted the composer of forty-three operas, Paër in his turn provided Chopin with another letter, this time to an official at the passport office. 'This young man,' he wrote, 'has been warmly recommended to me and I ask you to protect him. He is Polish, deported during the Warsaw revolution, went to Vienna, where he was highly appreciated by the press and society. He has quality and is well educated.' The requisite papers were duly issued and from that moment onwards, Frédéric Chopin was a Parisian.

Such nostalgia as he may have felt for his native land was greatly alleviated by the presence in Paris of a thriving Polish community, many of them, like himself, recent arrivals, and some already known to him. Even the most abortive wars create refugees, and Chopin was only one of 8,000, each seeking asylum in neighbouring or sympathetic countries. Paris was the natural rallying point for the dispossessed aristocracy of Poland, many of whom had had the foresight to invest their capital with the Rothschilds, a family who, as it turned out, were to play an important part in the Frenchification of Chopin.

Little can most of the émigrés have guessed that their newfound home was in fact an indirect beneficiary of the disaster that had occasioned their exile. Ever since the overthrow of Charles X in the July Revolution of 1830, Tsar Nicholas I had dreamt of assisting his restoration through a major assault on Paris in alliance with the armies of Austria and Prussia. With this in mind, he had begun massing forces in Poland while waiting for a decision from his allies. It was only the uprising in Warsaw, with the consequent deflection of his troops, that drove the assault on Paris from his mind. Even so, Chopin was to witness mass disturbances on the streets of the city which had their own resonance for the Polish émigrés in its midst. The arrival in Paris of General Ramorino, an Italian revolutionary who had materially helped the Poles, had provoked a number of violent clashes between anti-government agitators and the police. It was Chopin's first sight of revolutionary politics in action and he looked on in horrified fascination.

A huge crowd, not only of young people but of townsfolk, which assembled in front of the Pantheon, made a rush for the right bank of the Seine. They came on like an avalanche, increasing their numbers with each street they passed through, until they reached the Pont Neuf where the mounted police began to break them up. Many were arrested, but all the same a huge body of people collected on the boulevards under my window, intending to join up with those advancing from the other side of the town. The police could do nothing against the tightly packed throng; a company of infantry was brought up, hussars and mounted gendarmes rode along the pavements, the national guard showed equal zeal in dispersing the inquisitive and murmuring populace. They seize and arrest free citizens, panic reigns, shops are closed, crowds gather at every corner of the boulevards, whistles are blown, reinforcements are rushed up. . . . You cannot conceive what impression the menacing voices of the rebellious populace made on me.

Fortunately, such eruptions were exceptional and had no effect on Chopin's acclimatization to his new surroundings.

From the moment of his arrival in the city, he had thrown himself into its social and cultural life with an enthusiasm that eclipsed for the moment all thought of exile, despite his almost daily contact with the burgeoning Polish community, which soon included the Czartoryskis, the Platers, the Wodzinski brothers and two former classmates from the Conservatory, Orlowski and Fontana, who were all old friends. So, too, were Prince Valentine Radziwill, the poet Mickiewicz* and Countess Delfina Potocka, with whom Chopin was to be romantically linked by generations of biographers whose taste for apocrypha exceeded the stringency of their research. Between 1832 and 1836 these were joined by hundreds more, representing a rich cross-section of Polish society.

To the public, however, he would remain unknown until a suitable concert could be arranged, and this was by no means as straightforward an operation as it is today. In 1831 the solo recital as we know it was still a thing of the future. Not until Liszt in 1840 did a pianist have the effrontery to monopolize a public concert;† the very term 'recital' was

---

† It was Liszt who, single-handedly, established the model on which the life of the concert pianist is based to this day. His tours were near legendary, taking him not only to Paris, Vienna and Budapest, but to Spain, Portugal, Germany, England, Poland, Rumania, Turkey and Russia – and this was before the advent of widespread railways, let alone the aeroplane. He was the first pianist to play whole programmes from memory, the first to embrace the entire keyboard literature, as then known, from Bach to Chopin, the first consistently to place the piano at right angles to the platform, so that its lid opened outwards towards the audience, and the first to play to gatherings of 3,000 and more.

likewise due to him. Prior to his example, the public concert was almost by definition a high-class variety act in which it was not unusual for a symphony to be dismembered and delivered piecemeal, interspersed with songs, piano solos, vocal quartets, operatic arias and so on. Nor were the individual movements of a masterpiece necessarily immune to the fashion. The violinist Franz Clement has gone down in history not primarily because he gave the first performance of Beethoven's Violin Concerto but because, in the process, he entertained the audience by such edifying feats as playing on one string with the fiddle upside down, albeit between movements.

It was not until 26 February 1832, after four postponements, that Chopin's Parisian début took place, and the list of participants allowed for no doubt that this was an important occasion. Prior to Chopin's first appearance came a performance of Beethoven's C major Quintet, op. 29, given by some of the finest string players in Europe, among them the violinist Baillot,★ in Chopin's view a serious rival to Paganini, and the remarkable Belgian musician, Chrétien Urhan, an artist equally adept as an organist, violinist and viola-player.† The two singers who then contributed a duet to the proceedings, Mlles Tomeoni and Isambard, were of lesser distinction but had the good grace to appear well clad. Next, Chopin played his F minor Concerto, filling in the orchestral parts at the piano, and was joined after the interval by Messrs Hiller, Stamaty, Osborne, Sowinski and the composer for a performance of the monstrous Introduction, March and Grand Polonaise for six pianos by the German pianist, composer and teacher Friedrich Kalkbrenner.★ This was followed by an operatic aria, sung by Mlle Isambard, and an oboe solo played by a Monsieur Brot, and the concert ended with Chopin, again unaccompanied, playing his 'Là ci darem' Variations. 'All Paris,' the Polish violinist Antoni Orlowski wrote home, 'was stupefied! Our Fritz mopped the floor with every one of the pianists here.' In fact, 'all Paris', even figuratively speaking, had been otherwise engaged. The audience, numbering little more than a hundred, had barely filled a third of the hall. Nevertheless, every important pianist in Paris was there, including Liszt, who befriended Chopin almost

---

† Devoutly religious, Urhan had planned for a time to become a monk, but one week in a Trappist monastery was enough to disabuse him of that ambition. Nevertheless, he dressed always in blue (an obeisance to the Virgin), fasted daily until 6:00 pm and exacted from his employers at the Paris Opéra a promise that whenever he played in the orchestra he would be permitted to turn his back on the stage, lest he glimpse the sinful displays of the female form vouchsafed by the tight-fitting costumes of the dancers. In all his years at the Opéra he never saw a single one of its productions.

immediately upon his arrival in Paris, and Mendelssohn, who was passing through. The long-deferred concert established Chopin, beyond doubt, as one of the greatest musicians of the day. As Liszt put it: 'the most vociferous applause seemed insufficient for the talent that was opening a new phase of poetic sentiment and presenting happy innovations in the substance of his art.' The Polish community were out in force, and Chopin's triumph did no harm to his social standing with them, indeed from then on he was to be regarded by them as a kind of unofficial crown prince. The most influential member of the audience, however, was the esteemed musicologist François Joseph Fétis,* founder and chief critic of the *Revue Musicale*.

Composer, scholar, professor and librarian at the Paris Conservatoire, Fétis was among the most learned and penetrating listeners of his time. His reactions to this début concert, therefore, tell us more about Chopin's historical and artistic significance than all the bravos and cheers of the composer's friends and colleagues put together. Most importantly, they urge us to listen afresh to music whose subsequent popularity may have deafened us to its revolutionary nature.

Piano music is generally written in certain conventional forms that may be regarded as basic, and that have been continually reproduced for over thirty years. It is one of the defects of this kind of music, and our most skilful artists have not succeeded in ridding their works of it. But here is a young man who, surrendering himself to his natural impressions and taking no model, has found, if not a complete renewal of piano music, at least a part of that which we have long sought in vain, namely an abundance of original ideas of a kind to be found nowhere else. . . . I find in M. Chopin's inspirations the signs of a renewal of forms which may henceforth exercise considerable influence upon this branch of art.

Prophetic words. Fétis was mistaken, however, in suggesting that Chopin had no models. He had, but they were not pianistic. In the development of his unique style of piano-writing and piano-*playing* it would be hard to overstate the importance of opera, a passion with him long before his infatuation with Constantia Gladkowska.

In Paris Chopin indulged that passion to the hilt. Within a few weeks of his arrival there he made the acquaintance of Cherubini* and Rossini and became a regular visitor to all the Parisian opera houses, large and small. His letters on the subject are as vivid and revealing as those of Mozart half a century earlier. To Titus in December:

Never have I heard the *Barber* [Rossini's *The Barber of Seville*] as last week with Lablache, Rubini and Malibran, nor *Otello* [also Rossini] as with Rubini, Pasta and Lablache; or again, *Italiana in Algeri* [Rossini again]. Now, if ever, I have *everything* in Paris. You cannot conceive what Lablache is like! They say that Pasta has gone off, but I never saw anything more sublime. Malibran impresses you merely by her marvellous voice, but no one *sings* like her. Miraculous! Marvellous! Rubini is a really excellent tenor. He sings true notes, never *falsetto* and sometimes his ornamental runs go on for hours (but sometimes his decorative passages are too long and he deliberately uses a tremolo effect, besides trilling endlessly – which, however, brings him the greatest applause). His *mezza voce* is incomparable.

And a fascinating account of *Otello*:

Schröder-Devrient is here – but she's not such a sensation as in Germany. La Malibran* played Othello and she was Desdemona. Malibran is small while the German lady is huge – it looked as if *she* would stifle Othello! . . . The orchestra is marvellous, not to be compared, however, with the real French Opera, the Académie Royale. If ever magnificence was seen in a theatre I doubt whether it reached the level of splendour shown in *Robert le Diable*, the very latest five-act opera of Meyerbeer. It is a masterpiece of the modern school, in which devils (the huge chorus) sing through megaphones and spirits arise from their graves in groups of fifty or sixty. On the stage there's a diorama in which, towards the end, you see the inside of a church and the whole church itself all lit up, with monks and congregation seated, with censers and, what's more, a grand organ whose sound, when heard on the stage, enchants and amazes one and practically drowns the whole orchestra. No one will ever stage anything like it! Meyerbeer has made himself immortal!

And this from a man renowned for his reserve! Chopin's veneration for Mozart and Bach, like his sporadic unease with Beethoven, was entirely genuine, but to be properly understood it must be seen in a context which includes his responses to Meyerbeer.

Less surprising was his reaction to two of the biggest wheels in Parisian musical politics, both of them immigrants, like himself. One was the Italian Cherubini, the other was the renowned Bohemian composer, Antonin Reicha. Chopin had been particularly eager to meet this remarkable musician but was rapidly warned off. As he wrote to Elsner:

I know a few of his pupils who have completely changed my ideas of him. It appears that the man doesn't even like music – he doesn't even go to the Conservatoire concerts. He refuses to discuss music with anyone, and during his lessons he does nothing but look at his watch, etc. It's the same with Cherubini, who only rambles on about the cholera and revolution. These gentlemen are dried-up puppets: one must regard them with respect and use their works for purposes of study.

In any case, Chopin, and Paris, could get along without them.

The crowd of people concerned with all branches of the art of music is quite amazing. There are three orchestras: those of the Académie, the Italian opera, and the opera in the Rue Feydeau are excellent. Rossini is the director of his own opera, which has the finest stage-production in Europe. And Lablache, Rubini, Pasta, Malibran, Schröder-Devrient, Santini etc. enchant their fashionable audiences three times a week. Nourrit, Levasseur, Dérivis, Mme Cinti-Damoreau and Mlle Dorus are the stars of the Grand Opera. Cholet, Mlle Casimir and Prévost are the stars of the Opéra-Comique: briefly, it is only here that one can fully understand what singing really is.

Yet when it came to original composition, Paris was almost as flat and as featureless as the plains of Mazovia. It is one of cultural history's greatest ironies that in the midst of this unprecedented ferment of art and letters, music in France, with the sole exception of the Paris Opéra, was at its lowest ebb for centuries. Apart from a few revolutionary contributions from Berlioz, no symphonic works of lasting substance were composed there, there was no chamber music of any distinction and, where native-born Frenchmen were concerned, no instrumental music either. Nor even when he had acquired wealth and fame did Chopin himself add anything to the wider realms of music: he left no symphony, no opera, no string quartet, no choral works, and his indifference to the orchestra, even in his own works, has already been noted.

Yet while the piano remained, with few exceptions, the sole repository of his creative thoughts, it would be wrong to conclude, as many have, that he had no interest in any other instrument. He wrote a number of highly idiomatic works for or involving the cello, and there are many passages in his music which might well have been inspired by the sound of the cello. Nor, of course, was he indifferent to the human voice. His actual songs are curiously few, and of relatively minor importance, but the sound of Italian *bel canto* flows through his nocturnes and ballades. The role, specifically, of Bellini's operas, on the other hand, has repeatedly been exaggerated, and in the face of the most elementary evidence. The most evidently 'Bellinian' features were a well-integrated part of Chopin's style years before he even knew the composer's name, much less his operas. Indeed no work by Bellini was ever performed in Warsaw until 1841, fully a decade after Chopin's departure, and no evidence has yet surfaced to support the once popular claim that Chopin wished to be buried near Bellini in the cemetery of Père-Lachaise. That both men, who later enjoyed a cordial and mutually admiring friendship, were influenced by Italian opera in general is beyond argument. If there was any single composer who most influenced them both, it would almost certainly be Rossini, but in Chopin's case the roots go back to Mozart, who had, after all, provided the theme for his first great success, the 'Là ci darem' Variations. As mentioned earlier, the operatic diet in Warsaw was based almost entirely on works from the great Italian tradition, of which, ironically, Handel the German and Mozart the Austrian were the two greatest exponents. Stylistic genealogy is among the most speculative of musical studies, but it may broadly be said that the peculiar curvaceousness of Chopin's melodies, like their arabesque ornamentation and their textural sweetening by thirds and sixths (a time-honoured standby of vocal duets), derives more from opera than from any other source.

Among the strangest aspects of Chopin's early years in Paris was his abiding admiration for Friedrich Kalkbrenner, a former prodigy who had made his formal début when he was five and graduated from the Paris Conservatoire when he was thirteen. Widely deprecated by many of his colleagues as a charlatan of overweening vanity and conceit, this shrewd and obviously able executant was extolled by the twenty-one-year-old Chopin as 'the leading pianist of Europe – the only one whose shoelaces I am not fit to untie'. And elsewhere: 'I simply long to play like Kalkbrenner. If Paganini is perfection itself, Kalkbrenner is his equal. In truth, he is superior to all the pianists I have ever heard.' Whether Kalkbrenner concurred is not recorded, although it seems likely. What is well documented, however, is his astonishing offer to take the young Chopin in hand and, in a three-year course of lessons, to 'make a real artist' of him. Still more astonishing was Chopin's initial enthusiasm for the idea and his apparent total lack of pride:

Kalbrenner has convinced me that I can play splendidly when I am inspired but abominably when I am not – something that never happens to him. When he had observed me closely he declared that I had no 'school', that I am going along fine but might take the wrong turning. He added that after his death, or when he completely gives up playing, there will be no representative of the great school of piano-playing left. He says I couldn't create a new school, even if I wanted to, since I haven't yet mastered the old one, and sums me up thus: I have not a perfect *mechanism*, and the free expression of my ideas is thereby cramped.

On the evidence available, and there's no reason to doubt it, Chopin, who had by that time composed most if not all of the op. 10 Études, was already a pianist with no superior. Yet when he shared a multi-piano concert with Kalkbrenner in December, the German chose for himself 'an enormous *pantaleon* of an instrument', while Chopin, whose generally small tone had redounded to his disfavour in both Warsaw and Vienna, had to make do with 'a monochord piano which is tiny but whose tone carries – like little bells on a giraffe'.

Unsurprisingly, Chopin's family were more than a little bemused by this strange infatuation, and the conservative Elsner was naturally suspicious, suggesting, persuasively, that Kalkbrenner was motivated by vanity and the prospect of claiming Chopin as his pupil. Worse, he suspected a jealous desire to cramp Chopin's self-evident genius, 'to hold back that which Nature herself might push forward'. He was worried, too, by the essential naïvety that underlay Chopin's sophistication and quiet self-confidence. 'He is a good lad. He has no vanity, nor any desire to push himself forward – and he is easily influenced' (a curious, and revealing, thumbnail sketch of one of the most original creative artists who ever lived). As it happens, he *was* easily influenced in the matter of Kalkbrenner's proposal, and politely declined the offer while retaining an affection and admiration for the older man which stood the test of time. Years later, according to his not always reliable pupil Wilhelm von Lenz, Chopin offered a substantially different account of the whole affair, explaining: 'All that was when I had just arrived in Paris. You must remember that Kalkbrenner then reigned supreme; it was necessary to pay court to him a little.'

Elsner's concern for Chopin, however, went beyond the immediate question of Kalkbrenner's offer. He was also deeply concerned that Chopin should not be lured away from composition by the more glamorous life of the successful concert pianist. Nor, he kept insisting, should

the piano be allowed to dominate Chopin's compositions. It was in the
realm of opera, Elsner argued, and there only, that Chopin would find
the key to artistic immortality. Chopin, for his part, resisted the suggestion, while thanking his teacher for his concern and encouragement.
From a purely practical point of view, he felt obliged to make his mark
as a pianist, thereby acquiring the money necessary to everyday life –
Chopin was hardly an ascetic when it came to creature comforts – and
the experience necessary to the composition of a great opera, or indeed
of anything else. He cited the dozens of gifted young composers from
the Paris Conservatoire who were wasting away, 'waiting with folded
hands for someone to produce their operas, symphonies or cantatas,
which no one but Cherubini or Leseur have even seen in manuscript'.
Then, too, he added, even an artistic success in one of the smaller
theatres could result in very little reputation for its composer, however
worthy. To be sure, there was some practical wisdom in all this – and
Chopin gently let his teacher glimpse that cosmopolitan Paris was a very
different world from provincial Warsaw – but there was undoubtedly an
element of rationalization here. The truth is that Chopin had no desire
to write an opera or a cantata or a symphony. And if he had, he knew
that this was neither the time nor the place in which to do it. In any
case, he had more pressing concerns.

The temptations of Paris were many, particularly to one of Chopin's
spendthrift nature, and as yet he had found no means of securing his
livelihood. His much deferred concert had itself been expensive to
mount, and while it had undoubtedly been a *succès d'estime*, it had
done little for his financial prospects. Only two weeks later, on 13
March 1832, he had addressed a letter to the Société des Concerts
du Conservatoire, demonstrating that the politics of grovel were still
alive and well:

> Gentlemen of the Committee, I am exceedingly desirous of the favour
> of being allowed to appear at one of your admirable concerts and beg
> to submit an application for the same. Though I may have no special
> claim to put forward, I have confidence in your generous disposition
> towards artists and I venture to hope that my request will be favour-
> ably received. I am, Gentlemen, Your humble and obedient servant,
> F. Chopin.

A note was scrawled in the margin, presumably by the secretary:
'Request too late. Answered.' And the rest is silence. It was to be a
matter of some years before the Société deigned to accommodate this
upstart Pole.

Chopin was now twenty-two years of age, and still, from his own point of view, embarrassingly dependent on the financial support of his parents. 'It's a real problem to find students here,' he reported, quite accurately, '– almost as difficult as to organize a concert.' In the letters to his family he often concealed his anxieties and misfortunes, not out of shame but for fear of alarming them. We get a glimpse of the reality, however, from a letter written to his own parents by Antoni Orlowski:

> Dear Chopin sends you his warm greetings. He has been so depressed of late that sometimes when I go to see him we haven't the heart to say a word to each other. He is homesick. But please don't mention this to his parents. The truth is, things are bad here. There is great poverty among artists. The cholera is causing rich people to flee to the provinces. The worst of all is that none of the musicians, although they are as numerous as dogs, look like dying. If half of them would, the others might do better. Well, there's still time for it to happen.

There was, and it did. With memories of the summer still in his mind, Chopin might be forgiven for imagining that the disease was stalking him, and this time, interestingly, he makes no mention of the epidemic in any of his letters. Within three days of its outbreak in Paris, more than 300 cases were reported, and the situation rapidly worsened. In the hospitals the sick and the dying outnumbered the beds by three to one, and the daily toll grew so fast that the press ceased to report it. By mid-April it had reached 2,000 a day in Paris alone. The coffin-makers could not keep pace, and as George Sand notes in her auto-biography:

> The great movers' conveyances, now become the hearses of the poor, followed each other without let-up. Elsewhere, bodies were stuffed into old sacks and stacked pell-mell like so many lifeless bundles on carts, furniture vans, or any vehicle that could serve as a makeshift hearse. But what frightened me most was not the corpses but the absence of any kin behind these tumbrels; it was the drivers whipping up the horses, and quickening the pace with a curse; it was the passers-by, rushing frightened from the hideous cortege, and the despondent or apathetic expressions that stupefied all faces.

The worst casualties were sustained in the working-class districts in the east of Paris, where it was whispered that the plague had been deliberately unleashed to forestall a proletarian uprising. It would have been a remarkably short-sighted ploy. The cholera was no respecter of class, nor was any district immune. The evidence was all-pervasive: the most fashionable streets in Paris were blanketed with the contaminated clothes, linens and personal effects of the dead and the dying. Amazingly, given his frail constitution, Chopin escaped unscathed. His prospects, however, were hardly encouraging. Having weathered the July Revolution, Paris, indeed the whole of France, was plunged again into a sea of political turbulence and social unrest. The cholera had claimed 20,000 lives and devastated the economy, leaving much of the country in a state of poverty bordering on famine. Riots flared up all over Paris that summer, compounding the havoc already created by the cholera. The National Guard was called out to suppress the disruptions, and its fierce retaliation simply inflamed the situation all the more. As Jules Sandeau recalled:

> All Paris smelled of gunpowder, as though in the immediate aftermath of battle. The air was alive with a feeling of revolt, and a spirit of insurrection haunted streets, books and theatres. . . . Everything was called into question: social as well as religious institutions, husbands as well as gods and kings. All one heard was blasphemies against the laws, the savage ridiculing of marriage, and wild aspirations for a better future. Public places teemed with twenty-year-old legislators who found Christ somewhat aged and who wanted to supplant him in the task of guiding mankind.

The response of the authorities to this new threat of sedition was swift and merciless. The National Guard left in its wake a trail of bloodied corpses, hacked to death by bayonet and sabre or cut down in a hail of bullets. The morgue, its windows choked with stacks of human heads, quite literally overflowed. From beneath its doors, a thick red ooze ran like some infernal tributary over the embankment and into the Seine, itself already awash with bodies. The stench of putrefaction filled the air, and the stain of blood on streets and bridge could still be seen long after the rebellion had been crushed.

The consequences of all this were potentially devastating for Chopin. Of the few pupils he had managed to acquire, most had already fallen away, and the time was hardly ripe for another concert. Nor was he inclined to mount one. Quite apart from the nervous ordeal of the performance itself, he hated the prerequisites: the haggling with theatre managements, the hawking of tickets, the cajoling of singers and rehearsing of orchestras. In any case, Paris was in escapist mood. The only musicians who flourished in the summer of 1833 were to be found in the dance orchestras who plied their trade amongst the outdoor cafés on the Champs-Élysées. And playing a central role in their repertoire was a dance that Chopin was soon to make distinctively his own.

Interlude: Chopin and the Waltz

No form more typifies the glitter and grace of the Parisian salons than the waltz, and the Chopin waltz in particular, but in citing a certain symbiotic relation between them one must be wary of generalizations. There was no more equality among the Parisian salons than in any other social sphere, nor were they the sole progenitors of Chopin's waltzes. At some the guest list read like a *Who's Who* of the arts and sciences; at others the emphasis lay more on substance than on personalities, celebrities or otherwise. Whatever their status, however, they shimmered on the surface of a society in ferment. For the first time in European history, the commercial middle classes, not the landed aristocracy, were setting the pace: culturally, socially and economically. Where once the nobility had used art, and music in particular, as an agent of political distraction (and, indirectly, of oppression), the bourgeoisie now flaunted their ascendancy with an ostentation rivalling that of Louis XIV. The most conspicuous citadel of their taste for the spectacular was the Paris Opéra, dominated by Meyerbeer and reflected in the operatic pot-pourris that engorged the repertoires of virtuoso instrumentalists and in a worship of bravura that found its more individual expression in the institution of the benefit concert, to which Chopin was a sporadic and reluctant contributor.

More significant for music in general, however, and for Chopin's in particular, was the booming domestic market. No middle-class home worthy of a second glance could afford to be without a piano, and preferably a pretty daughter or a comely wife to play it. The ambitious bourgeois husband had a vested interest in the idleness of his women-folk, a wife with a job being the surest sign of an inadequate bread-winner, and few things could proclaim their homebound leisure more agreeably than a dainty demonstration of feminine 'accomplishments' at the keyboard. Nor were their attentions by any means confined to the demure and frothy. Cashing in on the mania for opera, a burgeoning music industry put out thousands of operatic medleys, variations on favourite scenes and arias and other confections rather more remotely associated with the stage. And for those unable to aspire to such heights, the publishers disgorged a torrent of pieces with no operatic connection whatever but which lured the prospective customer with the false promise of dramatic and arresting titles. In the humbler reaches of bourgeois aspiration, Paris in the 1830s resounded to the strains of *The Aeronauts – an Aerial Barcarolle*, and all for a price of two francs. A slightly greater outlay could net you more substantial fare, a particular favourite being *A Grand Characteristic Fantasy for the Piano, on the principal personages of the novel 'The Mysteries of Paris', dedicated to Monsieur Eugène Sue by T. Latour, formerly pianist and composer to his late Britannic Majesty King George the Fourth*. The novel in question consists of a lurid sequence of murders, frauds, seductions, rapes and suicides. Monsieur Latour's music, purporting to illustrate all this, consists of twenty-two solid pages of waltzes. At the same time, there was a curious inverse snobbery in the making, whereby an increasingly redundant aristocracy began to ape the habits and to cultivate the tastes of their increasingly powerful social inferiors. Indeed the rise of the waltz was itself a manifestation of this tendency.

Emanating originally from Austria and southern Germany, the taste for it swept across Europe like a kind of benign counterpart to political revolution and the ravages of cholera. Its benignity, however, was hotly disputed. The much-travelled musical historian Dr Charles Burney described the waltz as 'a riotous German dance, of modern invention'. And he continued,

> The verb 'walzen', whence this word is derived, implies to roll, wallow, welter, tumble down or roll in the dirt or the mire. What analogy there may be between these acceptations and the dance, we do not pretend to say; but having seen it performed by a select party of foreigners, we could not help reflecting how uneasy an *English* mother would be to see her daughter so familiarly treated, and still more to witness the obliging manner in which the freedom is returned by the females.

The objection, of course, was to the waltz's physical not its musical attributes. But Chopin himself had poured scorn even on these. 'Here,' he had written contemptuously from Vienna only months before, 'they actually call waltzes "works".' So, eventually, did he.

His own waltzes undoubtedly reached their finest flowering in Paris, but it was in Warsaw that he had first discovered and explored the form. Like the mazurka and many other folk dances, it was a dance in triple time with a characteristic emphasis on the second beat, and some of

Chopin's earliest examples might easily be confused with urbanized mazurkas. Curiously, they also anticipate the tone and style of composers whose works were unknown to him. The beautiful A flat Waltz of 1830, for instance, sounds remarkably like Brahms (as yet unborn), while the slightly earlier E major might almost be Schumann. Chopin's Polish waltzes have little of the dash and bejewelled elegance of his Parisian works, and unlike most of their later siblings could easily be danced to, the notion of the idealized 'concert' waltz then being in its infancy. They retain something of the formalized grace and slower speeds of the minuet, with its courtly undertones, and follow their simpler structure. Only in the brilliant E minor of 1830 do we get a real foretaste of the Chopin waltz in its fullest maturity. With its cascading introduction, the panache of its almost militaristic repeated notes and its virtuoso coda, it found its way for many decades into the repertoire of virtually every performing pianist and belongs there still.

With few exceptions, the poignant A minor, op. 34, no. 2, foremost among them, Chopin's mature waltzes are sparklingly extroverted affairs, shamelessly ingratiating, pianistically elegant and emotionally refined. Shrewdly designed for the ears of the salonistes and the fingers of the more advanced dilettantes, they assured Chopin's success both socially and commercially, and more perhaps than any of his other works have enjoyed a popularity that shows no sign of abating. That they have survived the surfeit of dross that once threatened to submerge the bourgeoisie of five continents is due entirely to the art that lies behind them and to their Mozartian reflection of hidden depths beneath the surface. The ever-popular C sharp minor is both fashionably wistful and genuinely profound, but requires an artist of special reserve and insight to reveal both dimensions (different as they are, the recordings of Lipatti, Rubinstein and Horowitz are unsurpassed in this regard). That the A minor should ever have been published as a 'Grande valse brillante' is a spectacular offence against the celestial Trade Descriptions Act and a perfect example of nineteenth-century commercialism at its crassest, the only accurate term in the title being 'valse'. In spirit and technique, it lies closer to Mozart's equally subtle Rondo in the same key and, like that work, requires restraint, variety and technical control in equal measure if it is not to sound merely coy. That Chopin himself gave the title to what was avowedly his favourite waltz is both interesting and revealing, the compromise between art and Mammon being blatant but solely verbal. If the A minor is unique in tone amongst Chopin's waltzes, it is wholly characteristic in its refinement. With a handful of unimportant exceptions, the Bolero, Tarantella, bourrées, écossaises, Galop marquis and maybe one or two others, Chopin made no qualitative distinction between 'light' music and any other. Sketches, alternative versions and anecdotal evidence indicate that he lavished almost as much care, attention and energy on these outwardly frivolous pieces as on his most cherished and hard-wrung works.

Where lesser composers, and some less fastidious greater ones, were often content to string together a sequence of waltz tunes like so many beads, Chopin took special pains over the structure and continuity of his waltzes, and the organic principle of developing variation lies in one way or another behind most of them, even when they appear unashamedly sectional. Musical analysts can expose layer upon layer of thematic correspondences and derivations, some of which are useful in revealing the inner, often unconscious logic of the compositional process, many of which are content with arid observation, and all of which are irrelevant to all but the pedant if their functions are not audible. When Mark Twain observed that 'Wagner's music is better than it sounds' he scored a neat, critical bullseye.

One of the miracles of Chopin's waltzes is the variety of utterance that he discovers within an outwardly rigid framework, dominated by the square, relentless four-bar phrase, with its equally relentless oom-pah-pah accompaniment. Where his mazurkas revel in jagged rhythms and asymmetrical groupings, the waltzes flow with an apparently seam-less regularity, a foreground of steady quavers often veiling a kaleido-scope of rhythmic and melodic shapes which will emerge under the hands of all but the most typewriterish players. And as usual, Chopin casts his net wide, drawing on the luscious thirds and sixths of Italian opera and combining them with the elusive cross-rhythms and harmonic ambiguities of the mazurka. No 'respectable' waltzes were ever more replete with syncopations. Like Beethoven, Chopin was a master of rhythmic synthesis, using time-patterns to connect what was formerly separated and to extend what formerly seemed complete. A case in point is the very first waltz, op. 18, where the temporal motto of the first main group (♩ ♫ ♩) serves to underpin the contrasting second group, thus providing an organic link between the two. More characteristic still, however, is his reversal of its original rhythmic function. Where before it had an upbeat, forward drive, it now assumes a passive, backward-looking role, thereby enhancing the new section's nostalgic character. Like Beethoven, too, Chopin often tellingly exploits the shift-ing tensions of the scale (though never quite so explicitly as Beethoven in, say, the finale of his First Symphony, where their varying degrees of expectancy are illustrated with characteristic clarity and wit).† In the waltzes, Chopin often uses the phenomenon to countermand the metre, with its implacable tripleness, achieving in the process an extraordinary flexibility. Take, for instance, the intrinsic duality of the right hand in bars 17–20 of the F major, op. 34, no. 3, or the entire opening section of the A flat, op. 42, from bar 9 onwards. In the waltzes, as elsewhere, Chopin's creation and deployment of contrasting characters (both related and discreet) is hardly less vivid or subtle than Mozart's, and requires no less subtlety from the performer. No composer understood better than Chopin that in music context alters content. The pianist who 'merely' repeats what Chopin *appears* to repeat is playing only half the music.

Perhaps the most characteristic feature of Chopin's waltzes is their combination of rhetorical gesture and intimate reflection, again, a typical Mozartian trait. It was never his intention that they should be performed as a cycle, *à la* Schumann, but the fact that they can be is a tribute to the extraordinary resourcefulness of his imagination.

† These can be felt even without Beethoven's rhythmic teasing, simply by following his melodic sequence on the piano, beginning with C: 1–2–3; 1–2–3–4; 1–2–3–4–5; 1–2–3–4–5–6 and so on, each time assessing the relative sense of completeness accruing to the last pitch of each segment.

— 5 —

The Dandy and the Dilettantes
1833–1837

At this point Chopin's biography becomes somewhat muddled. Two stories have successfully weathered a century and a half of Chopin scholarship, despite the fact that no evidence has come to light to substantiate either. One tells us that Chopin in desperation now contemplated travelling to the United States, as a number of other prominent pianists had done; the other has it that a chance meeting with Prince Walenty Radziwill led to a dinner at the home of Baron James de Rothschild, after which Chopin's playing so moved the Baron's wife that she implored the young Pole to accept herself and her daughters as pupils. After that, the story concludes, no young lady worthy of the name could afford *not* to have lessons with Chopin. It could have happened, although the absence of evidence is puzzling. Whatever the reason, Chopin's fortunes did take a dramatic upward turn at about this time. From then, he derived most of his very considerable income neither from performing nor from the publication of his music, but from teaching.

As the new year dawned, Chopin could hardly believe his luck. In mid-January he wrote to a friend:

I have found my way into the very best society; I have my place among ambassadors, princes, ministers – I don't know by what miracle it has come about, for I have done nothing to push myself forward. But today, all that sort of thing is indispensable to me.

As a consequence, he gave it his unremitting attention:

I have five lessons to give today. You will probably imagine that I am making a fortune – but my coach and white gloves cost more than that, and without them I should not have a *bon ton*. I am all for the Carlists, I hate the Louis-Philippe crowd; I'm a revolutionary myself so I care nothing for money, only for friendship.

In one thing only was Chopin a revolutionary, and that was his music. With every step closer to the citadels of fame and fashion, he grew outwardly more conventional in his manner, appearance and conduct. Not only his gloves and coach, but his clothes and coachman, his man-servant, his hairdresser (a daily requirement), the decoration of his apartment, to say nothing of its location, all these required a heavy outlay of the money he professed to disdain.

Chopin's rapid progress to the hub of Parisian society conferred on him a unique distinction. Even when appearing at the houses of the great and mighty, professional musicians in 1833, and for many years thereafter, were traditionally ushered in at the tradesmen's entrance. Nor were they then expected to mix with the company or partake of the provender (in London, and still later in New York, even the most famous artists were sometimes literally cordoned off at one end of the drawing room, like so much livestock). That Chopin was excepted from these rituals is revealing. There is a direct and significant conflict between the very fact of his social ascendancy and the claims, noted in Chapter 2, that beyond the essentials of a general education he was interested in, and knowledgeable about, little other than music. The aristocrats of Paris, French or otherwise, were more than merely wealthy; they were highly educated, broadly cultured and uniquely cosmopolitan in both outlook and experience. Is it likely that they would have welcomed into their midst, and for many years, a provincial musician whose interests barely exceeded the means of his own liveli-hood? It is true that Chopin stood largely apart from the Romantics' obsession with literature, but not, as has often been suggested, that he was insensitive to it: his nine-year liaison with George Sand, one of the century's most prolific and versatile writers, should be evidence enough of that. As a child, partly because of the infectious enthusiasm of his sisters, he showed a keen interest in poetry, both Polish and French, and occasionally attempted it himself. While never aspiring to the role of poet, he enjoyed writing verses, much as he enjoyed mimicry and caricature. The enthusiasm waned somewhat as he grew older, but there was one notable occasion in his adult life when he drew up precise instructions for the furnishing of his home, written entirely in verse. Despite his own talent for drawing, his enjoyment of painting and sculpture seems to have been casual rather than intense, but he showed considerable discrimination in the choice of pictures which he displayed in his rooms. He was not, strictly speaking, an intellectual himself, but he was at ease in their company, as they were in his. If he was not as widely read as his colleagues Berlioz, Liszt and Mendelssohn, he was far from ignorant. He read regularly at night, and a book was always by his bedside. But these were incidental virtues, for those who chose to see them in that light. What counted more with them was Chopin's quick intelligence, his charm, his ready wit – and, of course, his music. Or more to the point, his playing of it. At the keyboard he was a sorcerer.

On no one, however, did the young Chopin have a more profound effect than on Liszt, his exact contemporary and likewise an immigrant from eastern Europe. Also a former child prodigy, Liszt was a more complete virtuoso at the keyboard, if only by dint of a range that embraced the extremes of tempo, volume, mood and texture with equal, and unprecedented, mastery. And Chopin was unhesitating in his acknowledgement. As he famously put it in a letter to Ferdinand Hiller,★ a mutual friend: 'I write to you without knowing what my pen is scribbling because at this moment Liszt is playing my studies and putting honest thoughts out of my head: I should like to rob him of the way to play my own studies!' As a composer, however, Chopin's creative odyssey was already well advanced while Liszt still paddled in the shallows. He might well have returned the compliment by wishing he could steal from Chopin the way to *write* such studies. From the beginning, their friendship was tainted by a mixture of admiration and envy that precluded genuine intimacy. To a man of Chopin's fastidious cast of mind there was something repellent in Liszt's incorrigible showmanship, the more so for a competitive streak alien to Chopin's nature. Indeed, while he enjoyed the admiration and friendship of such various colleagues as Mendelssohn, Berlioz and Schumann, he was never able fully to reciprocate it. He could enjoy their company, but not their music or their aspirations. Nor could he fully enjoy their praises, which arose, in his view, from a misconception of his purpose. With the basic tenets of Romanticism – the exaltation of feeling over form, the cultivation of literary, autobiographical or programmatic allusions, the pursuit of sensuality and the picturesque – he was fundamentally at odds. As a gregarious expatriate Pole, living in Paris with halting French amid a crowd of idolatrous admirers, he nevertheless felt himself, at some level, to be three times isolated: geographically, socially and artistically.

At the same time, Chopin's avid cultivation by the Parisian aristocracy was a threefold blessing. In addition to its obvious social benefits, it provided him with a guaranteed and appreciative audience for his

pianistic and compositional accomplishments – an audience whose very
selectivity pandered at once to his innate elitism and relieved him of the
need to mount further public concerts, always an ordeal for him.† Most
importantly, however, it ensured a steady stream of affluent pupils
whose fees enabled him to live comfortably in the style to which he
had all too rapidly become accustomed. That most of them were high-
born and admiring young ladies was a double bonus, which appealed
to his vanity and nourished his innate snobbishness.

Nowhere, perhaps, has Chopin been more misrepresented than as a
teacher. The picture of him as a languid dandy, taking the easy option
by humouring the aspirations of comely dilettantes on their way to the
fashionable altar, is both inaccurate and unfair to his pupils. True, many
of them were not immensely talented, but virtually all of them were
serious about their studies. And Chopin reciprocated, treating them
with the seriousness they deserved. Nor, in accepting them, did he feel
demeaned or compromised as a teacher. Indeed there are few more
inspiring musical exercises than the study of his pupils' reminiscences.
Of those who left detailed accounts, none was more influential than
Karol Mikuli, who was struck from the outset with Chopin's dedication.

> Chopin daily devoted his entire energies to teaching for several hours
> and with genuine delight. Was not the severity, not so easy to satisfy,
> the feverish vehemence with which he sought to raise his pupils to
> his own standpoint, the ceaseless repetition of a passage till it was
> understood, a guarantee that he had the progress of the pupil at heart?
> A holy artistic zeal burnt in him then, every word from his lips was
> stimulating and inspiring.

Was it, perhaps, this 'holy artistic zeal' that made Chopin so uneasy
about receiving his pupils' fees? Whatever the reason, his students, by
prior arrangement, discreetly left their payment on the mantelpiece,
thus sparing him the embarrassment of confronting a business trans-
action. The alliance of Art and Mammon, so essential to his chosen
mode of life, made him conspicuously uneasy throughout his career,
despite his often rancorous dealings with publishers. Although the
'genuine delight' cited by Mikuli was a highly variable commodity,
there can be no doubting Chopin's commitment to his pupils. As Maria
von Harder recorded: 'Chopin was a born teacher; expression and con-

---

† Here again we find him a chip off the old Zywynian block – a man whose
sensibilities were often firmly rooted in the aesthetics of the eighteenth century.
'Concerts,' he once said, 'are never real music. You have to give up the idea of
hearing in them all the most beautiful things in art.'

ception, position of the hand, touch, pedalling, nothing escaped the sharpness of his hearing and his vision; he gave every detail the keenest attention. Entirely absorbed in his task, during the lesson he would be solely a teacher, and nothing but a teacher.' Nor did he subscribe to a single approach. While he often worked closely with the student at improving the performance of a work just played, there were also lessons where, like Liszt in later life, he would teach almost wholly by example. Entire lessons often passed without the pupil playing more than a few bars. And the deciding factor was rarely the performance just given; more often it was determined by a particular student's mood and psychological make-up. As Émilie von Gretsch put it at the time:

> It's wonderful to see how tactfully Chopin puts one at one's ease; how intuitively he identifies, I might say, with the thoughts of the person to whom he is speaking or listening; with what delicate nuances of behaviour he adapts his own being to that of another. To encourage me, he tells me among other things 'It seems to me that you don't dare to express yourself as you feel. Be bolder, let yourself go more. Imagine that you're at the Conservatoire, listening to the most beautiful per-formance in the world. Make yourself want to hear it, and then you'll hear yourself playing it right here. Have full confidence in yourself. Forget you're being listened to, and always listen to yourself. I see that timidity and lack of self-confidence form a kind of armour around you, but through this armour I perceive something else that you don't always dare to express, and so you deprive us all. When you're at the piano I give you full authority to do whatever you want; follow freely the ideal you've set for yourself and which you must feel within you; be bold and confident in your own powers and strength, and whatever you say will always be good. It would give me so much pleasure to hear you play with complete abandon that I'd find the shameless confi-dence of the "*vulgaires*" unbearable by comparison.'

But his practical approach could be just as illuminating and more immediately applicable than his psychological perceptions, however subtle. One of Chopin's outstanding virtues as a teacher was his meth-odical demonstration of practice technique. He taught his pupils how to work, and with clear results. Gretsch discovered that, too, and in some of the most technically demanding music ever written: 'Chopin showed me the best way of practising his études – and what a special joy it was to me to be able to play easily what had previously seemed to involve the most perilous difficulties.' He had, too, an intuitive (indeed prophetic) grasp of problem-solving psychology, advising his pupils never to practise too long at a time, but rather to interrupt their practice sessions with frequent, mind-refreshing breaks, whether it was reading a good book, studying some masterpiece of art or sculpture or simply taking a walk. He understood both the activity and the passivity of learning and regarded excessive practising as positively dangerous. He advocated a maximum of three hours' daily practice (including exercises, études and repertory pieces), and when one of his pupils boasted of practising six, he was treated to a rare display of Chopin's anger. At the same time, elsewhere in the city, Liszt was practising, and making his pupils practise, three hours a day on finger exercises alone. Only then did they begin on repertoire. Here, as in much else, Chopin and Liszt were poles apart. Indeed Chopin had a horror of mechanistic practising in any form. Like Liszt and virtually every other teacher, he did assign his pupils certain exercises, but stressed at all times that they were not to be regarded as mechanical in any way. The simplest five-finger exercise was to be treated as music and was of only limited use unless it claimed the entire concentration and imagination of the pupil. It was first and foremost an exercise in hearing – more than that, of listening. It was only by this means that one acquired true muscular control and relaxation. From the beginning, Chopin's definition of technique was centred on sonority: a mastery of the piano's tonal properties was for him the necessary precursor of virtuosity. As he wrote himself: 'One needs only to study a certain positioning of the hand in relation to the keys to obtain with ease the most beautiful quality of sound, to know how to play long notes and short notes and to attain unlimited dexterity. . . . The only well-formed technique, it seems to me, is one that can control and vary a beautiful sound quality.' This, indeed, is the very essence of Chopin's approach not only to teaching but to every aspect of pianistic life. The experience recollected by one pupil was the experience of all: 'He made me practise first of all constantly varying the attack of one single note, and showed me how he could obtain diverse sonorities from the same key, by striking it in twenty different ways.' Chopin's entire approach to playing the piano, as to writing for it, was highly individual, and currently unfashionable. 'Everything,' he wrote, with characteristic simplicity, 'is a matter of knowing good fingering. . . . Just as we need to use the conformation of the fingers, we need no less to use the rest of the hand, through the wrist.' His views on the 'conformation of the fingers' were both original and heretical.

For a long time we have been acting against nature by training our fingers to be all equally powerful. As each finger is differently formed, it's better not to attempt to destroy the particular charm of each one's touch but on the contrary, to develop it. Each finger's power is determined by its shape: the thumb having the most power, being the broadest, shortest and freest; the fifth-finger as the other extremity of the hand; the third as the middle and the pivot; then the second, and finally the fourth, the weakest one, the Siamese twin of the third, bound to it by a common ligament, and which people insist on trying to separate from the third – which is impossible, and, fortunately, unnecessary.

The third finger, being the longest and most central finger, was, for Chopin, best suited to the kind of broad, singing tone that he revered above all others and whose model is to be found in the human voice.

He did not confine his piano-teaching to the instrument itself, however, but recommended that his pupils should also have singing lessons, and insisted that they undertake basic theoretical studies as well, if they were not already so grounded. Any work selected for study, Chopin's or otherwise, was carefully analysed for its formal structure, as well as for the feelings and psychological processes which it evoked. These analyses were not only illuminating in themselves but trained the pupil never to dissociate technique from mental work. In effect, if not in words, Chopin anticipated Theodore Leschetizky's evergreen injunction: 'Think ten times, and play once.' The testimony of his pupils repeatedly suggests that there was no aspect of piano-playing which Chopin did not address: posture at the piano, phrase structure, the singing tone of a musical line, dynamic contrasts, rhythm, the principles of ornamentation, and perhaps most crucially of all where his own music was concerned, the uses of the pedals. 'The correct employment of the pedals,' he would say, again and again, 'remains a study for life', and significantly, he advised his pupils to use them 'with the greatest economy'.

It would be interesting, if ultimately futile, to explore the degree to which Chopin's revolutionary approach to writing for the piano was determined by the accident of his particular physical characteristics. '*Souplesse avant tout!*' he would reiterate. Nor did his requirements stop with the hand and arm. He advised his pupils, 'Have the body supple, right to the tips of the toes.' As his pupil Dubois reported: 'Suppleness was always his greatest object. He would repeat, ceaselessly, "*facilement! facilement!*" [easily! easily!]. Stiffness quite exasperated him.'

Chopin's own suppleness bordered on the freakish, particularly in the context of his celebrated improvised mimes. According to his friend and pupil Gutmann★ 'he could, like a clown, throw his legs over his shoulders', while Stephen Heller recalled how amazing it was: 'to see one of those small hands expand and cover a third of the keyboard. It was like the mouth of a serpent which is going to swallow a rabbit whole. In fact, Chopin appeared to be made entirely of rubber.' As more than one witness observed, his fingers seemed to be without any bones. And surprisingly, given his generally fastidious and demanding nature, he could be as flexible in his attitudes as in his joints. He was quite capable of saying, as he did to the fourteen-year-old Karl Filtsch, admittedly his most brilliant pupil: 'We each understand this music differently [his own E minor Concerto], but go your own way, do it as you feel it, it can also be played like that.' It all depended, however, on what day you happened to catch him. From Lenz we hear: 'Chopin could not bear anyone to interfere with the text of his works. The slightest modification was a gross error for which he would not pardon even his closest friends, not even his fervent admirer Liszt.' On the other hand, as another pupil repeatedly discovered, you could adhere with religious fervour to his printed markings and still incur his disapproval:

> Over six months I played this Nocturne [op. 15, no. 2] at Chopin's and every time I began to play it as Chopin had shown me at my previous lesson, he would sit down at the piano himself, saying 'But it's not that at all!', and he would play it completely differently from the time before.

Many others confirm the impression that for Chopin, composition was a continuously evolving process, that the inspired improvisation through which many of his works came into being never ceased, despite his best efforts. As the same time, he was rigorous to the point of pedantry in his approach to other men's music. Camille Dubois witnessed a striking case in point:

> I remember once seeing Chopin in a blue rage over a fermata in Liszt's transcription of [Beethoven's] *Adelaide*, a dreadfully platitudinous fermata, a stain deposited by Liszt on Beethoven's marvellous cantilena. Chopin had just received the *Gazette musicale* issue containing this transcription, and his anger would not subside, he just could not get over this wretched pause, he railed on and on about it. He seemed to feel a kind of indignant regret towards his former comrade-in-arms.

Of all composers, the one whose name he most invoked in lessons was Bach. 'Practise Bach constantly,' he would tell his pupils. 'This will be your best means to make progress.' But there were others too, of course. Hummel, Field, Clementi and Scarlatti also played a central part in Chopin's teaching.

Karol Mikuli spoke for many when he wrote: 'One can say without exaggeration that only Chopin's pupils knew the pianist in his entire, unrivalled greatness.' And after them came those lucky enough to hear him in the close quarters of the salon. There he was in his element. It would be a mistake, though, to assume that because Chopin shunned the public concert he was inattentive as a teacher to the requirements of projection in performance. However lost to the world he may have appeared to be while playing, Chopin was never unaware or disrespectful of his audience. While never storming the heavens as Liszt did, he fully understood the needs and applications of rhetoric, and addressed them in his lessons. As Mikuli recalled:

> On declamation and performance in general, he gave his pupils invaluable and sensible instructions and hints, and conveyed his meaning by repeatedly playing not merely single passages but whole pieces, and this with a conscientiousness and enthusiasm that listeners in a concert hall could never have had the opportunity of hearing.

Not least because Chopin seldom gave them the chance. Not once in 1833, his first year as the uncrowned darling of the salons, did Chopin play a solo work in public. Nor, according to our present knowledge of Chopin chronology, did he write much of any consequence, with the exception of a handful of mazurkas (op. 17 and op. 24). On the whole, he matched the character of his music to the character of his heady new circumstances. The elegantly virtuosic Variations brillantes, op. 12, and the Introduction and Rondo in E flat, op. 16, are salon music *par excellence*: solid gold compared with the confections dispensed by such minor salonistes as Herz and Hünten, but dross, albeit high-class dross, compared with his own nocturnes (op. 9) and études (op. 10) of the preceding year.

Unlike Clementi,* Hummel, Czerny and Liszt, Chopin did not create any kind of a 'school' or establish a tradition. Partly, perhaps, because he did not live long enough, partly too because, as Liszt put it, he was 'unfortunate in his pupils'. This isn't to say that they were necessarily second-rate. Princess Marcelina Czartoryska, one of Chopin's most faithful disciples, for instance, was by all accounts a quite extraordinary pianist. But she was a princess, and like Chopin's other aristocratic pupils, her social rank ruled out any kind of professional career, whether it was playing or teaching. She and her kind simply were not in a position to establish and nourish a pianistic tradition. As for the professionals, or those who might have been professionals, several died young (Karl Filtsch was dead at fifteen) or they chose other paths. But then Chopin's teaching was no more oriented towards the concert life than he was himself. In no sense did he regard himself as either a trainer or a coach. His fame as a teacher spread all over the world and people travelled great distances in the hope of having lessons with him. At one time or another his pupils came not only from France and Poland but from Russia, Bohemia, Austria, Germany, Switzerland, Britain and Scandinavia. Many other hopefuls never got near him. He was heavily protected by his admiring friends, and just getting to meet him was something of an accomplishment.

Chopin divided his year equally between teaching and composition. From October to May he taught virtually without a break, every day, from eight o'clock in the morning until early evening, with lessons ranging in length from forty-five minutes to several hours, depending on the talent and stamina of the individual pupil. There is no doubt that Chopin's teaching was significantly influenced by the fact that as a pianist he was basically self-taught (Zywny having been principally a violinist) and though he always acknowledged his compositional debts to Elsner, his real masters, when it came to composing, were Mozart and Bach. One of the keys to understanding Chopin's music is a recognition of his debt to Bach in particular. Because his style is so much his own, and so different in character from Bach's, it is easy to overlook the degree to which it too is polyphonic. Polyphonic textures pervade his music, most rigorously in the development section of the B minor sonata's first movement, but also in such popular dance forms as the mazurka: the end of the C sharp minor mazurka, op. 63, no. 3, for instance, is hardly less striking in its contrapuntal weave.

The mazurkas contain some of Chopin's most original and elusive music, and he played them, apparently, with a subtlety of rhythm that not even his most gifted students could approach. According to several witnesses, he would lengthen the first beat of the bar to the point where the piece sounded almost as if it were in duple rather than triple time, a pulse of two or even four in a bar rather than the pulse of three, which is actually written. There is a famous account of Meyerbeer dropping in on a lesson while Chopin was teaching the Mazurka, op. 33, no. 3, and casually pointing out that Chopin was both teaching and playing in 2/4 time. Chopin icily denied it, Meyerbeer stood his ground and if

Chopin had been a bigger and stronger man the pair of them might have come to blows. Meyerbeer, apparently, was never forgiven. Yet the same thing happened some time later with the pianist Charles Hallé, but on that occasion Chopin just laughed and explained that the ambiguity was a national characteristic of Poland, and a particular feature of the original folk dance.

Since Chopin himself was so compounded of irony and contradictions and so often indecisive in life, it seems somehow appropriate that one of the lynchpins of his teaching, and his playing, should have been ambiguity. Or rather, and this may well be the single most important function of the interpreter, the *control* of ambiguity. With Chopin it was almost always a case of rhythm. Part of the secret of his particular kind of songfulness lay in the potential for complete independence of the hands. And that boils down to rhythmic independence. Meyerbeer's problem with that mazurka crops up in many different kinds of pieces. The second étude in Chopin's op. 25 set is most obviously a study in delicate tone-painting, but, more importantly, it is a study in rhythm. As written, it is a combination of two contrasting groups of three: a slower group of three in the left hand set against a faster group of three in the right hand. But because of the way in which they interact it is almost impossible to prevent the ear from hearing the right hand part as a sequence of fours. And that's the trick.

Another feature of Chopin's teaching, as of his playing, and his writing, was a quite new concept of sound, which depended absolutely on the use of the sustaining pedal. The effect was sometimes of a pianist with four hands, but again the object was never out-and-out virtuosity. It was colour, contour, legato – and freedom. Not an arbitrary freedom, but the soaring flexibility of the great *bel canto* singers. Again and again Chopin urged his pupils to study the great opera stars and to emulate them. Indeed he used to tell them point blank: 'You have to sing if you wish to play.'

Interlude: Chopin and the Étude

Chopin's twenty-seven études mark the summit of all works composed with an overtly didactic purpose. Every one of them is first and foremost a work of art, no two are alike, and almost all of the first set, the twelve of op. 10, were completed before he reached the age of twenty-one. Many of them, and the underlying concept of them all, can be traced to his early immersion in Bach, the only other composer to have combined so consistently the requirements of art and instruction at the very highest level. Like most of the preludes (many of them studies in all but name), the études are predominantly focused on a single technical problem – the rapid expansion and contraction of the hand (as in op. 10, no. 1), quicksilver scales and trills in double thirds (op. 25, no. 6), the combination of two or more outwardly conflicting rhythms (op. 25, no. 2) and so on – and on a single musical idea.† This emphasis on singularity, rather than on a sequence of contrasting themes, is a direct throwback to the Baroque; Baroque, too, is the high incidence of polyphonic writing and a degree of harmonic daring, often achieved through melodic suggestion rather than in chordal blocks, which is both worthy of Bach and prophetic of Wagner, Debussy and even Schoenberg (op. 10, no. 6, for example). Harmonically speaking, Chopin was the most subversive composer of his day, extending chromaticism to the brink of atonality at a time when such procedures were unheard of.

As in his playing, so in his music, Chopin lacks the range of Liszt, and, contrary to widespread belief, his études are by no means all-encompassing in their scope. Pianists wanting to shore up the cracks in their trills, tremolos, broken octaves, hand-crossing and chordal skips and the *martellato* alternation of the hands will do better elsewhere – Liszt really *does* deal with all the principal categories of a pre-twentieth-century technique. Chopin's études, as befits the descriptions of his playing, are preponderantly studies in various forms of legato. Where Liszt exploited the essentially percussive nature of the piano, which is,

---

† There are exceptions, however. Op. 10, no. 12, for example, contains as many as eight different pianistic figures.

after all, an instrument in which strings are struck, and in which every note begins at its loudest and then rapidly diminishes in strength, Chopin does all in his power to transcend it. In many ways he seems to anticipate Debussy's ideal of the piano as an instrument without hammers.† To this end, he requires the almost continuous use of the sustaining pedal as a primary source of colour, though he will very seldom employ it as what Artur Schnabel used to call 'pedal glue': Chopin's legato is to be achieved by the fingers alone, the pedal being more a source of ever-shifting light, sometimes helping to emphasize the harmonic rhythm, sometimes deliberately blurring it. Interestingly, there is no instance of his ever having called in the score for the *una corda* (or 'soft') pedal, though its use is prescribed with some frequency by Beethoven, and still more so by Schumann and Liszt. But the études are by no means confined to the study of legato. Op. 25, nos. 4 and 9, for instance, are primarily studies in the fine control of staccato, and the middle member of the *Trois Nouvelles Études* is devoted specifically to the combination of legato and staccato articulation.

Like Bach's didactic works, Chopin's are music first and studies second. Not one has a hint of the schoolroom. If the Étude in A minor, op. 10, no. 2, sounds like glorified Czerny, its basic point has been missed, and the same can be said for the C minor Prelude from Book I of Bach's *Well-tempered Clavier*. But while Bach's cover a wide expressive range, they have nothing like the emotional intensity of Chopin's. The 'Revolutionary' Étude, op. 10, no. 12, is as powerful as emotion gets, within the confines of a work of art. No 'study' had ever been asked to contain such tragic force before, and the C minor which closes the op. 25 set equals it, while achieving, if anything, a still greater rhetorical sweep. The simplicity in the Étude in E major, op. 10, no. 3, is of heartbreaking poignancy if played with suitable restraint (sadly, it is probably the most abused of all the études), and the dramatic excitement and drive of op. 10, no. 4, is of breathtaking immediacy – unusually for Chopin, the two hands here have almost identical material, deployed in an alternating sequence of right and left. Nowhere does Chopin's love of opera find more eloquent testimonial than in the Étude in C sharp minor, op. 25, no. 7. Nor has the left hand ever been entrusted with a more bewitching exercise in sustained cantilena. This

---

† Indeed, more than any composer before him, Chopin revealed the hitherto untapped resources of so-called 'harmonics' – that rainbow of overtones released through the sympathetic vibration of strings not struck themselves but set in motion by the striking of a single note or group of notes below.

extended operatic *scena* for the keyboard is the work of a master colourist, a melodist without superior and a harmonic visionary at the height of his inspiration. Never was an étude less étude-like. No less masterly, though less obvious in their challenges, are the *Trois Nouvelles Études* of 1839, originally intended for inclusion in the *Méthode des méthodes*, masterminded by Fétis and Moscheles. Here the accent is on the subtlest ramifications of rhythm, colour and articulation.

At the time of their composition, the Chopin études constituted the most idiomatic music ever conceived for the piano. They have earned their place in history through their unflagging ingenuity in the context of the highest artistic aspiration, for their intrinsic beauty, and *variety* of beauty, and for their implacable rejection of crowd-pleasing tricks like Thalberg's famous 'three-hand' illusion. They set a standard by which all subsequent études must be measured.

— 6 —

Priming the Pump
1834–1836

Success in society did nothing to lessen Chopin's ambivalence when it came to performing. If anything it only strengthened his dislike of public concerts. After the privacy of his own apartments, the aristocratic Parisian salons, with their hand-picked audience and their relative intimacy, were his favoured venues, but even there he could be curiously retiring. Ferdinand Hiller remembered one such evening:

> The conversation was quite animated, and everything would have been fine had it not been for poor Chopin who sat timidly in a corner, almost unnoticed. But Mendelssohn and I knew that he would soon have his turn, and we anticipated it with pleasure. The piano was opened; first I played, and then Mendelssohn. When we asked Chopin to give a sample of his art too, everyone looked at us and him with surprise. But the moment he had played a few bars, everyone present, and above all Schadow, stared at Chopin with amazement – there was no doubt that they had never heard anything like it. When he finished, all were entranced and implored him to play again and again.

And by that time he generally obliged.

While Chopin played no solo concerts in 1833, he did appear several times in combination with others, most notably with Liszt, whose flamboyance was already putting a strain on their friendship. Nor can one rule out a measure of envy: had he been *able* to dominate orchestras and public alike with even half of Liszt's success, who is to say he would not have enjoyed it? As it was, he clearly prided himself on his superior education and took comfort in the fact that his natural refinement gave him an entrée into the highest circles, where Liszt, for all his acknowledged genius, was still regarded by many as a presumptuous social climber.

Justly or not, Liszt in his early manhood was never far from the whiff of sexual scandal. Dazzlingly handsome and incomparable as a pianist, he was also dangerously attractive to women, who often lost all restraint in his company, particularly after hearing him play. Women threw their jewellery on to the stage, they shrieked in ecstasy, they fought, scratched, bit and kicked each other over the gloves he contrived to leave on the piano or the snuff-boxes which he happened to mislay. One lady succeeded in retrieving the butt of a cigar Liszt had smoked and sequestered it in her bosom to her dying day (in what condition one daren't enquire).† And like most sexually attractive men, he returned the compliment, not always very discreetly. His unauthorized use of Chopin's flat for the seduction of another man's wife‡ did irreparable damage to their friendship.

Chopin, while altogether more retiring and guarded, could no longer fail to notice that he too was attractive to women, although not, generally speaking, the same women, and not in the same way. Where Liszt fired their loins, Chopin engaged their hearts. There was something mysterious and fascinating in the aura surrounding him, an elusive air of self-containment and hidden depths that was clearly reflected in his looks. It was at around this time that the critic Ernest Legouvé came to know him, 'an elegant, pale, sad young man, with brown eyes of an incomparably pure and gentle expression, and chestnut hair almost as long as Berlioz's and falling on his forehead in the same way'. 'Chopin,' he wrote, 'can best be defined as a *trinité charmante*. His personality, his playing and his compositions were in such harmony that they could no more be separated than can the features of one face.' Anyone doubting the accuracy of this perception need only turn to the nocturnes of 1835 (the C sharp minor and D flat major, op. 27, nos. 1 and 2) for confirmation. If ever one could 'see' a composer's face in his music, it is here – the haunting, dispossessed brooding of the former matched by the sensual melancholy and delicacy of the latter. Each finds Chopin in his finest, most uncompromising vein. The subtle, iridescent harmonies, the variety and originality of texture, the masterly integration of

---

† Even when he was a wen-covered, white-haired old man in a cassock, his effect on women was mesmeric. His power, however, transcended matters of gender. When he left Berlin after a series of concerts in the 1840s, he rode in a special carriage drawn by six white horses and was accompanied to the city limits by thirty coaches-and-four, packed with students, while thousands of others swarmed around him on foot. Not only were the streets and squares crowded with people but all the windows along the way were filled with spectators.

‡ Marie Pleyel, née Moke, an accomplished pianist herself and wife of the piano manufacturer Camille Pleyel.

contrasts, and above all, perhaps, the depth and directness of emotional utterance are light years beyond the reach of John Field. In no other composer, with the possible exception of Debussy, do we find a similar combination of temperament, intellect and sensuality contained within a framework of such perfectly proportioned craftsmanship. Small wonder that Debussy admired Chopin above all others.

To deny Chopin his sensuality would be a form of false piety. But it was an idealized, not a carnal sensuality. And few who encountered this *trinité charmante*, male or female, would have questioned its essential purity. From the very beginning of his years in Paris, Chopin had been much fussed over by women, who found in his combined sophistication and unworldliness, as in his elegant reserve and implicit vulnerability, a charm it was difficult to resist. Reciprocating their innocent flirtation without succumbing to seduction, he fast became an adept in the politics of sex. He appears to have found great satisfaction in the silent, mutual acknowledgement of libidinous desire without any intention of carrying it further. Unlike the carnivorous Liszt, he was no seducer. The thought appeared more pleasing to him than the act. Husbands, and not only the jaded (of which there were many), looked on with unconcern. Even had Chopin desired to take things further, his highly developed sense of gentlemanly behaviour, buttressed by a natural inhibition and that fear of rejection common to all shy people, would not have allowed him to proceed. There is, in any case, nothing to suggest that Chopin during this period was anything other than chaste. Indeed his sexuality remains for the most part a closed book, proof against the massed pryings of biographers and psychologists alike. Beyond two cryptic references in his letters to the unidentified 'Teresa' and the 'lady vocalists' who would willingly 'join in duets', there's no indication of any kind that Chopin in his mid-twenties wasn't still a virgin. Such evidence as has been cited in the past has now been authoritatively discredited, but it retains its diehard adherents, and because it tells us something interesting about Chopin by emphasizing what he was not, it justifies a brief digression. It concerns an allegedly torrid affair, marked by an almost complete abandonment of inhibition, with a woman who certainly played a part in Chopin's life and was among those present at his death.

Not the least of Delfina Potocka's appeal for Chopin was the fact that she was Polish; nor did it hurt that she was titled. For all that he loved Paris and the life it had to offer, it was only in the company of his fellow Poles that he could feel completely relaxed, all the more so when they were musicians – and the Countess Potocka was certainly that.

Eugène Delacroix was only one of many who were enchanted by her: 'I have heard her sing twice before,' he wrote in his journal, 'and thought I had never met with anything more perfect, especially the first time, when it was dusk, and the black velvet dress she was wearing, the arrangement of her hair, in fact everything about her . . . made me think she must be as ravishingly beautiful as her movements were grace-ful.' Indeed she had a way with men. In the words of another admirer,

> Here is a woman in the prime of her years, stately as a Greek statue; her nose has a strangely delicate contour, her eyes are gentle and sweet, on her lips there is a passionate desire for kisses that promise a heaven of delight, and above all this, a sombre, high forehead, as though veiled by a cloud of mourning; whether it is furrowed by a whim or by the thorn of disappointment remains an unsolved and all the more tempting mystery.

The writer Zygmunt Krasinski took a wider and more cynical per-spective:

> She is a Don Juan in petticoats, a woman whose ardent, strong soul, truly endowed in highest measure with all the gifts that God has lavished upon Polish women, has been spoilt by Paris and London etc. . . . Nevertheless, in this soul there remain smouldering fires that become volcanic explosions when memory or some very strong pain fans them; there remains a passionate long desire . . . for a higher con-dition in the world, a nobler sphere for the mind. . . . When these fires die out or slumber, however, she is unbearably capricious, incapable of uttering two serious words, obsessed with a need to laugh and joke in order to escape the terrible boredom that gnaws at her.

Interestingly, the 'evidence' of Chopin's fling did not surface until 1945, when a Polish scholar, Pauline Czernika, claimed to have unearthed a series of hitherto suppressed letters (or typed copies thereof) in which Chopin refers in the most forthright language to their sexual adventures, using the key of D flat as a codeword for the Countess's notoriously hospitable vulva, and directly attributing his own artistic inspiration to sexual abstinence, a view of creativity put forward by Freud (the concept of 'sublimation') many years after Chopin's death, but well within the lifetime of the mentally unbalanced Mme Czernika, in his monograph on Leonardo and elsewhere. 'Chopin' speaks here of 'husbanding [his] strength and life-giving fluids': 'Let the creator, whoever he may be, drive women away from him, and the strength collecting in his body will not go into his cock and balls but will return to his brain in the form of inspiration. Think,' he allegedly goes on, 'how much of that precious fluid and strength I have lost, ramming you to no purpose. . . . God knows how many of my finest inspirations and musical thoughts have been lost forever. Perhaps Ballades and Polonaises, even a whole concerto, have all vanished up you.'†

A remarkable number of scholars and biographers seemed ready to accept Czernika's evidence at face value. Yet what evidence was there? Not a single original document, nor any photograph or facsimile thereof; nothing but typescripts allegedly copied from originals, which then conveniently vanished into thin air. Now there is no doubt whatever that many people's sexual lives are strikingly at variance with their appearance and demeanour. Conversations, propositions, acts and words are regularly shared and spilt between the sheets of lovers who betray no hint of such 'depravity' in any feature of their public life. There is thus nothing inherently implausible in the idea that Chopin, in the fever of sexual arousal, might have uttered any or all of the things attributed to him by Mme Czernika. Would such behaviour, however, have been confined to his relations with Delfina Potocka? There is no evidence that he ever approached this sort of abandon with George Sand, with whom he lived for nine years and who was already notorious for her own sexuality when he met her. Nor was she ever reticent in talking or writing about sex. That her daughter Solange openly talked about 'No-sex Chopin' is hardly conclusive evidence for anything, but added to the whole picture it is not without interest. And does the following passage ring true as the words of the man who suffered his love for Constantia Gladkowska in painful silence rather than brave rejection by declaring himself?

I always look at lovely women with admiration and if one of them inflames me into a passion I pull her into my bed. . . . To these women I used to give my bed, my body and a little life-giving fluid, but none of them had my heart.

Ironically, it is when they stray outside the bedroom that the Czernika letters are most suspect. Nowhere in his extensive correspondence, not even to his most intimate friends (male or female), does Chopin ever

† If the Freudian theories ostensibly espoused by him in the Czernika letters are true, they serve only to undermine the case for Chopin's 'ramming' of Delfina, since the period during which he is alleged to have done so coincides with the production of some of his most powerful and significant works: the B flat minor Sonata (whose Funeral March had been composed two years earlier), the op. 37 nocturnes, and the op. 41 mazurkas, to name only a few.

refer to George Sand by her baptismal name, yet here we find repeated references to 'Aurore', and still more improbably 'Sandowa' (a term unknown in any other context). Rarely in his authenticated correspondence does Chopin discuss his own creative processes, and even then with great brevity and reluctance. In the Czernika letters we find repeated references to his 'creation', in one case using the Polish word *tworczosc* almost forty times within a few pages. The term is not to be found once in the authentic correspondence. Similar inconsistencies abound. At many of the times when Chopin and Delfina are supposed to have been devouring one another in bed, she has been proved beyond doubt to have been elsewhere. In fairness to Czernika, however, it should be said that rumours of Chopin's sexual relations with Potocka were current at the time. Otherwise he would not have taken the trouble to deny them to Liszt and others.

*   *   *

No such denials were necessary in the well-documented case of Maria Wodzinska, the youngest sibling of three brothers who had boarded with Nicholas Chopin in Warsaw. On Chopin's several visits to the Wodzinski estate in his teens he had formed the friendliest relations with the entire family, and had enjoyed giving piano lessons to the little Maria, who was nine years his junior. Following the abortive revolt of 1830, the family had escaped its immediate aftermath, some of them moving to Switzerland, one to Dresden, another, eventually, to Paris. In 1834 Chopin received an invitation to visit the family in Geneva. This proved impracticable, for lack of funds, but some months later, by way of a goodwill message he sent a copy of his most recent waltz (op. 18), inscribed 'To Mlle Marie, from her former teacher'. In his memory she was still a little girl of twelve. Eleven months were to pass before he discovered for himself the difference wrought by five years in a young girl's development. In the meantime, his travel plans were dictated by welcome and unexpected news.

In the summer of 1835, Chopin's parents left Warsaw on a trip to Carlsbad in Germany, the first time either had journeyed outside Poland. They arrived at the spa late on the night of 15 August to find Frédéric already installed at their hotel. At four in the morning they roused him from his sleep and after a tearful reunion embarked upon a month of unalloyed happiness. Later that day they joined in a collaborative letter to Ludwika and her husband (she had married in 1832 and now had two children). 'Our joy,' wrote Chopin, 'is indescribable.'

We never stop embracing one another – what more, after all, can we do? But oh what a pity we can't all be together here. Yet how good God is to us! I simply can't write sensibly – better not to try and think of anything today, only bask in the happiness that we all feel! I find our parents exactly the same, though a trifle older, of course. We go for walks arm in arm with darling Mama; we talk endlessly about you all, we imitate the tantrums of my little nephews, and we tell each other again and again how much we've all been thinking of each other. I am at the summit of my happiness! In my joy I smother you with kisses, you and my brother-in-law – my dearest friends in all the world.

Three weeks later, Chopin accompanied his parents on the first leg of their homeward journey. They parted at Tetschen, near the Polish border, never suspecting that it was the last time they would see one another. It was here, too, on 15 September, that Chopin wrote out his first draft of the entrancing A flat Waltz, which we know today as op. 34, no. 1, a work that captures his mood at the time with a wonderful precision: youthful energy and joy, coupled with a selfless exaltation at his own powers, but with passing hints, too, of the melancholy and nostalgia that come with parting. We get a charming thumbnail sketch of him at that time from the daughter of their host at Tetschen, Count Anton Thun-Hohenstein: 'Chopin,' she wrote, 'is an extraordinarily decent, modest and merry human being, and he kept us all in stitches with his talent for imitations – especially his mimicking of an Englishman who spoke broken French.'

The departure of his parents was quickly succeeded by another reunion, whose earlier postponement he had already marked with another waltz, of equal grace and ebullience. On his return to Paris he passed through Dresden, where the Wodzinski family were visiting a relative. Here Chopin discovered with a body-wide blush that the little Maria had matured into an extremely attractive young woman – and, what is more, a highly accomplished pianist. He was not the first to fall in love with her on sight (the poet Slowacki had preceded him, producing one of his finest works in the process; so had Charles Louis Napoleon Bonaparte, the future Emperor of France), but fall in love he did, and it was not long before she reciprocated. By the time he resumed his homeward trip in mid-September, Chopin may not have declared himself verbally (shades of Constantia), but he left Maria with two musical mementos of their days together: one was another waltz in A flat, like its predecessor, although in other ways it could hardly be more different, the other was a fragment, the opening bars of which were to become his most popular nocturne, the one in E flat, op. 9, no. 2, which he had written some three years earlier. The waltz, later published as op. 69, no. 1, is full of tender yearning and dream-sweet melancholy; the nocturne, too, is distinctly lovelorn, despite the message to Maria scribbled at the top: 'Soyez heureuse' ('Be happy'). It is interesting that he should have chosen to write it in French, especially in view of her pride in his Polishness.

They were to meet again, with important consequences for both, but for the moment Chopin tried to focus his mind on the immediate future. En route to Paris he stopped in Leipzig, where he renewed his friendly acquaintance with Mendelssohn and met Schumann for the first time. There, too, he heard the sixteen-year-old Clara Wieck* (later Schumann's wife) and later declared her to be 'the only woman in Germany who can play my music'. With Schumann himself, the first non-Pole to recognize his importance and hail him publicly, Chopin never felt very comfortable. He could not reciprocate Schumann's enthusiasm for his music, which he felt, in any case, that Schumann did not understand, nor, despite his profession of friendship, could he greatly warm to the man, as he did to such a disparate spirit as the flamboyant Berlioz. With Mendelssohn there was mutual affection and respect, and mutual ambivalence. Despite his sometimes disturbingly inconsistent accounts, there is no doubting the scale of Mendelssohn's enthusiasm. In the immediate aftermath of Chopin's visit, he wrote to his sister Fanny,

> There is something fundamentally personal and at the same time so very masterly in his playing that he may be called a really perfect virtuoso. . . . It was a joy to be once again with such a real musician, and with someone who has his own perfectly defined manner. And if that manner is far removed from my own, I can nevertheless get along with it splendidly. . . . It really was a sight to be seen on Sunday evening when I had to play him my oratorio [St Paul] while inquisitive Leipzigers crowded on tiptoe so as to be able to say they had seen Chopin. Between the first and second parts of the oratorio he dashed off his new studies and latest concerto to the astonishment of the Leipzigers, and then I went on with my St Paul just as if an Iroquois and a Kaffir had met and conversed!

And he adds, interestingly: 'Before he left, my copies of Handel's works arrived and Chopin showed a quite childish joy over them.' Chopin's curious combination of sophistication and childishness remained with him all his life – another bond with Mozart. Like Mozart, too, he was irredeemably unworldly when it came to the management of money, hence his earlier inability to visit the Wodzinskis in Geneva. In faraway Warsaw, his father grew steadily more anxious:

> I must go on repeating that as long as you've not put a couple of thousand francs to one side, I shall regard you as one to be pitied, notwithstanding your talent and all the compliments you receive. Compliments are so much smoke, which will hardly keep you alive in times of need. May God preserve you from poor health, or else you will be reduced to poverty in a foreign country. Such thoughts often trouble me, for I see that you spend as fast as you earn and can't take the slightest little trip at your own expense, even within France itself. Don't go and think I want you to be mean; not at all: I simply want to see you less careless of the future.

Almost as if to bear his father out, at Heidelberg, *en route* at long last from Leipzig to Paris, Chopin fell seriously ill with bronchitis. When near the end of October he recovered sufficiently to complete his journey, he was still far from well; in November he suffered a second and worse attack, this time coughing up blood and succumbing to feverish hallucinations. Holed up in his apartment, he kept himself so secluded that he was widely rumoured to have died. Just how widely is indicated by an entry in the *Warsaw Courier* as late as 8 January 1836:

> We wish to inform the many friends and admirers of the eminent talent of the virtuoso Frédéric Chopin, that the reports of his death which have been circulating are without foundation.

Chopin's response to this unnerving item was to write a will. To this day there is nothing to explain why he should suddenly have ceased to communicate with his family and friends. Was he distracted by thoughts of Maria Wodzinska? Had he grown so self-centred that the anxiety of his parents, from whom he had parted so fondly in September, never entered his head? Or could it be that he was already daydreaming about marriage to Maria and wanted to conceal his ill-health from his prospective in-laws? If those were his thoughts, then he was premature. When in the following autumn, after a blissful month in Maria's company, he did in fact propose, Mme Wodzinska, in the absence of her husband, expressed delight at her daughter's acceptance but enjoined the pair to secrecy while putting Chopin to a test he could ill afford to fail. Fearful of her husband's anxiety over Chopin's health (not assuaged by the published rumours of his death), and knowing that it must be allayed if his consent were to be forthcoming, she warned Chopin to stay well, *'for everything depends on that'*.

> Until all is settled, I ask you to say nothing. . . . Rest assured that I am on your side, but we must take precautions if my wishes for you are to be fulfilled. We must allow time for the feelings of both parties to be tested. . . . You must go to bed by eleven and drink only *eau de gomme* [an aromatic syrup]. Do keep well, dear Fryderyk. I give you my solemn blessing like a loving m. . . . [mother?]

How long this period of probation was to be she did not say, but two weeks later she returned to the theme with a hint of reprimand:

> I gather that you were not telling the truth when you solemnly promised to obey my orders, for you don't say a word about wearing woollen stockings with your slippers or going to bed before eleven. You speak only of Kunzel lying. Speaking of whom, he is now back, and sulking because you did not go to see the Kaskels. Moreover, a number of people are now angry at me, thanks to you, and I am losing my good name on your account. . . . I will write more from Warsaw, but now I must repeat: Take care of your health, if all is to be well.

As a prospective mother-in-law she was already wearing thin. But she had a point. Despite his somewhat feeble protestations to the contrary, Chopin was not following Wodzinska's orders, nor was he ever likely to. His gregarious habits were too deeply ingrained. Come winter, he paid the price and fell ill again, this time with influenza, against which his own mother had specifically warned him. With Maria's brother Antoni in Paris, word of Chopin's illness swiftly reached Poland, to which the Wodzinskis had returned in November. From this point onwards, it becomes clear from the surviving correspondence – and the lack of it – that Chopin the suitor had lost. From the beginning, Maria herself seems to have communicated almost exclusively through post-scripts to her mother's letters. From the outwardly passive role she appears to have adopted in these 'secret' negotiations, it is difficult to detect anything more intense on her part than a passing and reasonably diverting infatuation. On the other hand, as the teenaged daughter of an aristocratic family in the 1830s she would have been expected to keep her feelings to herself, and to submit entirely to the will of her parents. The effect of the whole affair on Chopin may be gauged by the fact that he gathered together his letters from the Wodzinskis, binding them into a packet labelled *'Moja Bieda'* ['My Misery'], and preserving it among his papers for the rest of his life.† It would seem to be no coincidence that the Funeral March, which was to become his most famous composition as the heart of his B flat minor Sonata, was composed at around this time. Mingled with the pain of his dashed hopes was a newly intensified sense of his own Polishness and of his self-elected exile. The reunion with his parents at Carlsbad and the Wodzinskis in Dresden can only have heightened in him that sense of apartness, which, ironically, ruled out his return to Poland, for like them, he could now have gone back without fear of reprisal. Artistically, he had long since outgrown Poland and yet would never see himself as French. Despite his celebrated talents as a mimic, he spoke his adopted language with a pronounced foreign accent and never acquired anything like the fluency of a native. Marooned, as he felt, by fate, and with his hopes of matrimony dashed, he turned again to the piano and produced in the B major Nocturne, op. 32, no. 1, a musical parable of love and loss whose surprise tragic ending is as powerful, in its way, as anything he ever wrote. It was neither the first nor the last time that he turned a minor musical heritage into a major artistic achievement. As an alchemist he was without superior.

† Maria's marriage in 1841 to Count Joseph Skarbek was unhappy and ended in divorce eight years later. Her second husband was, like Chopin, tubercular but lived on for many years, Maria herself dying in 1896 at the age of seventy-seven.

Interlude: Chopin and the Nocturne

From the very beginning of the published sequence it is clear that Chopin's nocturnes inhabit a world of inspiration and resourcefulness quite beyond the dreams of John Field, whose own examples, extraordinarily insipid by comparison, initially inspired them. From Field Chopin took the name and the general concept of a dreamy melody over a broad-spanned, lilting harmonic accompaniment, relying on a liberal use of the sustaining pedal and offset by a contrasting middle section before a reprise of the opening material. Like Field's, they cultivate a lyrical, non-virtuosic style (with one stupendous exception), and conform to the taste for moodscapes that persists to this day but that then enjoyed a fashionable novelty. Comparisons of Chopin's earlier nocturnes with some of Field's leave no doubt that the influence was both real and conscious, but the qualitative difference is incomparable. In the subtlety and power of their harmonies, the extraordinary flexibility of their rhythmic invention and the unprecedented suppleness and significance of their ornamental melody, Chopin's nocturnes are in a class of their own. That identity of style and substance, which blossomed so luxuriantly in his youthful concertos, reaches its apotheosis in the nocturnes, and their far-reaching effects on composers as distinctive and distant as Scriabin, Debussy, Rachmaninov and Ravel are clear to anyone with the analytical tools to explore them. That they do not lend themselves easily to verbal elucidation is demonstrated by the well-meaning and highly informed attempts of innumerable worthy academics whose prose is as heavy as their books. Nor are performers always as helpful as they might be. In concert and on record, the nocturnes are frequently confined in a metrical strait-jacket which obscures the very feature that renders them most miraculous: their transcendence of that 'fearful symmetry', to borrow Blake's phrase, which has menaced the unimpeded flow of music ever since the thirteenth century. In his nocturnes Chopin accepted the four-square, rhythmically divisive constraints of the poetic stanza and proved them capable of almost infinite manipulation. His Mozartian conception of rubato was born of an intuitive understanding that freedom, even the concept of freedom, derives both its nature and its power from the perception of order and that constraint at some level is, indeed, a prerequisite of freedom.

Taken as a whole, the nocturnes may not give us Chopin at his most adventurous. Many of them are the work of a supreme craftsman who has shrewdly gauged his audience, of an artist who is readier to seduce than to provoke, although at no cost to his musical integrity. Nevertheless, they also contain some of the most beautiful and resourceful music he ever wrote, and in at least one instance a stroke of originality that places him in the avant-garde of his day. The C sharp minor Nocturne of 1830, a work of quite haunting beauty, was discovered among Chopin's papers after his death and remained unpublished for a further twenty-six years. Also known as the *Lento con gran espressione*, after the instruction that lies at its head, the work was dedicated to his sister Ludwika 'to practise before playing my Second Concerto', an indication of her own capabilities at the piano, born out not only by the difficulty of the concerto but by the extraordinary notation of a tune from it in the nocturne itself. In the original version the tune is written out in 3/4 time, as in the concerto, against an accompaniment in 4/4, the time signature of the nocturne – no mean feat to play, and a fascinating documentation of Chopin's Mozartian definition of rubato: that the metrical pulse sustained by the left hand should remain impervious to the rhythmical liberties allowed to the right. That Chopin should even have thought of such a notation in 1830 is remarkable in itself. This sort of polymetrical combination is normally regarded as a twentieth-century development. Chopin seems to have concluded that it was more than the average pianist could be expected to handle, and subsequently 'normalized' it. Apart from its revolutionary aspect, the piece is notable for one of Chopin's most poignant and inspired melodies, full of *gran espressione* yet of a simplicity and intimacy which linger in the mind long after the notes have faded. If Chopin's request that his unpublished manuscripts be destroyed had been heeded, we would have been without both this and another, earlier nocturne, the E minor already mentioned in connection with his sister Emilia's death. Quite apart from its intrinsic merits, there is something extraordinarily moving about the fact that this broad yet tightly disciplined elegy came from the pen of a seventeen-year-old.

The nocturnes are very much the children of their age, an age in which 'subjectivity' and the mood of the moment ruled supreme. They are as much studies in feeling as they are musical artefacts, and this, together with their relative freedom and simplicity of form, has rendered them the most imitable branch of Chopin's work and the most easily

abused. More than any other of his works they helped to establish
his reputation for soulfulness and manipulative sentimentality. This is
particularly true of those, like the famous E flat, op. 9, no. 2, in which
he remains closest to his Fieldian model. Here, *par excellence*, we find
the fashionably pallid poet, dipping his pen in moonbeams and flooding
the world with lovelorn melodies. The apotheosis of this strain is
undoubtedly the D flat, op. 27, which contrives, too, to be an unsurpassed jewel of craftsmanship in every sense: in its uniquely delicate and
seductive sonorities, in the extraordinary, *bel canto* elaborations of its
melody, in its harmonic subtlety and its Classical proportions. Its
immediate predecessor, op. 27, no. 1, in C sharp minor, is an altogether
different but in no way inferior marvel, daring, mysterious, anguished
(in its turbulent middle section), even sinister. It would be hard to
sustain a charge of sentimentality here. At the opposite pole to the early
E flat Nocturne is the late one, in the same key, which closes op. 55.
Here we find the apotheosis of Chopin's contrapuntal leanings. The
polyphony is worthy of Palestrina, the ingenuity of the part-writing and
the textural variety worthy of Bach, the rhythmic complexity worthy of
Messiaen. This is no longer 'salon' music, but a work of the very highest
sophistication and intellectual acumen, all the more remarkable for being
cast in a *bel canto* style fit to ravish the ear of even the least demanding
music lover. Here 'feeling' and 'mind' are indissolubly wedded in a
perfect manifestation of the art that conceals art. And it is precisely the
skill of the concealer that has led both to the widespread underestimation
of Chopin by generations of critics and to the near-universal popularity
that has been enjoyed by his music, without interruption, for more than
a century and a half.

— 7 —

Majorca, Misery and the Muse
1837–1839

On 13 December 1836 Chopin penned a brief note to a Polish friend, Joseph Brzowski: 'I am having a few friends here today, among them Mme Sand; moreover Liszt is to play and Nourrit† will sing. If it will give Mr Brzowski any pleasure I shall expect him this evening.' Not much of a note, perhaps, but an historic one nevertheless, for it marks Chopin's first mention of George Sand. Born Amandine Aurore Lucille Dupin in 1804, making her six years Chopin's senior, she was one of the most controversial and prolific novelists of her time and, with the sole possible exception of his mother, the most important woman in Chopin's life. From her very beginnings she was never far from the whiff of scandal (being the illegitimate daughter of Marshal de Saxe), nor did she make any attempt to escape it. When she was eighteen she married Casimir, Baron Dudevant, thereby acquiring a title and a husband whom she left nine years later, taking their two children, Maurice and Solange, with her to Paris, where she proposed to earn her living from literature. She derived her masculine pen-name from the first of her many lovers, the writer Jules Sandeau, and since 1831 had set Parisian tongues a-wagging with her forthrightly erotic novels *Indiana* (1832), *Valentine* (1832), *Lélia* (1833) and *Jacques* (1834).

On the face of it, she was the very antithesis of Chopin in almost every respect. Where Sand was flamboyant and volatile, Chopin was reserved, formal and a fastidious follower of fashion; where she was rugged and outdoorsy, he was polished, a little delicate and conspicuously urban; while she was descended from the nobility and cultivated the company of peasants, he was of humble origins but consorted with royalty; where she espoused socialism and egalitarianism, he clung to the badges of tradition and the aristocracy. Together they were to

† One of the great lyric tenors of the nineteenth century.

become one of the oddest couples of the century, but on first meeting, however, Chopin found her frankly repellent. Dressed in men's clothing and brandishing cigars, she cultivated controversy with an apparently compulsive bravado. 'When we went home,' Frederick Hiller wrote to Liszt, 'Chopin said to me: "What an unsympathetic woman! *Is* she really a woman? Almost, almost I doubt it."' He was neither the first nor the last. According to the Countess d'Agoult, her transvestism was curiously convincing.

> When dressed as a man she had a casual air, and even a youthful, virile grace. Neither the outline of her breasts nor the prominence of her hips betrayed her feminine sex. Nothing – be it the tight-fitting black velvet redingote, the high-heeled boots, the tie wrapped around her rather plump neck, or the man's hat cocked cavalierly over her thick locks of short hair – could detract in any way from her uninhibited manner or the nonchalance of her bearing. She gave the impression of quiet strength.

Opinion among men was sharply divided. To Gustave Flaubert, she was 'that man who calls herself George'; to the poet and playwright Alfred de Musset, another of her lovers, she was unambiguously 'the most womanly woman I have ever known', and he knew more than a few. Honoré de Balzac wavered; at one moment she was 'a writing cow' but later a 'nightingale in her nest . . . great-hearted, generous, devout, and *chaste*'. She was certainly chased. While not conventionally beautiful, she sparked the fascination and excited the desires of men and women alike, of many different ages and from widely divergent pasts. The German poet Heinrich Heine, one of the most penetrating observers of the Parisian scene, wrote about her at some length:

> Her forehead is not high, her delicious chestnut brown locks reach her shoulders. Her eyes are somewhat languid, at least they are not brilliant, and their fire may have been dimmed by many tears, or may have consumed itself in her works, which have lighted conflagrations in all the world, have illumined many a dark prison cell, but also set on fire some temples of innocence. . . . A good-natured smile usually plays around her lips, but it is by no means provocative. Only her somewhat protruding lower lip suggests sexuality. Her shoulders are beautiful, no, magnificent. Ditto, arms and hands, small like her feet. Her breasts I leave to others to describe, as I confess incompetence. Her body is a bit thick and seems too short. Only the head bears witness to her idealism and reminds me of the finest examples

of Greek art. In this connection one of our friends likened her to the Venus de Milo in the lower hall of the Louvre. Yes, George Sand is as beautiful as the Venus de Milo; she even excels her in some respects – for example, she is much younger. She speaks naturally and with great charm. . . . She possesses nothing of the bubbling *esprit* of her compatriots, and nothing of their verbosity either. Her silence, however, is not due to modesty or her absorption in somebody else's concern. She is monosyllabic because of pride, not thinking it worthwhile to waste her intellect on you, or because of self-centredness, taking in the best of your thoughts to incorporate them later in one of her books.

'And,' he adds, 'she endowed our much beloved Frédéric Chopin with a good deal of worldly wisdom.'

No less controversial than Sand's conduct and bearing was her writing. Many deplored her, yet Heine rated her above Victor Hugo. Her works were enthusiastically devoured by Dostoevsky, Thackeray, Henry James and Marcel Proust. To Elizabeth Barrett Browning she was quite simply 'the finest female genius of any country or any age'. Baudelaire was less complimentary: 'She is stupid, she is ponderous, she is long-winded. Her moral ideas have the depth of judgement and delicacy of feeling of those of concierges and kept women.' On the whole, it has to be said that posterity has sided with Baudelaire.

George Sand's entry into Chopin's orbit coincided with the disintegration of his marital hopes for Maria. He was vulnerable, and she was predatory. In October 1837 she returned to Paris from her country estate at Nohant in the Berry district and called on Chopin, who had attracted her interest from the start. She detected at once a change in his attitude to her. If it was true then, how much truer was it a month later when he confided to his journal, in reference to a meeting the details of which remain unclear: 'I was quite overcome; my heart was conquered. . . . She understood me. . . . She loves me.' The stage appeared to be set for a new act, but the leading lady then retired to the country so as not to arouse the suspicions of her current lover, the playwright Félicien Mallefille, who was installed at Nohant as her children's tutor.

In the meantime, Chopin (presumably unaware of Sand's present dilemma) carried on with his teaching, wrote relatively little and published less. In March he made one of his rare solo appearances as a pianist, reaping a harvest of praise the like of which even he had never experienced. As Ernest Legouvé put it: 'Chopin, once heard, can never be forgotten. . . . He left his audience stunned, moved and intoxicated. . . . Throughout the entire performance the hall quivered with electricity and rippled with murmurs of ecstasy and astonishment. . . . On, Chopin! On! . . . Henceforth when the question is asked "who is the foremost pianist in Europe, Liszt or Thalberg?" let all the world be able to reply, like those who have heard you, "It is Chopin!"!' It was during this period, too, that he received a signal honour from an unexpected source. The improbably named Russian Ambassador to France, Count Pozzo di Borgo, extended to Chopin an invitation to become court pianist in St Petersburg, a position which would guarantee his freedom from financial anxieties for the rest of his life. But the Russians had misjudged him. In terse terms, he declined the offer: 'Even if I did not take part in the Revolution of 1830, my sympathies were with those who did. Therefore I consider myself an exile: it is the only title to which I am entitled.'

At just what point he qualified for the title of 'lover' we shall never know. By April Sand had returned to Paris and was using Chopin's presence as a ploy for attracting distinguished guests to her dinner parties. To Delacroix, for example, she wrote: 'I must tell you that Chopin will play to a small group of us, quite informally; and it is at such times that he is really sublime.' They were seeing ever more of each other, but from an astonishing letter which she addressed in June to Chopin's most trusted friend in Paris, Count Wojciech Grzymala, it seems clear that Chopin, while tempted, was holding back. The letter, which extends over some forty-seven pages, is surely one of the most extraordinary documents ever to fall into a biographer's hands. It tells us more about both Sand and Chopin than any other single source, and it is therefore printed here, not complete but at length.

Let us state the question clearly, since my entire future behaviour will depend upon your answer. . . . Your gospel becomes mine when it ordains that one must put one's own happiness *last*, and banish it from one's mind when the happiness of those we love claims all our strength. Listen carefully, then, and give me a clear straightforward and categorical answer. This young lady [Wodzinska] whom he wants or ought, or thinks he ought, to love, is she the right one to secure his happiness or is she likely to deepen his sufferings and melancholy? I am not asking whether he loves her or whether she returns his love, or whether he loves her more than me. I have a pretty good notion, judging by my own feelings, of what must be going on inside him. What I want to know is which of the *two of us* he must forget or give up, if he is to have any peace or happiness or indeed any life at all, for his nature seems too unstable and too frail to stand up to great anguish. Had I known that there was a prior attachment in our dear boy's life and a feeling in his mind, I would never have bent down to breathe the scent of a flower intended for some other altar. He too would surely have warded off my first kiss if he had known that I was as good as married [to Félicien Mallefille, her lover at the time]. We did not deceive each other, we surrendered to the passing gale which carried us away for a while to another world.

For myself I refuse to give way to passion, although a very danger-ous fire still smoulders sometimes deep in my heart. The thought of my children will give me strength to crush anything that might part me from them or from the mode of life which is best for their edu-cation, health and well-being etc. . . . Besides, there is a noble crea-ture [Mallefille], *perfect* in respect of love and honour, *whom I shall never give up*, because he is the only man who, having been at my side for nearly a year, has not intentionally caused me a minute's pain, no, *not a single minute*. He is, moreover, the only man who has surrendered to me completely and absolutely, without regret for the past or reservations for the future. And then his nature is so good and kindly that I could in time bring him to understand everything and know everything [about her past]. *His happiness is sacred to me.* So much for myself: pledged as I am and bound up fairly closely for some years I cannot wish that our *dear boy* should for his part break the bonds which restrain him. Were he to come and place his life in my hands I should be greatly alarmed, for since I am responsible for another's happiness I could not take the place of someone *he* might have left for me. I feel that our love can only last in conditions such as those in which it was born, that is, that when from time to time a favourable breeze wafts us towards each other we should take a trip to the stars and then separate for the return to earth, for we are the children of Mother Earth and it is not God's will that we should follow our earthly pilgrimage side by side. Heaven is where we shall meet, and the fleeting moments we shall spend there will be so divine that they will equal a whole life spent in this vale of tears.

There is another supposition that it is right for me to mention. It may be that he no longer loves this *childhood friend* at all and may even feel a real repugnance to forming a lasting bond. . . . Be assured, my friend, that I who loathe seducers and am always on the side of women when they are seduced and betrayed, I who am called the defender of my sex, and glory in the title, I have in cases of necessity used my authority as a sister, a mother and a friend to break off more than one such engagement. As for the question of [physical] possession or non-possession, that seems to me one which is secondary to the question we are now discussing. It is, however, one which is important in itself since therein lies a woman's whole life, her dearest secret, her most carefully thought out system, her most mysterious seductiveness. . . . I have no preconceived notions, no fixed habits, nor, I think, any false principles either in the direction of licence or restraint. I have largely trusted to my instincts, which have always been noble. I have sometimes been mistaken about other people, but never about myself. . . . Above all, I have believed in faithfulness, as I have preached and practised it. Others have failed me in this respect, and I have failed them. And yet I feel no remorse because whenever I have been unfaithful I have been the victim of a kind of fatality, of my own instinctive urge towards the ideal, which compelled me to leave what was imperfect for something which seemed closer to perfection. . . . So far I have been faithful to whomsoever I have loved, perfectly faithful in the sense that I have never deceived anyone, and have never ceased to be faithful unless I had very strong reasons, which, through another's fault, had killed my love. . . . I am so used to giving my exclusive affection to one who loves me truly, so slow to take fire, so accustomed to living with a man without reflecting that I am a woman, that I was rather disturbed and frightened at the effect this little person [Chopin] had on me. . . . And since I am telling you everything, I wish to say that one thing only in him displeased me; namely, he had false reasons for abstaining. Until then, I found it beautiful that he should abstain out of respect for me, out of timidity, or even out of faithfulness for someone else. There was an element of sacrifice in all that, and hence strength and chastity, as properly understood. It was that which charmed and allured me the most in him. But at your house, just as he was leaving, and as if to overcome a final temptation, he said two or three words which did not at all correspond to my way of thinking. He seemed to despise (in the manner of a religious prude) the coarser side of human nature and to blush for the temptations he had had, and to fear to soil our love by a further ecstasy. I have always loathed this attitude to the final embrace of love. If this last embrace is not something as holy, as pure and as sacrificial as the rest, no virtue lies in abstaining from it. This phrase 'physical love', which is used to convey the idea of something whose name is known only in Heaven, *displeases* and *shocks* me as being at once a blasphemy and a false idea. Can there be, for lofty natures, a purely physical love, and for sincere natures a love which is perfectly intellectual? Can there ever be a love without a single kiss, and a kiss of love without sensual pleasure? *To scorn the flesh* can only have a wise and useful meaning for creatures who are nothing *but* flesh; but when two people love each other it is not the word *scorn* but *respect* that should be used when they abstain. In any case, those were not his actual words. He said, I think, that 'certain actions' might spoil our memories. It was foolish of him to say that, wasn't it. And can he mean it? Tell me, what wretched woman has left him with such impressions of physical love? Poor angel. They should hang all women who make vile in men's eyes that which in all creation is most holy and most worthy of respect, the divine mystery, the sublimest and most serious act of universal life. . . . Don't say a word to the boy [Chopin]. . . . I simply must have you at Nohant this summer. As soon as for as long as you can. You will see how pleasant it is: no spying, no gossip, no provincial neighbours; it's an oasis in the desert. There's not a soul for miles around who knows what a Chopin or a Grzymala is. No one knows what goes on in my house. As for the boy, he can come if he likes, but in that case I should like to be notified in advance because I shall dispatch Mallefille either to Paris or Geneva.

In her letter, Sand shows an almost Chopinesque ambivalence: should she keep Mallefille on as her lover, while snatching stolen moments with Chopin? Or should she abandon him and bestow her favours on Chopin alone? And what should she do while making up her mind? As long as he remained sequestered at Nohant, Mallefille was easy enough to forget, but when he chose to accompany Sand to Paris, where their liaison was well known, the logistics of deceit grew more challenging. George rented an attic room near the home of her friends the Count and Countess Marliani in the Rue Lafitte, under the pretence that she needed it for her work. More devious still was her adoption of a new identity. Her landlord and neighbours knew her only as Mme Dupin. Chopin, by now aware of his delicate position, and having, unlike Sand, a horror of scandal, was only too happy to fall in with the deception. By the time she dispatched the unsuspecting Mallefille and her delicate son on a tour of Normandy in August, it seems clear that Sand and Chopin had finally become lovers. Why else would this highly sexed and widely experienced woman now speak of 'the delicious exhaustion of a fulfilled love'? For a month they enjoyed unlimited access to one another, and in a letter to Delacroix she wrote 'There has not been even the slightest cloud in our clear sky, nor any grain of sand in our lake', adding, 'I begin to think there may be angels in the guise of men.' It was the first of her many 'heavenly' references to Chopin, and he returned the compliment in kind. With the reappearance of Mallefille in September, however, clouds and sand combined in an emotional tornado that had lasting consequences for Chopin's life and art.

Whatever his previous experience of sex, it was in the arms and bed of its self-proclaimed High Priestess that Chopin discovered the power of erotic possession. With Sand he discovered jealousy. While she, in June, could evidently contemplate two lovers, Chopin in September could not. The die was cast, and Mallefille was finished. To begin with, he was mortified. On belatedly discovering the truth, so legend has it, he became murderous. Accounts differ, however, as to the identity of his intended victim. In one version, he breaks into Chopin's room at night and is prevented from strangling him only by the timely arrival of Grzymala. According to the other, he lies in wait for Sand in the street outside Chopin's apartment. When at last she emerges he rushes forward to assault her but is frustrated by the sudden appearance of an enormous wagon, which momentarily separates them. Grasping her chance, she escapes, leaps into a passing cab and disappears round a corner, casting, presumably, one last glance at her jilted lover as he falls disconsolately to his knees. As the stories have nothing common except Mallefille, and in the absence of corroborating testimony from any of the leading players, it seems likely that neither is true. Would Sand really have left no first-hand account of her narrow escape or of that of her lover? She was never otherwise at a loss for words. Chopin's almost pathological abhorrence of scandal might explain his own silence in the matter, but is it likely that Grzymala, who outlived his friend by many years, would have maintained a lifelong silence on the attempted murder of a great and much-discussed composer? What almost certainly *is* true is that Mallefille, in these circumstances, at any rate, was no respecter of discretion. The time was ripe for the lovers to decamp.

*   *   *

At the time their affair was known only to a select circle of friends – the painter Delacroix, Wojciech Grzymala, the poet Mickiewicz, and the Count and Countess Marliani, two Italian expatriates. Ambivalent as ever, Chopin was unready to share the secret with his customary circle of Parisian acquaintances, many of whom regarded Sand with both distaste and suspicion. The idea of pursuing the affair without risk to his social position, let alone his life, held a natural appeal for Chopin.

Sand too savoured the prospect of a 'honeymoon' away from prying eyes and wagging tongues. All that remained to be decided was the venue. In view of Chopin's fragile health and Maurice's worsening rheumatism, it was decided that they should head south, remaining there throughout the coming winter and early spring. On the recommendation of friends who had not themselves been there, they opted for the island of Majorca, a sun-drenched, unspoilt haven in which they could write, compose, explore, frolic and make love to their hearts' content. Having arranged that a piano be sent for Chopin's use, they made elaborate plans to cover their traces. Unbeknownst to all but a handful of trustworthy friends, Sand would slip discreetly out of Paris in mid-October, Chopin joining her two weeks later at Perpignan, on the Franco-Spanish border, whence they would embark together on the holiday trip of a lifetime (the only snag, for honeymoon purposes, being the presence of Sand's two children).

At Barcelona, on the evening of 7 November, they boarded the ship that was to carry them to Palma. As they gazed upwards at the night sky and listened to the lapping of a quiet sea against the bows, the obvious rightness of their decision crowded all thoughts of Paris out of their heads. Chopin, 'fresh as a rose and as rosy as a beetroot', had brought little beyond his volumes of Bach, his uncompleted manuscripts and a sheaf of music paper. As he filled his lungs with the warm, scented air, he felt himself suffused with a pleasant admixture of contentment and excitement. Seven days later, the mood persisted. In time to catch the one postal collection of the week, he reported to his friend Julian Fontana in Paris,

Here I am at Palma, among palms, cedars, cacti, olive-trees, oranges, lemons, aloes, figs, pomegranates etc. – everything that is to be found in the hot-houses of the Jardins des Plantes. The sky is like turquoise, the sea like lapis lazuli, the mountains like emerald and the air as in Heaven. In the daytime, sunshine; everyone goes about in summer clothes and it's hot. At night, guitars and songs for hours on end. Enormous balconies with overhanging vines: Moorish ramparts. Everything, including the town has an African look. In a word, life here is marvellous. . . . It's settled that I shall live in a wonderful monastery on the most fabulous site in the world: sea, mountains, palm trees, a cemetery, a crusader's church, ruins of a mosque, olive-trees a thousand years old. Oh, my dear friend, I am really beginning to live. I am close to all that is most beautiful. I am a better man.

At the same time he wrote to Pleyel, complaining that while he dreamt of music he could compose none for lack of a piano – an interesting indication of the extent to which this most pianistic of composers thought and discovered with his fingers. Berlioz, by contrast, with his vivid orchestral imagination, would scarcely have known what to do with a piano if he had had one.

The euphoria of these first days in Majorca soon dissipated. Within a fortnight of arriving, Chopin wrote in some disgruntlement to Grzymala: 'This is the devil's own country as far as the post, the population and comforts are concerned. The sky is as lovely as your soul; the earth is as black as my heart.' As so often, his spirits reflected his physical condition. Sand reported: 'Chopin has not been well. He suffers from the frequent changes of temperature. At last we are getting a Homond stove, and may Heaven grant us its protection for there are neither doctors nor medicines here.' An odd place, under the circumstances, to have brought a consumptive. Nor, for the moment, did it favour her own work. 'We are still not settled,' she wrote in December, 'and have neither donkey, servant, water, fire nor any safe means of dispatching manuscripts. In such circumstances I am cooking, not writing.'

Chopin's health had in fact collapsed within days of their arrival. As he wrote to Fontana, in early December:

> I've been as sick as a dog for the past two weeks. I caught a cold in spite of the heat, the roses, the oranges, palms and figs. The three most celebrated doctors on the island have been to see me. One sniffed at what I spat, the second tapped where I spat from, and the third sounded me and listened as I spat. The first said I was dead, the second that I am dying, and the third that I'm going to die. It was all I could do to stop them bleeding me or applying blisters and setons.

But he remained optimistic that a changed venue would bring about a change:

> In a few days I shall be living in the most beautiful surroundings in the world: sea, mountains, everything. . . . It's a huge, old, deserted Carthusian monastery not far from Palma; indeed it's impossible to imagine anything more marvellous. I know I shall be alright there.

Two weeks later the travellers were ensconced in their new quarters at Valldemosa. It was, as Chopin put it:

> A queer place, situated between the cliffs and the sea, where in a cell with doors larger than any carriage-gateway in Paris you may imagine me with my hair unkempt, without white gloves, and as pale as ever.

The cell is shaped like a large coffin, the enormous vaulting covered in dust, the window small. Close to my bed is an old, square, grubby box which I can scarcely use for writing on, with a leaden candlestick (a great luxury in these parts) and a little candle.

It wasn't what he'd imagined. He was not all right there. Nor did his work flourish.

All this is having a wretched effect on the *Préludes* – God knows when you will receive them. . . . Meanwhile my manuscripts sleep while I get no sleep at all. I can only go on coughing and await the spring, or something else. . . . Nevertheless, I expect to send my *Préludes* and the *Ballade* [Op. 38] shortly. Go and see Léo. Don't tell him I'm ill, though, or he'll be worried about his thousand francs.

And the weather was hardly calculated to improve his mood. Three days after Christmas, Sand reported to Marliani: 'The rains here are such as one cannot imagine, frightening deluges, with the air so wet and heavy one cannot drag one's self about. . . . I am all rheumatism . . . And our poor Chopin is quite feeble and suffering. For his sake I await impatiently the return of the beneficent season.'

Now coughing badly and covered in poultices, Chopin continued to await the delivery of his piano, which had allegedly been in port for more than a week. Nor was its progress aided by Majorcan topography. 'I have travelled here from Palma many times, always with the same coachman but each time by a different route. This is a place where roads are made by torrents and repaired by landslides. You can't drive through this way today because it's ploughed up, tomorrow only mules can pass – and what vehicles they have!' And yet despite the frustrations, the poor state of his health and his generalized contempt for the local populace, his sense of enchantment persisted:

Tonight the moon is marvellous. Never have I seen it like this. Nature is kindly here, even if the people are scoundrels and thieves. . . . You can have oranges for nothing, but they demand an enormous sum for a trouser-button. All that, however, is a mere grain of sand when compared with the poetry which everything here exhales and the colouring of this most marvellous scenery, still unsullied by the eye of man. Few have ever disturbed the eagles which daily soar over our heads.

On the ground below, however, circumstances steadily worsened. As Sand later informed Marliani:

The climate at Majorca was becoming more and more deadly to Chopin and I hastened to get away. Just to show you what the inhabitants are like – I had three leagues of rough roads to cover between my mountain retreat and Palma. We knew ten people who have carriages, horses, mules etc., but not one was willing to lend them. We had to make this journey in a hired cart without springs, and of course Chopin had a terrible attack of blood-spitting when we reached Palma. And the reason for this unfriendliness? It was because Chopin coughs, and whosoever coughs in Spain is declared consumptive; and he who is consumptive is held to be a plague-carrier, a leper. They haven't stones, sticks and policemen enough to drive him out, for according to their ideas consumption is catching and the sufferer should therefore be slaughtered if possible, just as the insane were strangled two hundred years ago. What I say is the literal truth. We were treated like outcasts at Majorca – because of Chopin's cough and also because we didn't go to church. My children were stoned in the street . . . I should have to write ten volumes to give you an idea of the cowardice, deceit, selfishness, stupidity and spite of this stupid, thieving and bigoted race.

It was a relief to put the island behind them, but Chopin's condition was pitiful. By the time they reached the mainland, he was haemorrhaging badly and bringing up blood, as Sand put it, 'by the bowlful'. On their arrival, he was examined by a doctor who stopped the bleeding and administered a sedative before pronouncing, to the mixed puzzlement and relief of his auditors, that Chopin was not in fact suffering from consumption or from any other disease. His lungs were apparently sound, although the doctor diagnosed a 'weak chest', and the only prescription was rest. Sand's mood lifted at once, but as she indicated in a letter to Marliani, the curse of Majorca followed them to the mainland.

Here we are at last in Barcelona, which seems a paradise by comparison. We came by steamer, however, in the company of a hundred pigs whose stench didn't exactly help to cure Chopin. But the poor boy would have died of melancholy at Majorca and I had to get him away at all costs. Heavens, if you knew him as I do now, you would be still fonder of him. He is an angel of gentleness, patience and kindness.

Chopin reciprocated, almost to the letter. Writing to Grzymala some time later he remarks, 'If you could know her as I do today, you would love her still more.' And elsewhere:

My health is steadily improving – the blisters, diets, pills and baths and also the tireless nursing of my angel are putting me on my feet again – rather shaky feet. . . . I have gone awfully thin and I look wretched, but I am now eating to gain strength. In addition to my eternal coughing you can imagine all the rage which those Spaniards put me into, as well as the other similarly pleasant experiences. I had to look on while she, continually harassed, nursed me (the less said about those doctors the better), made my bed, tidied my room, prepared hot drinks. She deprived herself of everything for me, while all the time she was receiving no letters and the children needed her constant attention in these unusual circumstances. Add to this the fact that she was writing her books . . . and you have evidence of an iron will and a love beyond passion.

How (if at all) Chopin now envisaged his future with her we don't know. Nor can we deduce much from a passage which has tantalized biographers for more than a century and a half. In his first letter from the mainland, and after three paragraphs of business instructions to Fontana, Chopin suddenly writes

It is not my fault if I am like a mushroom which seems edible but which poisons you if you pick it and taste it, taking it to be something else. I know I have never been of any use to anyone – and indeed not much use to myself. I told you that in my desk, in the first drawer next to the door, there was a document which you or Grzymala or Jas might unseal. I now ask you, please, to take it out and burn it *without reading it* [sic]. I adjure you by our friendship to do this – the paper serves no purpose now.

From the timing, it seems likely that there was a direct connection between this mysterious document and Chopin's deepening relationship with Sand. But what? And why such urgency? Could the matter not have waited until Chopin's return?

Chopin's physical frailty and the distressing symptoms of his disease seem not to have affected Sand's pleasure in his company. They do seem, however (and not surprisingly), to have shifted the emphasis from the romantic and sexual to the maternal and vocational. Given Chopin's state of health and the constant proximity of her children in relatively confined quarters, the circumstances were hardly conducive to the passionate sexuality that seems to have characterized their first month together. That Sand's love for him only grew during their hapless

Majorcan winter seems clear in a letter written to the Countess Marliani at the end of April:

> This Chopin is an angel; his kindness, tenderness and patience some-times worry me, for I have the feeling that his whole being is too delicate, too exquisite and too perfect to exist long in our coarse and heavy earthly life. In Majorca, when sick unto death, he composed music full of the scent of Paradise; but I am so used to seeing him away in the skies that it doesn't seem to signify whether he is alive or dead. He doesn't really know on what planet he is living and has no precise notion of life as we others conceive and live it.

Perhaps not. But if Sand perceived the scent of paradise in the music he composed that winter, her understanding of Chopin's music was deficient from the start.

Interlude: Chopin and the Prelude

It was in Majorca that Chopin completed one of his most remarkable and innovative works: the set of twenty-four preludes, one in each key, on the model of Bach's *The Well-tempered Clavier* (a monumental work that Chopin carried in his memory and played, generally to himself, throughout his life). But which were composed in Majorca? Contrary to popular mythology, most of them appear to have been finished before Chopin arrived on the island. Nor is there any justification for the legend that the D flat Prelude, the so-called 'Raindrop', was inspired by the remorseless drips from the roof of the monastery. In any case, such speculation is largely irrelevant. Of all the romantic composers, none was more opposed to programmatic references than Chopin, a point emphasized by his almost provocatively non-committal choice of title. The headings nocturne, étude, polonaise, waltz, mazurka and scherzo may not tell us much, but at least they tell us something: a nocturne is likely to be lyrical; an étude will address itself to a specific, individual technical or interpretative challenge; a waltz is a lilting dance in 3/4 time; a mazurka will always be in three (even if it does not always sound that way), as will, at one level or another, a scherzo.

The only thing conveyed by the word prelude is an expectation that it will be followed by something else. Chopin's preludes, on the other hand, precede only one another, while the final, tempestuous D minor leads to nothing but applause, or to a resonating silence. 'Preludes to what?' people asked at the time.† Some musicians, noting the inconclusive endings to a number of these pieces pondered the unlikely possibility that Chopin had here provided a kind of glossary of introductions to other works altogether. Others, more persuasively, have sought by various analytical means to demonstrate the binding integrity of the set as a whole. This view of the preludes as a single, inviolable cycle remains so widespread that few pianists venture to dismember it. Chopin himself

---

† In terms of nomenclature Chopin was, once again, simply harking back to Bach, whose so-called 'Little Preludes' lead likewise only to each other.

was not so squeamish. He repeatedly played varying selections of preludes, mixed in with nocturnes, études and waltzes.

In several cases, the preludes are generically indistinguishable from
the études, many of them being exclusively addressed to a single
musical-cum-technical idea. Outstanding examples of this type are
no. 3, with its quicksilver figuration in the left hand (a kind of lightweight
counterpart of the 'Revolutionary' Étude); no. 6 in B minor (a miniature
cousin of the so-called 'Cello' Étude from op. 25); no. 8, the extraordinary
F sharp minor, with its premonitions of Wagner; no. 12 in G sharp minor,
reminiscent in the nature of its difficulties although not in mood of the A
minor Étude from op. 10; the dazzling, demoniacally exuberant B flat
minor, no. 16, one of the most sheerly exciting exercises in bravura ever
penned; and the fiendishly taxing, rhapsodic E flat, no. 19.

It is ironic that this most neutrally entitled opus by the nineteenth
century's most reluctant Romantic is among the most definitively
Romantic things he ever wrote. It lacks the sprawling grandiosity and
the allusiveness of the operatic and symphonic Romantics still to come;
it contains none of the sensation-drenched egotism of Berlioz, Liszt or
Richard Strauss; nor does it descend, as Chopin would have viewed it,
to the merely pictorial. Yet, in the startling brevity of its utterance –
almost half of the preludes last less than a minute – its subversion of
traditional tonality, its myriad colours and its spell-binding virtuosity,
Chopin's op. 28 could well be enshrined as a keyboard Romantic's
manifesto.

Those preludes that are not undercover studies in pianism are equally
striking studies in emotion: 'Dream Visions', Schumann might have
called them; some of them nightmarish. The starkly prophetic A minor,
no. 2, is among the bleakest meditations ever entrusted to the piano.
Hardly less disturbing is the E flat minor, no. 14. The nocturne-like D
flat, no. 15, the so-called 'Raindrop', with its veiled harmonic references
to Bach – the suspensions in the middle section, for instance – is one
of the most sensuously beautiful of all Chopin's works, fully justifying
its fame and popularity. It is also, at six minutes plus, far and away the
longest of the set, serving a function that, in the context of the cycle as
a whole may perhaps be seen as analogous to the twenty-fifth of Bach's
'Goldberg' Variations, itself one of the profoundest utterances in the
history of music. In both placement and tone the D flat Prelude serves
as a kind of timeless halt in the proceedings, an opportunity to withdraw
from the cumulative tension and momentum of the cycle thus far, to
take spiritual stock of what's gone before and to prepare for the climactic
moments still to come. In the context of the preludes as a whole, it thus

requires a degree of simplicity on the part of the performer, far removed from the sentimentality that so often disfigures it. On its own, however, or in a different context, an element of nocturnal reverie can be entirely appropriate.

In the uninhibited E flat Prelude, no. 19, we find Chopin at his most pianistically exultant. Few pianists, however, are fully equal to its colouristic challenges, which lead us straight to Debussy. When advising his pupils that 'the use of the pedals is a study for life', Chopin could hardly have done better than to direct their attention to this work, whose varied pedal markings tell one almost as much as the notes which they affect. No. 22 is brief, turbulent and terrifying. Aptly marked *Molto agitato*, it harks back to the torments of that verbal explosion in Stuttgart when Chopin learned of Warsaw's fall. The penultimate prelude, in F major, comes closest to justifying Sand's reference to 'the scent of Paradise'. Marked *Moderato* and *delicatissimo*, it is one of Chopin's most serene creations, and when combined with its successor it justifies, if ever anything did, the description, often misleading, of Chopin as a tragic composer. For no sooner does he soothe us with a vision of consolatory peace, than he plunges us into one of the most dramatic and doom-laden finales ever penned.

The cycle or collection debate raises important questions for the performer. If one subscribes to the cyclic approach – that is, if one sees the opus as a single, organic entity, with more binding it together than Chopin's chosen key-scheme – does that organic integrity suggest a different interpretation of each piece according to whether it is presented singly or in its wider context? Is there, for instance, a dramatic, even a rhetorical connection between the E that concludes the first prelude and the succeeding E that marks the melodic entry of the second, with its eerie, subversive harmonics? If so, does this juxtaposition, this transformation, give us fair warning at the outset that the set as a whole is conceived precisely in terms of its internal relationships, and that it derives much of its effect from that duality which was so deeply ingrained a part of Chopin's nature? Certainly each can be effectively presented in isolation or in varied combinations; but the only way in which we can discover their full import is through playing and listening to them in the particular combination which Chopin finally conceived for them.

His chosen key scheme encourages a cumulatively dualistic view. Unlike Bach, who proceeds through the '48' alphabetically, as it were (C major/minor; C sharp major/minor; D major/minor etc.), Chopin advances through the so-called circle of fifths (C–G–D–A–E–B etc.) in pairs of descending thirds, each major prelude being followed by one in its relative minor (C major/A minor etc.) – a scheme well suited to a plan of dramatic opposition. They proceed, on the whole, with a brevity seldom attempted by Bach.

Viewed as a single, continuous entity, the preludes amount to a tragic drama of exceptional power and conviction. As an unflinching self-portraitist, Chopin seems here to give of himself with an almost terrifying candour. He also renders largely irrelevant the biographical circumstances so often, and inaccurately, ascribed to the preludes' composition. The emotional and psychological truth of these miniature masterpieces is often so intense as to transcend the mere experience of a moment. Also revealed is the revolutionary originality of Chopin's mind. Even today, with all our experience of Debussy and Schoenberg, of Webern and Boulez, of Stravinsky and Stockhausen, the A minor Prelude retains its implacable and disturbing sense of modernity. Never did Chopin venture further from the world of the Parisian salons. In the preludes and the cumulative power of their unfolding, he turns his most pitiless and unflinching eye on the human condition and creates a drama whose tragic stature has seldom been equalled.

— 8 —

Rural Retreat
1839

For all his love and appreciation of Sand, Chopin's letters to Grzymala and Fontana during this period give vent, though not for the first time, to a misanthropic streak strikingly at variance with his impeccable conduct in public, let alone Sand's characterization of him as an angel. 'Bloody Germans!', 'rogues', 'swine', 'sharks', 'animals' are only a few of the bouquets strewn about his correspondence. In a single and not long letter of 12 March 1839 he refers to various of his friends, acquaintances and publishers as 'cheats', 'tricksters', 'swindlers', 'fools', 'imbeciles', 'Huns' and 'Jews', the last being his most common term of abuse.

> I didn't expect such Jewish behaviour from Pleyel. . . . And don't let Schlesinger take you in, like Pleyel. . . . This Pleyel, my God, who supposedly adores me! What scoundrels! . . . If we have to deal with Jews, let it at least be with orthodox ones. . . . Schlesinger has swindled me all along, but it's best to go carefully with him, for this Jew would like to cut a figure in the world. If Pleyel makes the slightest difficulty, go to Schlesinger and tell him he can have the Ballade for France and Germany at a price of 800 . . . Jews will be Jews and Huns will be Huns – that's the truth of it, but what can one do? I'm forced to deal with them. . . . The *Préludes* are already sold to Pleyel, so he can wipe the other end of his stomach with them if he pleases, but since they're all such a band of Jews, stop everything else till I get back.

To put such deeply unattractive behaviour in context, it must be said that, however repellent, the thoughtless, casual antisemitism evident in his correspondence was in no way peculiar to Chopin. It was common change among Poles of almost every class and political stripe. More revealing of Chopin's own character, and in some ways more disturbing, is his readiness to address the unsuspecting recipients of his abuse in terms of the sincerest friendship. Written at the same time as the above was a letter to Pleyel, which Fontana was instructed to deliver:

> I am vexed, my dear friend, that Fontana has been troubling you with my affairs. . . . I am writing him this very day to tell him not to bother you any more with this business. I wrote to you twice from Majorca and was grieved at receiving no reply. I learn from Fontana that you are still unwell, and that grieves me more than your silence. . . . I expect to return to Paris when the fine weather comes . . .
>   Au revoir, then, my dearest friend.
>   Yours devotedly,
>   F. Chopin

By the time he wrote the letters just quoted, Chopin and Sand had moved on from Barcelona to Marseilles, where they remained, partly on medical advice, for the next three months. The wonder is that they could afford it. The travails of their Majorcan winter had seriously hampered their creative activities, and their continued absence from Paris deprived Chopin of his principal income.

                              *   *   *

If the furnace of Chopin's creativity was indeed stoked by abstinence, the bellows are less likely to have been sexual than emotional. After the crisis in Stuttgart, the façade he presented to the world was all but impenetrable. Even in letters to his closest friends he adopts an air of sophisticated detachment when touching on subjects too painful to acknowledge. There is no reason to doubt Sand's word that he was almost unhinged by the suicide of Adolphe Nourrit, news of which reached him in Marseilles, yet his only recorded comment on the matter was a line to Grzymala on 27 March: 'What do you make of the Nourrit affair?' he asks. 'It gave us a great shock.' So cool, almost dismissive; so reserved and studiedly aristocratic. And soon followed by the kind of humorous small talk that often served to conceal his deepest feelings:

> Next month we're sure to move to Avignon and from there to Nohant. There we shall embrace you, not by letter, but complete with your moustache, unless your moustache happens to have met with the same fate as my side-whiskers. Kiss the hands and feet of your lady-friend (not your own) for me. Without being dead to the

most sublime feelings I may sign myself, for your sake, The genuine cloistered monk, Ch.

Its jocular, dissembling tone recalls Mozart.

As with Mozart, it can be a dangerous and misleading game to seek a meaningful correspondence between the substance of Chopin's music and the circumstances of his life. Mozart, in common with any number of other composers, was capable of producing at the same time works of completely opposite character. If composers, and especially opera composers, were required by the nature of their task to experience all the emotions and psychological conditions they portray, their lives would be not only intolerable but impossible. Music, like painting, affords its creators the opportunity to convey opposing states of mind not only sequentially but simultaneously. No art is better suited to reflect the ambivalence and ambiguity that lie at the centre of human experience. It could be argued that the reflection and resolution of ambiguity is a necessary precondition of the greatest music. It is in the Bach Passions, in virtually all the masterworks of Mozart, in the late sonatas and quartets of Beethoven – and in the best of Chopin. From this point of view, that paradoxical ambivalence of character that so bedevilled Chopin's life can be seen as a vital part of his creative genius.

On 22 May the travellers set off at long last to Nohant, where they arrived a week later. As Chopin reported to Grzymala: 'We had an excellent trip. The countryside here is beautiful: nightingales, larks – the only bird we lack is you.' It was now almost nine months since Chopin had last spoken Polish or seen any of his Polish friends. Sand well understood the importance of this to the course of Chopin's recovery and herself beseeched Grzymala:

> You really *must* come! I tell you, we *need* you. The boy's [Chopin's] health is still only so-so. I feel that he now needs less quiet, solitude and monotonous routine than life at Nohant offers. And, who knows – perhaps a little trip to Paris. I am prepared for any sacrifice rather than see him waste away in melancholy. Come and feel the pulse of his morale. Who can define the frontier between physical malady and dullness of spirits? He will never confess to me that he is bored. He has not been accustomed to such a strict mode of life, while I am gradually becoming a frightful matron and schoolmistress.

It was true. But her anxieties, at least on that score, were groundless. There is nothing to suggest that Chopin found the metamorphosis disagreeable. Indeed, if the works that now tumbled from him in profusion are any guide, he had at last found a mode of existence ideally suited to the requirements of his restless genius. There was a price, but at least for the moment he was happy to pay it.

*   *   *

On 19 June 1839, seventeen days after returning to her home, George Sand took a knife and carved the date into the wood panelling at the side of the window in her room. Why? The mystery vies with the immolation of Chopin's document in Paris three months before. She was not given to defacing her own property, least of all in her own bedroom. That the date was significant seems beyond argument. Two theories, both entirely conjectural, have stood the test of time. One proposes that it marked the first anniversary of the day on which Sand and Chopin consummated their love; the other that it marked the end of their sexual relations. In the case of the first hypothesis, the dates tally. But Sand had never seen fit to memorialize the start of any other affair – nor the end. On the other hand, none of her previous lovers had enjoyed the hospitality of her bed for so long, let alone against such odds. The second theory suggests a wilful decision on her part, an interpretation supported by her own claim, almost a decade later, that she had elected to withhold her favours for the sake of Chopin's health. In view of her well-aired libido, this would have been a remarkable sacrifice, the more so for her later insistence that she lived with Chopin for eight years in a state of perfect chastity. Whatever the truth, there is no doubting that their return to France marked the beginning of a new and important – in many ways the *most* important – chapter in Chopin's creative life. To the next few years would belong the majority of his finest works: the two great sonatas, the A flat and F minor Ballades, the F minor Fantasy, the A flat Polonaise, the Barcarolle and Berceuse, the Polonaise-Fantasie, the late nocturnes, and numerous mazurkas of prophetic originality.

Nohant itself had a potent charm. A gracious, eighteenth-century manor house, nestled comfortably on the outskirts of a modest village, it opened, in Sand's words, on to 'a parcelling out of fields, meadows, copses and communal paths, offering a variety of forms and nuances, within a harmony of sombre green relieved by a tint of blue; a jumble of luxuriant closures, thatched huts, hidden under orchards; curtains of poplars. . . .' Chopin was installed in a pleasant room on the first floor, whose charming red and blue Chinese wallpaper and southerly view over the lawn and its surrounding countryside can be seen to this day.

Its relative seclusion, however, from the point of view of a gregarious Parisian, was a two-edged sword. And in their very different ways, Chopin and Sand were both gregarious, if often as a means of escape from themselves. As Hiller remarked,

> He disliked being without company – a circumstance which he rarely allowed to arise. In the morning he liked to spend an hour by himself at his grand piano; but even when he practised – or how should I describe it? – when he stayed at home to play in the evenings, he needed to have at least one of his friends close at hand.

Sand, too, professed a dislike of solitude. 'I would rather play dominoes in a café,' she once wrote to a friend, 'than spend an hour of the afternoon alone. Alone! What horror!' Few writers, however, create in company, and Sand was no exception. While she reserved the afternoons for society and the mornings for sleep, she spent her nights in labour, writing for six or seven hours at a stretch and averaging a daily output of some twenty pages. Her use of ink and paper was as prodigious as her energy and concentration, and led to the production of some sixty novels, several plays, numerous essays, and sundry other published works, numbering 104 in all. In addition, she wrote almost 20,000 letters, some exceeding forty pages. At break of dawn, in summertime, she would set aside her pen and walk down to the river, where she would undress, hanging her clothes on a tree, and lie naked on the sand 'with the water up to my chin, smoking a cigar and looking at the reflection of the moon in the stream around my knees.' Then it was to bed to sleep till noon.

Chopin adopted a very different mode of life at Nohant. He would rise early, sometimes before Sand had gone to bed, work sporadically throughout the day, socialize in the evening when (as often) there were guests, and retire early. As Sand put it in a letter to Marliani: 'We lead the same monotonous, quiet, gentle life. We dine out in the open, friends wander over, first one, then another, we smoke† and talk, and in the evening, when they have gone, Chopin plays to me in the twilight, after which he goes to bed like a child, at the same time as Maurice and Solange.' Anyone doubting the congeniality of place and circumstance to Chopin's creative energies need only look at the works that flowed from his pen during this first, idyllic summer: the B flat minor Sonata (except for the Funeral March, which had been written two years

---

† Except for Chopin, who detested smoking in any form.

before), the three mazurkas, op. 41, the F sharp major Impromptu and the G major Nocturne, op. 37.

At Nohant in summertime, with its sunlit peace and gentle, scented breezes, the sounds of Chopin the creator mingled through open windows with those of nature. During this and other summers, guests at Nohant – Delacroix, for instance, Balzac, Grzymala, Louis Blanc and the Viardots – were privileged to eavesdrop on the mysterious alliance of art and instinct. It was something to which Sand herself had now become accustomed.

> His music was spontaneous, miraculous. He found it without seeking it, without previous intimation of it. It came upon his piano sudden, complete, sublime, or it sang in his head during a walk, and he was impatient to hear it himself with the help of the instrument. But then began the most desperate labour that I have ever witnessed. It was a succession of efforts, hesitations and moments of impatience to recapture certain details of the theme he could hear; what he had conceived as one piece, he analysed too much in trying to write it down, and his dismay at his inability to rediscover it in what he thought was its original purity threw him into a kind of despair. He would lock himself up in his room for whole days, weeping, pacing back and forth, breaking his pens, repeating or changing one bar a hundred times, writing and erasing it as many times, and beginning again the next day with an infinite and desperate perseverance. He sometimes spent six weeks on one page, only in the end to write it exactly as he had sketched at the first draft.

Certainly few composers have ever been more determined that their discarded ideas should remain undisturbed by prying musicological eyes. His crossings-out often consumed as much ink as the notes he spared.

With the 'fiasco' of Majorca behind him, Chopin's health seemed to improve with every passing day. No fewer than three doctors had examined him and pronounced him free of consumption; his creature comforts were provided with unflagging devotion by a woman who loved him and understood the throes of artistic creation as well as anyone; and surrounded by beautiful countryside under an azure sky, he composed and played without restrictions. In its outer aspect this summer was among the happiest of Chopin's adult life – would it have been so had Sand refused him her bed from 19 June? His music, on the other hand, often seemed to tell a different story, but on that subject he was as taciturn as a Trappist monk. Of one of his most astonishing and original compositions – largely a product of this idyllic summer – he writes to Fontana with a flat, matter-of-fact reserve:

> I am writing here a Sonata in B flat minor which will contain my March, which you already know. There is an Allegro, then a Scherzo in E flat minor, the March and a short Finale – about three pages of my manuscript-paper. The left hand and the right hand gossip in unison after the March.

These three pages, which Chopin so casually dismisses as gossip, may well constitute the most enigmatic movement in the entire history of the sonata idea. As a self-contained prelude, less than ninety seconds long, it would be astonishing enough; as the conclusion of a major virtuoso work of more than twenty minutes' duration, it simply takes the breath away. Its weirdness is timeless. Its restlessness eternal. If this is gossip, it is the gossiping of demons. The fate of the soul memorialized in the Funeral March seems hardly to be in doubt. If the work is to be understood symbolically, it must be ranked with music's most pessimistic utterances. Whether Chopin's Christian faith survived his Roman Catholic upbringing is difficult to say. That he accepted the Last Rites from a priest is inconclusive, for nothing is easier than to be a Christian on one's deathbed. The tone and placement of this 'gossiping' finale suggest that Chopin at least believed in the possibility of damnation. If he did not presume to depict the torments of Hell itself, nor did he flinch from its contemplation. To 'pictorialize' it, in the manner of a Liszt or Berlioz, would have struck him as unutterably vulgar and presumptuous. To portray the terrors of the imagination in the face of death was another matter altogether. But here we again encounter that strange lack of synchronicity that often separates a work of art from the external circumstances of its composition. This blackest of Chopin's creations surfaced in an environment of idyllic contentment and grace.

Interlude: Chopin and the Sonata

Chopin wrote four sonatas – three for solo piano and one for cello and piano – and a fifth if the Piano Trio in G minor of 1829 is included. Of these, only two hold a secure place in the repertoire today. The C minor Sonata, op. 4 (composed in 1827–8 and discussed in Chapter 2) was clearly a prentice work, designed mainly for the eyes and ears of Elsner, and in later life he effectively disowned it. His next sonata was begun in 1837, although Chopin at the time was not aware of this. It was only later that he decided to embed the previously free-standing Funeral March of that year in the midst of a major four-movement work. Chopin gave the name 'Funeral March' to two works only, but a number of others might well be described as funeral marches. The C minor Prelude, op. 28, no. 20, is probably the first most people encounter, if only because its relative ease has made it a favourite with piano teachers, but there are many others. The one that is effectively the cornerstone of the B flat minor Sonata is a special case, however. Conceived and composed two years before its sonata siblings, it has an almost hypnotic power which has made it the most famous funeral march in history. People who have never heard of Chopin can sing its first phrase. Its place at the heart of Chopin's most celebrated sonata is one of the relatively few instances in his music to reveal the direct and openly acknowledged influence of Beethoven. Beethoven's own so-called 'Funeral March' Sonata, the A flat, op. 26, was Chopin's favourite, and despite some deep-seated reservations about much of Beethoven's music, he taught and played the piece many times. On no other musician does this particular work seem to have made so overwhelming an impression. Part of its appeal must have been its unconventional form, beginning, like Mozart's A major Sonata, K.331, with a theme and variations, proceeding to the exceptionally fiery scherzo, before rather than after the slow movement, then giving pride of place to an imposing and quasi-programmatic funeral march before finishing with a *moto perpetuo* which seems to echo the studies of J. B. Cramer.* Chopin too puts his scherzo second and the march third, and ends with perhaps the boldest and certainly the weirdest movement he ever wrote – a colloquy of bats and witches darting over the keys in continuous parallel octaves (as Chopin put it, the two hands 'gossip in unison'). The whole movement is over in a mere ninety seconds, but its power to amaze, disturb and shock is hardly diminished even today.

Of all Chopin's major works, none has occasioned more abuse or more aggressive defence than this magnificent sonata. Much of it can be traced in one way or another to Schumann's remark that Chopin had here yoked together four of his maddest children under the same roof. The suggestion that there is no overall integrity unifying the work's four movements, and the controversy over Chopin's structural procedures in three of them, has led to the conventional wisdom, chanted like a mantra until the last third of the twentieth century, that he had little understanding and still less mastery of large-scale forms. The arguments, pro and con, are complex and highly technical, but the cause of them can be summarized fairly briefly: 'Sonata form', as taught in countless schools and academies the world over, is a ternary structure (A–B–A) based on the initial opposition but eventual resolution of two contrasting key centres (tonic–dominant; minor and relative major, etc.) each associated with contrasting themes. After the initial exposition of these effectively rival forces comes a central 'development' section, marked by continuous flux (melodic, harmonic, thematic), in which the basic ideas of the exposition are explored, combined, rejected and so on. This period of flux is then succeeded by a recapitulation of the original exposition, this time without the opposition of keys that characterized the opening. The whole concept of the form is essentially discursive. Long, unfurling rhapsodic themes are therefore frowned upon in favour of short thematic 'acorns' (my term), which lend themselves easily to development and variation. So goes the text. In fact, few great composers have slavishly adhered to this recipe, with the result that 'model' sonata-form structures have usually to be drawn from the works of the second rate. It should also be said that this principle is essentially representative of the Germanic tradition and plays a relatively minor role in the development of music in France, Italy, Spain, Russia and much of eastern Europe. It should be noted, too, that acorns are not the only seeds that lead to mighty structures, and oaks are not the only trees. Had Chopin called his B flat minor Sonata 'Fantasy, Scherzo, March and Finale' he might have saved himself and history a lot of fruitless trouble. In any case, his ostensible inadequacies here, and in the great B minor Sonata, seem to be of little or no concern to pianists and audiences.

The abuse meted out to the B flat minor Sonata in particular has prompted an army of knowledgeable musicians to take up the pen against the form-wielding Philistines in a welter of closely reasoned rebuttals, which have long since given the lie to Schumann's suggestion that the work's four movements enjoy no organic or thematic unity. The close scrutiny to which it has been subjected in our time has produced some unexpected and intriguing observations. Anatole Leikin, for instance, has found in the enigmatic finale a demonstrable link with Bach, and, more specifically, with the Prelude from his D major suite for unaccompanied cello. Here, too, is a *perpetuum mobile* of four quaver triplets per bar, one of whose principal motives bears a remarkable likeness to the main theme of Chopin's first movement. What is more, the finale itself can be seen as a kind of compressed sonata form.†

The influence of Bach and of other contrapuntists is more readily apparent in the great B minor Sonata, which was written five years later, in 1844. This was a time when Chopin's reverence for Bach was at its height, and his recent immersion in contrapuntal treatises by Cherubini and Kastner bore its most immediate fruit in the first movement of the B minor Sonata. No work by Chopin is more riddled with polyphonic devices, or more rooted in the aesthetics of a bygone age. Here, almost certainly, is to be found the explanation for the unusually impersonal character of the work's opening section and its later transformations. In the seventeenth and eighteenth centuries the character of themes was held to be subordinate to their subsequent, developmental uses. Given the strict requirements of such contrapuntal devices as augmentation, diminution, inversion, retrogression and so on, it was felt that too personal or expressive a theme would be subject to a counterproductive level of emotional distortion. In its overall design the B minor follows the essential layout of its predecessor. Again the scherzo comes second, and here, as in the first movement, the prevailing texture is strikingly polyphonic. There is nothing particularly noteworthy in the form of the slow movement, a more or less straightforward ABA pattern, other than the disproportionate length of the middle section, which practically dwarfs its flanking sections. The finale is one of Chopin's biggest and most stirring conceptions, light years away, in

---

† Leikin writes of the enigmatic finale: 'In a very fast rendition, the movement appears athematic, whereas in reality it has a system of tonal and melodic repeats that creates a tangible trace of sonata form. After the first four introductory bars, the principal section begins in B flat minor. It drifts away into the partially atonal transition, which leads to the secondary section in D flat major. A short development follows (bars 31–8), and the recapitulation opens with a return of the introductory passage in bar 39.'

almost every sense, from its counterpart in the B flat minor Sonata. In his entire output there is nothing more confident or more steadfastly affirmative than this thrilling, driving sonata-rondo in which he tweaks the ears of the pedants by allowing his main theme to return in the 'wrong' key.

Chopin's final sonata cost him untold effort. Written for his friend Auguste Franchomme, a musician for whom he had a great admiration, the Sonata in G minor for Cello and Piano, completed in 1846, is filled with interesting ideas and thematic ingenuity, but lacks the immediacy and emotional conviction of its two great pianistic siblings. It has never been a favourite, even among cellists, who are renowned for bewailing the limitations of their repertoire. Ironically, it is in this work, more than any of its flawed companions, that Chopin comes closest to answering the criticisms levelled at his earlier essays in the form. In overall design it repeats a number of their most controversial 'idiosyncrasies' (notably the omission of the first group in the recapitulation of the first movement), although the organic integration and development of thematic kernels is markedly more disciplined and inventive. But in many ways, it is not the work's formal procedures but its determinedly anti-Romantic character, especially in its outer movements, that sets it apart from the rest of Chopin's output. That, and another feature which is unique in the products of his maturity: as Leikin has persuasively demonstrated, the piece shows every sign of having a hidden agenda, based on a work by another composer, with whom Chopin has many affinities but who rates not a mention in his entire correspondence. Just as Schumann had used a song of Beethoven's as a kind of secret motto in his great C major Fantasy for the piano – a motto expressing his longing for union with his wife-to-be – so Chopin, in the first movement of this sonata, seems to have taken and developed not one motive but two from Schubert's greatest song cycle, *Die Winterreise*† (a work depicting the sorrows of a man parting from his loved one in despair). The parallel with Chopin's agonized separation from George Sand seems almost too obvious to mention, and Leikin suggests that it may have been for this reason, rather than from any musical considerations, that Chopin chose to omit the first movement from the only performance

† The first of the two *Winterreise* motives (of a rising and a falling semitone) appears in the opening song, 'Gute Nacht', and reappears throughout the cycle, notably in the vocal entries of 'Rast', 'Frühlingstraum', 'Einsamkeit', 'Die Krähe' and 'Das Wirtshaus'. The second, a rising from the fifth to the first degree of the scale, is sometimes combined with the first, as in 'Mut'. And there is a notable resemblance between the opening of the sonata and 'Gute Nacht'.

he gave of the work, with Franchomme in 1848. Had the sophisticated Parisian audience spotted the *Winterreise* reference and drawn the obvious conclusion, it would have been a matter of the greatest embarrassment to Chopin.

— 9 —

Sinfonia Domestica
1839–1842

If creativity is a barometer of spiritual health the auguries for Chopin's
return to Paris in the autumn of 1839 were more than promising.
Between bouts of composing he found renewed sustenance from a
familiar source.

> When I have nothing in particular to do I am correcting, for myself,
> the Paris edition of Bach, not only the mistakes made by the engraver
> but those which are backed by the authority of people who are sup-
> posed to understand Bach – not that I have any pretensions to a deeper
> understanding, but I am convinced that I sometimes hit on the right
> answer. Oh, you see now how I have gone and boasted!

The pattern of Nohant summers was much the same from year to year.
Guests would come and go, with no evident disruption of the creative
routine already established. Among them, from the summer of 1842,
was Delacroix, who savoured the experience.

> This is a delightful place and my hosts do everything in their power
> to make life agreeable. When we are not together for dinner, lunch,
> billiards or walks, one can read in one's rooms or sprawl on one's
> sofa. Every now and then there blows in through your window,
> opening onto the garden, a breath of the music of Chopin who is at
> work in his room, and it mingles with the song of the nightingales
> and the scent of the roses. . . . I have endless conversations with
> Chopin, of whom I'm very fond and who is a man of rare distinction.
> I believe he is the truest artist I have ever met. I asked him one day
> what *logic* in music consisted of. He made me realize what harmony
> and counterpoint are, and how fugue is, as it were, pure logic in
> music. I thought how glad I would have been to learn all that. The
> fact is that true science is not what people ordinarily understand by

that word; that is to say, something quite different from *art*, in the realm of knowledge. No; science thus envisaged and demonstrated by a man like Chopin is art himself. And on the other hand, art is not what the common herd imagine it to be – a sort of inspiration coming from I-know-not-where, something proceeding from chance and portraying merely the picturesque exterior of things. It is reason itself, adorned by genius but following a course determined and restrained by superior laws. Chopin told me that pupils usually learn about chords before they understand counterpoint, that is, the succession of notes which lead to chords.

When guests were not staying, Sand and Chopin would go on long outings in the surrounding countryside, 'he riding on his donkey, I on my own legs, for I feel the need to walk and breathe'.

In the summer of 1839, however, there were pressing reasons to return to Paris. Beneficial though the country air and leisurely pace at Nohant may have been to his health, Chopin's financial position was doomed to worsen the longer he stayed away. As it was, the abandonment of his pupils had already cost him something in the region of 13,000 francs. Sand, too, who had shouldered the heaviest part of their financial burden, was increasingly hard-pressed, and there was still the education of her children to be settled. Before they could return, however, they had to find accommodation. To this end Chopin subjected Grzymala, and more particularly Fontana, to a barrage of detailed instructions, couched more in terms of orders than requests. Nor was the task made easier by Sand's subversive countermanding of them:

CHOPIN: Take the small apartment, but if we are too late then rent the large one – it doesn't matter which, provided I have one of the two. Regarding the one for her, she thinks it's too expensive and I will never convince her that it is better to pay more rent than have a lot of other tenants in the house.

SAND: Don't pay too much attention to the boy's [Chopin's] nasal arguments. It's stupid of him to want to save on the rent. He must have somewhere to put his manservant, and room to turn round in himself. If in your opinion the little apartment isn't spacious enough, never mind what he says.

The rooms for the grown-ups must face south. That is most important for the boy, and for my rheumatism too. . . . The main thing is that the lay-out of the rooms should be as required (*you know what I mean*).

The requirement referred to was that Sand's bedroom was to be well separated from those of her children. But there were others:

SAND: All the rooms need not be large and fine. The children's rooms, for example, can be small, provided they have fireplaces. . . . As I never entertain more than twelve people at any one time, I don't need a fine large drawing-room. It is important that the whole place should be clean and fresh so that we can move straight in without any further expense except for furnishings.

CHOPIN: Choose a wallpaper like the one I used to have, dove-grey but glossy and shiny for both rooms, with a narrow dark-green strip as a border. Choose something else for the vestibule, but neat and respectable. I prefer something smooth, very quiet and neat rather than commonplace vulgar and petty-bourgeois. As to the furniture, it would be best if *you* deal with that: collect and install it. . . . And another point: you must write to Wessel and tell him I have six new manuscripts, for each of which I am asking 300 francs [could Chopin not easily have written himself?]. Let me know whether Probst is in Paris, and engage a manservant for me – if possible, some honest, steady Pole. Settle with the man that he shall get his own food and be paid not more than 80 francs a month. The rubber mattress for my bed should be sent for repair. Have the chairs and everything beaten well.

Fontana, having successfully carried out Chopin's instructions, was now presented with a further list, this time on behalf of Sand:

She would, as far as possible, like to have something *detached* – a small detached residence for example, or else something in a court-yard, looking onto a garden. She requires: three bedrooms, two of which should be next to each other and the third separated by, for example, the drawing-room. Next to this third bedroom should be a well-lighted study for her. Also a suitable drawing-room and dining-room, a large kitchen, two servants' rooms and a cellar. Parquet floors, of course, fresh decorations and as far as possible no repairs needed. It must be quiet, *silent*, with no blacksmiths in the neighbourhood, no ladies of the street etc. Let me repeat: *it is absolutely necessary* that the third bedroom [Sand's own] with its adjoining study should be away from the others [the children's], and if possible, the study or third bedroom should have a separate door leading outside. Have a good look, *and let us keep the matter between ourselves.*

Having dealt with the matter of lodgings, Chopin now turned to more intimate accoutrements:

> I forgot to ask you to order me a *hat* from my hatter Dupont, whose shop is in your street. He has my measurements and knows what sorts of light hats I need. Tell him to make it in this year's fashion, but not exaggerated, for I have no idea what sort of things you men are wearing just now. There's something else: as you go past Dautrement's, my tailor on the boulevards, call in and order a pair of grey trousers, to be made at once. You yourself choose a dark grey – winter trousers, something decent, without stripes, and close fitting. . . . I need also a simple black velvet waistcoat with no more than some kind of tiny, discreet pattern – something combining great elegance with simplicity. If he has no suitable velvet let him use black silk, but it must be handsome yet simple. I am relying on you. The waistcoat must not be too open in front, of course. And find me a valet if you can.

He could, and he did. If Chopin ever paid Fontana for his endless, uncomplaining services, no evidence has survived to tell the tale. A further gloss on Chopin's attitude to him is revealed in a note to Grzymala in which he blithely states: 'If you need somebody to help you or go running about for you, use Fontana. He'll do anything for me.'

On 10 October 1839 Chopin and Sand finally returned to Paris after an absence of just under a year. Despite an excellent recovery during the summer, Chopin was visibly frailer than when he left. Weighing a mere 95 pounds (42.75 kilograms), and plagued with a near-permanent cough, he tired easily and still gave the impression of a convalescent, regularly mopping his brow with eau-de-Cologne, and sipping at gum-water laced with sugar and opium. The evidence provided by his Scottish pupil Jane Stirling, however, that 'he no longer mimicked his friends or seemed to enjoy life' is demonstrably inaccurate.

Unfortunately, all Fontana's efforts to find suitable accommodation for his friend were largely wasted. While at first professing himself content with his new apartment at 5 rue Tronchet (behind the Madeleine), Chopin later decided that it was both too cold and too distant from Sand's new quarters, a double-mews flat at the back of the rue Pigalle, to which he himself now adjourned, having already spent most of his nights there in any case. He quickly discovered not only that his liaison with Sand was well-known but that its acknowledgement carried with it none of the opprobrium of which he had been so afraid a year earlier. Nevertheless, he had his own quarters, where he could receive friends, pupils and colleagues, and the couple maintained a discreetly independent stance.

> A few fine ladies protested that the rue Pigalle was too far from their elegant districts. He answered, 'Ladies, I give much better lessons in my own room and on my own piano for twenty francs than I do for thirty at my pupils' homes, and besides, you have to send your carriages to fetch me, so take your choice.' Several of them have chosen to come to him; several others pay thirty francs and send their carriages to fetch him and bring him home. The dear boy is not sufficiently interested in money for him to have thought of this himself. It was I who suggested it, and I have had a lot of trouble to make him agree to it. But I'm glad I did it, for with his poor health he must earn money at a high rate so as to be able to work less.

Chopin could hardly conceal his pleasure at returning to the hub of Parisian society, and the continuous contact with like-minded people shook him out of that listlessness that had begun to overcome him during his final weeks at Nohant. Shortly after his return he made the acquaintance of Ignaz Moscheles, fifteen years his senior and one of the most famous musicians of the day. Chopin himself had played much of Moscheles's music and the two men found an instant rapport. For Moscheles, who had hitherto found Chopin's music impossibly elusive, the composer's playing was a revelation.

> Now, for the first time, I understood his music, and could also explain to myself the great enthusiasm of the ladies. The sudden modulations that I could not grasp when I myself played his works no longer bother me. His *piano* is so ethereal that no *forte* is needed to create the necessary contrast. Listening to him, one yields with one's whole soul, as to a singer who, oblivious of accompaniment, lets himself be carried away by his emotion. In short, he is unique among pianists.

And so being, he was promptly commissioned by Moscheles to compose three études for a comprehensive 'Piano Method' (confidently entitled *La Méthode des Méthodes*), which Moscheles was compiling with Fétis. The result was the set of *Trois Nouvelles Études*, which are strikingly different from Chopin's other contributions to the genre, despite a strong family resemblance in terms of thematic material between the first, in F minor, and the second from the op. 25 set, in the same key.

All three are of great beauty and originality, but they scrupulously avoid all invitations to bravura display. The first is a perfect example of Chopin's very individual approach to counterpoint, in which the combining of melodic strands is complemented by a cohesive rhythmic tension between the parts. The second, like the A minor, op. 10, no. 2, is a study in combining detached and legato articulations, while the third deals with the dovetailing of duple and triple rhythms. Above all, however, these are studies in colour and characterization, calling for the maximum of subtlety and a minimum of rhetoric.

Throughout the early months of 1840 Chopin and Sand worked tirelessly to regain the financial security ravaged by their Majorcan adventure of the previous winter, Chopin often giving as many as eight lessons a day. Much has been made of Sand as the comforter and supporter of the ailing Chopin; we should do wrong to forget that it was reciprocal. If Chopin on returning to Paris was surprised at the lack of scandal attending their relationship, it was partly because his influence had rendered Sand herself less scandalous. Gone were the ostentatious cross-dressing, the brandished cigars and the *frisson* of her reputed nymphomania. In both appearance and manner she had grown markedly quieter since the beginning of their affair. For the moment, at least, she seemed to have outgrown the need to shock. As the opening night of her play *Cosima* approached and her nervousness increased, she confessed in a letter to her half-brother: 'Without his [Chopin's] perfect and delicate friendship I would often have lost heart.' Not even a perfect friend, however delicate, could have saved her the disappointment and hurt occasioned by *Cosima*'s failure (it closed within a week). Nor was the effect only emotional. Largely because of insufficient funds, the following summer was spent in Paris, although a brief excursion by Sand alone resulted in one of the few of her letters to Chopin that have survived. Its maternal tone indicates to what extent their relations had changed since the rapturously erotic 'honeymoon' of the year before.

Cambrai, 13 August 1840

Dear boy,

I arrived here at noon, very tired, for the distance from Paris is forty-five leagues, not thirty-five. We shall have fine stories to tell of the Cambrai *bourgeoisie*. They are a handsome stupid race of shop-keepers – perfect specimens of the type. . . . We live like princes, but oh what hosts, what conversations, what dinners! When we are by ourselves it makes us laugh, but facing the enemy we cut pitiable figures. I no longer wish for you to come here: I am longing to get away, and now I begin to understand why my Chop. hates giving concerts. . . . I wish I were well away from the ladies and gentlemen of Cambrai.

Good night, Chip-Chip. Good night Solange and Bouli [her son Maurice]. I am ready to drop and must go to bed. Love your old mother as she does you.

Back in Warsaw, Chopin's real mother and her husband were growing ever more curious about their son's relations with this notorious woman. As Nicholas put it in a letter of 9 January 1841: 'We are glad that you are being well looked after but we should very much like to know something of this intimate friendship.' It proved a largely vain request. Chopin was disinclined to enlighten them, and they were to remain more or less in the dark for another three years.

The one great event for Chopin that year was announced in curiously self-conscious style by George Sand in a letter to their friend Pauline Viardot in London:

A great, astounding piece of news is that little Chip-Chip is going to give a Grrrrand Concert. His friends have plagued him so much that he has given way. However, he imagined that it would be so difficult to arrange that he would be obliged to give it up. But things moved more quickly than he bargained for. Scarcely had he uttered the fatal *Yes* than everything was settled, as if by a miracle. Three-quarters of the tickets were sold even before any announcement was made. Then he woke up, as if from a dream. There is no more amusing sight than our meticulous and irresolute Chip-Chip compelled to keep his promise. . . . This Chopinesque nightmare will take place at Pleyel's rooms on the 26th. He will have nothing to do with posters or programmes and does not want a large audience. He wants to have the affair kept quiet. So many things alarm him that I suggest he should play without candles or audience and on a dumb keyboard.

There can be few performers who do not sympathize with him, although one who would not have was Liszt, on whom the presence of an audience acted like a drug and whose temperament was in many ways the opposite of Chopin's. Most biographers believe that it was partly or even principally Liszt's own spectacular success in Paris that year that stimulated Chopin to emerge from his unofficial retirement. There is no real evidence, either general or specific, that Chopin was sufficiently competitive to be motivated by such a pretext, but the same could not be said for many of his friends and associates. With or without his approval, there was a groundswell of partisanship among his supporters, and Parisian society loved nothing so much as a showdown. Liszt's own triumphs that year were in direct response to the successes in Paris of the Austrian virtuoso Sigismond Thalberg★ – 'the man with three hands', as he was widely known. On Liszt's return to the capital, the two men had met in a pianistic duel whose nature and outcome were succinctly represented by the Princess Belgiojoso, who had arranged the event. 'Thalberg,' she said, 'proved that he is the best pianist in Europe; Liszt that he is the *only* one.' Of such substance are royal *bons mots* made. The whole affair can only have confirmed Chopin's growing belief that Liszt's genius was beset by a fatal vulgarity. Liszt's attitude to Chopin may be gauged by his lengthy and revealing account of the concert that 'Little Chip–Chip' consented to play on 26 April 1841. Whether it reveals more of Chopin or of Liszt is for the reader to judge.

On the evening of the performance an audience of nearly 400 wended its way up the graceful double staircase at Pleyel's. From the bare shoulders and slender necks of the ladies radiated the soft glow of pearls and the sparkle of precious stones while their perfumed hair flutters with 'golden ribbons' and 'delicate blue veils'. Here and there above the brilliant assemblage towered the military plumage of an officer or one of those 'awful black hats' shaped like a stove-pipe which men of fashion had then taken to wearing [a curious tense to adopt, as though he were quite conscious of writing for posterity]. . . . Having arrived in France around ten years ago, Chopin never competed in any way for first or second place among the horde of pianists who surge around us today. He has seldom allowed himself to be heard in public; the eminently poetic nature of his talent is not suited to that. Similar to those flowers which open their fragrant calyces only in the evening, he requires an atmosphere of tranquillity and composure in order to yield up the melodic treasures which repose within him. Music was his language [a still more interesting choice of tense, putting Chopin firmly in the past], the divine tongue through which he expressed a whole realm of sentiments that only the select few can appreciate. As with that other great poet Mickiewicz, his compatriot and friend, the muse of his homeland dictates his songs, and the anguished cries of Poland lend to his art a mysterious, indefinable poetry which, for all those who have truly experienced it, cannot be compared to anything else. . . . The piano alone was not sufficient to reveal all that lies within him. In short he

is a most remarkable individual who commands our highest degree
of devotion.

Less eminent but more conventional critics were unanimous in their
praise. *La Revue Musicale* reported:

> Chopin has broken new trails for himself. His playing and his compo-
> sition, from the very beginning, have won such high standing that
> in the eyes of many he has become an inexplicable phenomenon. . . .
> No one as yet has tried to define the special character and merit of
> those works, what distinguished them from others, and why they
> occupy such a high place.

And the critic of *La France Musicale* wrote:

> The one has done for the piano what the other [Schubert] has done
> for the voice . . . Chopin is a pianist of conviction. He composes for
> himself, plays for himself . . . and everyone listens with interest, with
> delight, with infinite pleasure. Listen how he dreams, how he weeps,
> with what sweetness, tenderness and melancholy he sings, how per-
> fectly he expresses the gentlest and loftiest feelings. Chopin is the
> pianist of sentiment *par excellence*. He may be said to have created a
> school of playing and a school of composition. Nothing indeed equals
> the lightness and sweetness of his preluding on the piano, nothing
> compares with his works in originality, distinction and grace. Chopin
> is unique as a pianist – he should not and cannot be compared with
> anyone.

On this there was universal agreement.

There must have been times when Chopin envied Liszt his obvious
enjoyment of performing. With a single appearance at the Salle Pleyel,
Chopin's bank balance soared to the tune of some 6,000 francs, a sum
surpassing his normal income from three months' teaching. A further
bonus was a huge rise in the sale of his works.

By the beginning of summer Sand's income, too, had regained its
former level, and in June they decamped to Nohant, after an absence
of some eighteen months. Their Parisian summer of the previous year
was the only break in a pattern that characterized their lives for the next
six years: after eight or nine months of activity in Paris – she writing,
indefatigably, he teaching and occasionally performing – they would
spend the summer and early autumn at Nohant, where Chopin gave
his full attention to composition during the days and to socializing with
a steady stream of house guests in the early evenings. At eight, rarely

later, he would retire to his bedroom, not to be seen again until the following morning.

To the summers of 1841 and 1842 we owe such masterworks as the F sharp minor Polonaise, the A flat Ballade, the op. 48 nocturnes, the magnificent trilogy of mazurkas, op. 50, the G flat Impromptu and, perhaps most importantly of all, the F minor Fantasy. There's general agreement that this is among the greatest products of Chopin's imagination, but words, unsurprisingly, have proved inadequate to explain why. The title itself is intentionally imprecise, but any thought that it suggests a loosely assembled ramble of spontaneous ideas soon disappears when one begins to explore the music. Alan Walker has persuasively demonstrated the organic unity of the piece, almost all of which derives in one form or another from the opening: a three-link chain of falling fourths, which themselves outline a falling sixth, presented in stark octaves with an ominous, march-like rhythm. He further suggests that the piece, despite its title, is a fully worked out sonata form. Among its most characteristically Chopinesque features is the fact that it begins in one key, F minor, and ends in another, A flat major, which also serves as the tonal anchor for most of the work's main ideas. But no amount of description can convey the sombre, haunting beauty of the piece or its near tragic power. And as with the B flat minor Sonata, we have here another predominantly turbulent work arising from what would seem to have been one of the happiest and most stable periods of Chopin's life.

A year later he returned to this same, dramatic, sombre key for a still more remarkable and gripping work, the great F minor Ballade. Indeed, the summer of 1842 was a vintage year for Chopin. Among its other products was the astonishing A flat Polonaise (the guns, in this case, pushing right through the flowers) and the sunny E major Scherzo, which is one of the happiest and most capricious of all his major works. In quantity it is not, perhaps, a very prolific output for two years, but its quality remains a source of wonderment.

For all but one of the above-named forms, there were instrumental precedents. Keyboard fantasies, in reality too nebulous to constitute a 'form', had been around as long as keyboards; nocturnes of one kind or another were plentiful long before Field claimed them for the piano; impromptus owed their place on the musical map to Schubert, while the mazurka and the polonaise were well established by the turn of the eighteenth century. The instrumental ballade, however, was the special creation of Chopin himself.

Interlude: Ballades and Scherzos

Although they stand today as a kind of family, and not without reason, the ballades were never envisaged as a group, and nor do they establish or develop any particular form to which the title 'ballade' might provide a clue. This was entirely intentional. Chopin preferred his titles to be without the baggage of formal or programmatic expectations, and, on the whole, his works are most interesting when they are least constrained. His greatest, certainly his subtlest, polonaise is the most equivocally entitled, the Polonaise-Fantasie; his richest nocturne is hidden behind the evocative but imprecise title Barcarolle; his most impressive experiments with the principles of sonata form are not in the works to which he gave that title. He liked his listeners to be free of preconception. Like every composer of genius, Chopin discovered early on that form in music is essentially self-generating; that it is the result rather than the cause of musical events. And that above all else it must be audible.

The first Ballade, in G minor, occupied Chopin, on and off, for four years. Begun in the spring of 1831, well before his departure from Poland, it lay untouched for many months after the crisis of Stuttgart that autumn. No work cost Chopin greater effort, but he had no doubt in the end that it was as fine as anything he had done. Nothing is more subjective in music than its characterization, but few would deny that we have here a work of genuinely tragic stature. If the agonies of Stuttgart were initially responsible for its abandonment, they may also have provided it with vital nourishment. In its control and deployment of passion, in its combination of immediacy and inner logic, it shows us not once but repeatedly how art derives order from chaos. The intensity of utterance in the G minor Ballade is hardly less than in the half-crazed outpourings of Chopin's journal, yet its impact is infinitely more powerful for the discipline and psychological acumen that control it. But if we are to make any sense of Chopin's title, used here for the first time in the history of purely instrumental music, we must presume that he intended a specifically narrative (hence dynamic) form of musical continuity. Considering his sensitivity on the subject of titles generally, it seems safe to assume that the choice of 'ballad' was not taken lightly. What, then, were the definitive features of the word as Chopin understood it?

A ballad is a song or verse that tells a story, often of an epic character. It has its roots in the folk tradition, in which the history of a person, a family, a community or a people is relayed from generation to generation to emphasize the identity and continuity of those acts and values that give a society its cohesion. It tells a story, but is fundamentally a poetic medium. And poetry in the folk tradition is something more than art. It uses art as an aid to memory, as a means of engraving its sense and substance on the consciousness of its auditors. It has a mnemonic function, and thus a symbolic as well as an aesthetic dimension.

What, then, is the nature of the symbolism in Chopin's ballades? If it conforms to no programme, how does it justify the 'narrative' expectations aroused by the title? If these four remarkable works are more notable for their differences than for their similarities, why are musicians and connoisseurs united in feeling they are bound together to the exclusion of all others? The Barcarolle may be a nocturne in all but name, but one looks in vain through Chopin's music for a corresponding, undercover ballade. Among the similarities that might be felt as definitive is an element of rhythmic ritual, which is one of the hallmarks of the folk ballad. Its claim on our memories is inseparable from its strongly metrical cast. Each of Chopin's ballades is characterized by an almost hypnotic grouping of beats in units of six. Nowhere is this more immediately apparent than in the openings of the second and fourth ballades, yet these units are neither monotonous nor musically separable. Through such devices as overlapping phrases – the ending of one serving also as the beginning of the next, as in the opening of the F major Ballade – the use of asymmetry within a metrical context and the deployment of ambiguity, both melodic and harmonic – the opening of the G minor Ballade keeps us guessing, constantly shifting our perceptions and expectations – Chopin rivets the attention, creating and manipulating a kind of suspenseful continuity, which is clearly comparable with that of verbal narrative.

The second ballade was begun in 1836 and finished in Majorca three years later. Its most obviously remarkable feature is its juxtaposition of tender, lilting innocence and the most violent passion, intensified by the opposition and eventual reconciliation of two contrasting keys, F major and A minor. It was evidently a favourite with Chopin, who often played it, yet seldom in the same version, sometimes ending it in F, sometimes in A minor and often leaving out the fast sections altogether. The episodic nature of the piece which allowed for such treatment was presumably behind Ferruccio Busoni's startling and rather daring declaration that the work is 'remarkably badly composed'. According to the Germanic notion of music as 'developing variation', there is no doubt that, strictly speaking, Busoni had a point. By the highly subjective and intrinsically dramatic standards of the time, on the other hand, that property – the apparently episodic juxtaposition of extreme contrasts – can be construed as a virtue. Whatever else it may be, the work as Chopin wrote it is a perfect illustration of the kind of mood swings that seem to have characterized his daily life. No one who has ever suffered from a manic depressive illness will find anything remarkable in the cheek-by-jowl alternations of the F major Ballade – nothing, that is, but the notes themselves, which add up to some of the most anguished music Chopin ever wrote as well as some of the most serene. More remarkable than the extremities of contrast, however, is the astonishing way in which Chopin later combines elements of both, rewarding the attentive listener with a combination of psychological insight and intellectual sleight-of-hand that wholly belies the work's more obviously 'Romantic' gestures. In its organic synthesis and integration of two magnetic poles, as in its masterly deployment of stability and flux, this work, like its companions, has its most fundamental roots in the Classical sonata principle, which, by 1836, was widely, if wrongly, thought to have run its course.

The A flat Ballade is a far gentler affair, taken as a whole, and its disproportionate popularity for many decades relative to its companions may owe as much to its less fearsome pianistic demands as to its intrinsically musical properties, beguiling though they are. Whereas few amateurs can hope to master all the challenges of the first two ballades, the third is a perfectly reasonable proposition for the moderately advanced player. As usual with Chopin, the music says far more for itself than anyone has yet been able to say for it, which has not, of course, prevented it from being saddled with all manner of extra-musical associations. Among the most picturesque is a drawing by Aubrey Beardsley depicting an elegant lady on a rocking-horse, an image that tells us rather more about the piece than the analyses of innumerable pedants. That said, the work, from its very outset, is a perfect example of the way in which Chopin could apply the contrapuntal lessons learned from Bach in a manner and style entirely his own. Pianists wanting to master Chopin's unique sonorities could do worse than to start here and to discover, thereby, the extent to which the secret lies in an essentially polyphonic ear. Here, too, we find the Classical sonata idea at the very centre of Chopin's thematic procedures, and at the centre of the work itself: the 'development section', to fall back for a moment on academic terminology, is as neat an example of Classical synthesis as one could reasonably hope to find in 1841.

Although it was unpopular to begin with (and there are very few pieces by Chopin of which *that* can be said), the last ballade, in F minor, has long since come into its own as one of his greatest achievements. And again the form is true unto itself alone. Appearing at first to be a series of variations on an inward-looking, almost circular theme, unfurled near the beginning, it builds to a climax through the pursuit of altogether different material, although determined analysis can demonstrate that it is not as wholly different as it may at first appear. Few works in any medium so deftly combine a sense of the inevitable with such apparent freshness and unpredictability. And we find here, too, a characteristic example of Chopin's lifelong flirtation with paradox: as in the G minor Ballade, he combines some of his most profoundly felt and thought-out music with the trappings of a style renowned for its sensual frivolity – the waltz, whose stereotyped accompaniment plays an important role in his music as a whole. But this was part of his secret. The near-universal appeal of his music, to listeners ranging from the novice to the near-omniscient, derives in part from a unique combination of sophistication and a deep-rooted, wholly uncondescending sense of the popular. Within the framework of the waltz, the polonaise and the mazurka, he used extraordinary craftsmanship to address realms of experience seldom hinted at in any of these forms before.

* * *

When it comes to etymology, Chopin's four scherzos are elusive. Before it was appropriated for artistic purposes, 'scherzo' was simply the Italian word for 'joke'. Haydn used the term to denote a much-accelerated minuet in the context of a sonata design, but it was Beethoven who gave it pride of place in the musical history books. Beethoven's scherzos, like Haydn's, were conceived as parts of a larger design, and they contain, on the whole, enough good-humoured energy to justify their label on etymological grounds. Chopin's scherzos, on the other hand, are self-contained works, more notable for their alternating intensity and lyricism than for any spirit of playfulness – although an exception must be made for the Fourth, in E major – and the dance element is largely submerged in favour of an epic, 'narrative' style, drawing loosely and idiosyncratically on the basic principles of so-called sonata form.

The first, in B minor, had been conceived back in the spring of 1831, when Chopin was twenty-one and still based in Warsaw, although there is reason to believe that it underwent drastic revision after his crisis in Stuttgart that autumn. The work leaves no doubt whatever of its essentially tragic character. The powerful, discordant opening bars, like the ensuing rejection of melodic or harmonic 'themes' in favour of tumultuously driven rhythmic figurations, establish the work's spiritual turbulence and seriousness of purpose at the outset and explore the use of texture as a primary element of musical design, which was later to become a cornerstone of Chopin's mature style and a formative influence on such later composers as Debussy and Ravel. The use for the consolatory middle-section of a Polish Christmas song, 'Lulazse Jezeniu' ('Sleep, little Jesus, Sleep'), is all the more affecting in the light of the loneliness and nostalgia experienced by Chopin in the earliest phase of his exile. And is it fanciful to find in the repeated F sharps an echo of the cowbells that can be heard to this day in the Tatra mountains? The overlapping of this brief idyll with the return of the opening's anguished cry is one of Chopin's greatest masterstrokes as a psychological dramatist. The discovery of order in the throes of emotional chaos is among the fiercest challenges a composer can face, and Chopin achieves it here with an intensity which is little short of terrifying and that should render the structural strictures of latter-day academics as offensive as they are irrelevant. We take it for granted at our peril. This is not music one wants to 'get used to'.

Curiously, the second scherzo, written six years later, begins with exactly the same discord as the first, but with what a difference of effect! The prevailing tone is altogether more buoyant and positive, and Chopin's lyricism so airborne and well balanced that one quite forgets the skill and discipline that lie behind it. And again, whatever may be said of the work's design, the dramatic pacing is superbly crafted, the thematic development is full of surprises – the little triplet upbeat figure proves astonishingly fertile – and the sense of spontaneity is sustained right to the end of the brilliantly integrated coda – a typical, Chopinesque apotheosis serving as a kind of dramatized curtain-call for the work's principal ideas. When this scherzo first appeared in London in 1837 it bore the ludicrous and wholly inappropriate title 'La Méditation'.

The third scherzo, as already noted, followed in 1839, the same period as the bulk of the B flat minor Sonata, with its almost inconceivably modern finale. The form is about as near as Chopin ever gets to the straight ABABA structure favoured by Beethoven, and its harmonies are both daring and occasionally prophetic. In the virtually keyless

introduction, all twelve notes of the chromatic scale appear, thus antici-
pating the serialism of the Second Viennese School by some three-
quarters of a century. The opening rhythm, too, is a classic example of
Chopinesque ambiguity: two bars of four beats each, at the outset of a
scherzo! After such revolutionary stuff, the second main theme can
sound extraordinarily trite unless played with a Lutheran simplicity and
reserve. Attempts to render the tune itself meaningful are generally
counterproductive. The most remarkable feature of this opening section
is precisely the contrast between the stolidity of the 'chorale' (my term,
not Chopin's) and the iridescent shower of overtones it releases in the
upper register – a characteristically unprecedented exercise in tone-
painting, which few players even attempt to explore *in tempo*, generally
coming in late with the shimmering cascade and divorcing it further
from its progenitor by beginning it with an accent. Both procedures
impede the continuity, which is itself part of the magic.

If its companions represent Chopin at his most intense, the fourth
scherzo, in E major, finds him at his sunniest. Subjective descriptions
of Chopin's music almost invariably lead to contentious ground, however. One of his many biographers, Kasimir Wierzynski, found the
work embodying 'an emotion so perfectly sublimated that one can find
in it whatever one pleases: joy or grief, happiness or despair'. It is said
that misery loves company, but the listener who finds grief or despair
in the E major Scherzo may well be doomed to solitude. In keeping
with its serene good humour, it lacks the extreme contrasts that characterize its siblings. Indeed, few works of such length have been so restricted in their dynamic range. Only rarely does Chopin suggest anything
stronger than *piano*. Most of the work's components are audibly related,
the phrasing is generally straightforward and spacious, the repetitions
are without embellishment and the climaxes few and benign.

Fame, Fear and Family
1842–1846

Following the success of his single concert appearance in 1841, Chopin was persuaded to undertake another, once again at the Salle Pleyel. On this occasion he was joined on the platform by two colleagues who were to play a significant role in his life. The mezzo-soprano Pauline Viardot,★ a committed friend to both Sand and Chopin and one of the most remarkable musicians of her time, and the cellist-composer Auguste-Joseph Franchomme. Viardot, who inspired Meyerbeer, Gounod, Brahms and Saint-Saëns to write works for her, achieved fame only as a singer, but she was also a professional organist, pianist, actress and composer who enjoyed the lifelong devotion of such literary luminaries as Turgenev, de Musset (the latter proposed marriage to her) and, of course, Sand herself. She set a number of Chopin's mazurkas to words and sang them with the wholehearted approval of the composer. Franchomme, although a minor composer, was a cellist without superior and a musician whose faultless intonation and singing tone spoke directly to Chopin's heart. The observation of one critic that 'he remained almost invisible when he played, as if he were part of the instrument' could well have been applied to Chopin himself. No two colleagues, then, could more perfectly have graced Chopin's second concert at the Salle Pleyel, which took place on 21 February 1842. It was to be his last public appearance for six years.

As before, it was a brilliant success and equally lucrative. But it came with a price. In its immediate aftermath Chopin, increasingly wraith-like in appearance, succumbed to exhaustion and took to his bed for two weeks, complaining of aching mouth and tonsils. According to Sand, he was not a good patient. She spoke with the voice of unrivalled experience when she wrote of him:

Gentle, cheerful and charming, Chopin could bring his intimates to despair when he was ill. There was no nobler, more delicate nor disinterested soul, there was no man more loyal and faithful in daily relationships. No one could surpass him in wit and gaiety; no one had a fuller or deeper understanding of his art. But unfortunately no one ever had a temperament so uneven, an imagination more deranged and gloomy, a sensitivity so easily wounded, and emotional demands so impossible to satisfy. Nothing of this was his fault. It was all the fault of his illness.

Yet the nature of that illness remained elusive. Three doctors had now pronounced Chopin free of consumption, and Sand herself increasingly took the view that his ailments were psychologically rather than physically based. From the standpoint of medical knowledge in the late twentieth century it is clear that they were mistaken, although hypochondria, of course, is not incompatible with genuine illness. Sand's reluctance to accept the reality of his disease may have sprung from two sources. Hypochondria and a pervading sense of malaise are not fatal conditions and their eventual cure do not require the attentions of trained physicians. In her refusal to acknowledge the physical portents of his condition, Sand was at least partially released from the contemplation of his early death while preserving for herself the role of potential saviour.

Thoughts of death were never far from Chopin's own consciousness, but he was soon to encounter the reality with a shocking force. As Sand put it in a letter to Pauline Viardot at the end of April:

A Polish friend, a doctor and former schoolmate of Chopin [Jan Matuszynski] died in our arms after a slow and cruel death-agony which caused Chopin almost equal suffering. He was strong, courageous and devoted – more so than one might have expected from such a fragile being. But when it was all over he was utterly broken.

It requires no great imagination to presume that in witnessing the protected suffering of his friend Chopin saw portents of his own end. His subsequent collapse, now characteristic of his response to death, must have been occasioned as much by fear as grief. With the death of his father in 1844, also from tuberculosis, the former may even have replaced the latter as the dominant emotion. But this is to anticipate.

That Chopin was growing increasingly petulant seems clear, but the causes are harder to divine. Some may have been directly related to the disease that, true to its nineteenth-century nomenclature, was slowly but inexorably consuming him. Others may only have been exacerbated by Sand's increasing maternalism, a tendency that, ironically, she largely withheld from her own children. It has been suggested that Sand's caretaking instincts, evident in many of her relationships, may have psychologically unmanned Chopin. His music tells a different story. The epic B minor Sonata, the A flat Polonaise, the Barcarolle and the Polonaise-Fantasie are hardly the products of an emotional eunuch. If music be the guide, Sand's influence can be regarded only as benign. It was she more than anyone who created and maintained the circumstances in which Chopin's peculiar genius could flourish. If, in the process, she unsheathed the spoilt child in him, posterity can forgive her. For Chopin's contemporaries it was not always so easy. That she treated him *like* a child is amply evidenced by her letters. Even before they drifted into an indolent asexuality she openly referred to him as 'the little one', 'the boy', 'little Chip-Chip' and so on. As the years wore on he became 'the poor child', and later even 'my son'.

Perhaps significantly, we find little or no evidence of the spoilt child in the letters and reminiscences of his boyhood and youth. While subject throughout his life to cyclical alternations of euphoria and depression, he seems in no way to have been an exceptionally 'difficult' child, still less a conceited or demanding one, despite the numerous privations occasioned by his fragile health. Prior to his departure from Poland his background was one of great stability and warmth. He enjoyed the security of an orderly, close-knit family in which, as the only son, he was unstintingly adored by mother and sisters alike; he commanded the admiration of his elders and reciprocated the affection of his peers; and he shared with his compatriots an abiding and bonding pride in belonging to the community of the Polish nation, a pride that embraced Poles of every class and type. In the autumn of 1831 he had chosen to cut himself adrift from all of this. His friendships forged in France were many and lasting but, barring that with Sand, they never approached the intimacy and shared identity of those he formed in Poland. Not even with the émigré community of Poles in Paris did he find that depth of familial security that had nurtured his most formative years. As that age of love and innocence receded, his sense of isolation grew. So too did his dependence on the surrogate family provided by Sand and Nohant. With the deaths of his father and of Matuszynski the links with his lost youth became more tenuous. Whatever the state of his libido or Sand's reasons for abstaining, the removal of sex from their relations was likewise undermining. Throughout the period of his early to mid-thirties, he showed signs of intensifying neurosis, significant chinks beginning to appear in his armour of genteel imperturbability. Displays of temper and impatience erupted suddenly and unpredictably.

Nor was Sand by any means the only witness. Increasingly, his students bore the brunt of his unease. Of these, none has left a more telling portrait than Zofia Rozengardt, a young Polish girl who travelled from Warsaw to Paris expressly to study with Chopin. Describing him as 'a weird and incomprehensible man', she goes on:

> You cannot imagine a person who can be colder and more indifferent to everything around him. There is a strange mixture in his character: vain and proud, loving luxury and yet disinterested and incapable of sacrificing the smallest part of his own will or caprice for all the luxury in the world. He is polite to excess, and yet there is so much irony, so much spite hidden inside it. Woe betide the person who allows himself to be taken in. He has an extraordinarily keen eye, and he will catch the smallest absurdity and mock it wonderfully. He is heavily endowed with wit and common sense, but then he often has wild, unpleasant moments when he is evil and angry, when he breaks chairs and stamps his feet. He can be as petulant as a spoiled child, bullying his pupils and being very cold with his friends. Those are usually days of suffering, physical exhaustion or quarrels with Madame Sand.

Yet even here there was a curious element of self-control and calculation. The lash of Chopin's tongue was reserved for his professional pupils. The well-born ladies of Parisian society who provided the bulk of his income witnessed nothing of this. Sand undoubtedly did. And if a nineteen-year-old student was attributing Chopin's behaviour to 'quarrels with Madame Sand', it is unlikely that she was alone in her suspicions. It would be premature, however, to speak of an impending rift in their relationship at this stage. Whatever tensions may have coloured their private life, they remained outwardly devoted, and there is no evidence from this period to support a charge of hypocrisy against either of them. That there were certain unbridgeable chasms in the topography of their relations can hardly be doubted. Sand almost certainly perceived them first. Chopin's, on the whole, was the wisdom of the ostrich. To us, with the wisdom of hindsight, his behaviour in crisis may speak volumes; to Sand and Chopin both, in the 1840s, it seemed to speak in riddles and continued so to do for some considerable time.

In May 1844 Nicholas Chopin died in Poland at the age of seventy-three. On hearing the news, his only son, now thirty-four, turned his back on solace and locked himself into his apartment, where according to Sand he remained immured and silent for days, speaking only and briefly to his servant Jan until toothache compelled him to admit a doctor. For weeks afterwards he remained morose and morbid. His obsessive curiosity as to the manner of his father's death smacked more of fear than grief, and while his experience of bereavement was undoubtedly both genuine and deep, his sense of loss was symbolic as well as filial. With the loss of his father, whom he had not seen for nearly a decade and with whom he had never been particularly intimate, an important part of Chopin's Poland died. Bereavement inevitably looses the floodgates of memory, and there was hardly a cranny of Chopin's Polish life in which his father had not played some part. Throughout his years in Poland Chopin had remained financially dependent on his father, his actions were very largely determined by his father's fund of practical good sense, and he owed the most lasting friendships of his life to the fact that his father kept a boarding-house.

Finding herself unable, as she put it, 'to break in on his grief', Sand wrote movingly to Chopin's mother, who ended her reply:

> You understand how I must feel, Madame, and it needed a mother's heart to realise this and to understand how to pour true consolation into mine. And so Fryderyk's mother thanks you sincerely and entrusts her dear boy to your maternal care. Be, Madame, his guardian angel as you have been an angel of consolation to me, and accept our respectful gratitude which you may be sure equals your valuable devotion and care.

Any lingering suspicions of impropriety between her son and a scarlet woman had obviously been well allayed. Justyna was not to see her Fryderyk again, but the high point of his summer that year was a visit to Paris and Nohant by his sister Ludwika and her husband, neither of whom he had seen since leaving Poland fourteen years before.

Unexpectedly, in view of its traumatic start, the summer of 1844 proved in many ways to mark the apex of Chopin's creative and emotional life. His sister's visit was a joy to Chopin, not least for her warm approval of his life with Sand and the obvious affection and esteem that they felt for one another from the start. When they parted at the end of August, Chopin, notwithstanding the pangs of farewell, was spiritually much restored. The crisis of his father's death had passed, Ludwika's visit had enriched the creative soil of his freshly recollected youth, and when he returned to Nohant on 4 September it was with renewed self-confidence and energy.

*   *   *

The glow of summer continued to illuminate a productive and generally peaceful autumn, and not even Chopin could fail to notice that he was at the peak of his artistic powers. Of all arts, music is perhaps the most manipulative. For this reason alone its biographical significance can be highly suspect. It seems safe to assume, however, that Chopin's B minor Sonata gives a broadly accurate picture of his state of mind during this period. In its proud self-assurance and wealth of melodic invention, in the Olympian skittishness of its scherzo, the rapturous serenity of the slow movement and the noble striding of the finale, it gives us Chopin not only at his most masterful but at his most spiritually healthy. Never was he less deserving of Field's contemptuous description of him as 'a sickroom talent'. No other composer of the time was writing music of more natural and unprotesting virility. Certainly none of comparable stature housed so great a spirit in so fragile and delicate a shell.

Almost more remarkable, even than the B minor Sonata, was a piece whose duration in performance seldom exceeds five minutes: the entrancing Berceuse (or Cradle Song) of 1844, a small miracle of musical embroidery, based on a premise that by any logical reckoning ought to have proved suicidal – a progression of finespun variations over a tonic (D flat) pedal point, maintained unaltered for fully sixty-eight bars beneath a simple, one bar, tonic-dominant *ostinato* in the left hand, which is then repeated, unchangingly, no fewer than fifty-four times. At that point, even the dominant drops out, to be replaced by four bars of reiterated tonic with no change of texture. A mere twelve bars from the end, the *ostinato* figure finally yields to the subdominant for two bars only, pays its final respects to the dominant for a further two bars before subsiding on to the tonic until the penultimate bar, when the work's first real cadence brings the piece to a close. On paper, the harmonic interest is virtually non-existent. Glimpsed through the apparently effortless kaleidoscope of melodic filigree, however, it seems both inexhaustibly fascinating and profoundly calming. The seamlessness of the successive variations is complemented by a characteristically asymmetrical phrase structure, present, almost from the outset, in Chopin's unusual opening phrase, which extends from the beginning of the piece to the end of bar thirteen in the autograph score, an 'error' thoughtfully corrected in the Paderewski edition. As the Chopin scholar Arthur Hedley rightly remarked, the Berceuse attains a level of musical poetry that utterly defies analysis. 'Who will open the nightingale's throat,' he asked, 'to discover where the song comes from?'

*   *   *

Whatever the diagnosis of his doctors, let alone Sand, who persisted in her scepticism, Chopin was growing progressively weaker. As 1844 drew to an end he more than once had to be carried upstairs or lifted into his carriage. In only a few more years he would come to rely on such services.

Despite her later claim to have lived with Chopin 'in perfect chastity', Sand's sexual appetite demanded some form of release, and it was during this period that she found solace between the sheets of Louis Blanc,★ a socialist firebrand, one year Chopin's junior, whose revolutionary writings had made him a hero of the French proletariat and a thorn in the flesh of the Orléans dynasty. The affair was purely physical and posed no threat to Chopin, with whom Sand was planning to spend the winter in Italy. The real threat to Chopin was Chopin himself. Long outworn as a lover – his physical condition alone would have seen to that – he was less and less a soulmate to Sand. In marked contrast to the previous year, the summer of 1845 was one of increasing indolence and mindless fatigue. Apart from the splendid triptych of mazurkas, op. 59, he produced no music at all that year. The charms of Nohant were wearing thin, and he did little to counter the enervating boredom that now assailed him. His cultivated, incisive mind began to atrophy through lack of nourishment. If he wrote hardly any music of his own, still less did he study that of others. If Bach and Mozart did not come to his rescue, it was only because they were unbidden. The library at Nohant housed some of the greatest thought and literature of humankind, yet there is nothing to suggest that Chopin read a single volume. Sand, for her part, sought his company less and less, confining herself to her room and writing for longer and longer periods.

At thirty-five, Chopin was beginning to resemble an elderly relative, kept on in the house as a kindness but largely ignored. And who was there to amuse or converse with him? His most faithful companion was an enormous dog called Jacques, like him a fixture in the house for years. And what of Sand's children, with whom he had endured the Majorcan adventure and many other chapters of their collective lives over more than half a decade? What was he to them or they to him? They were born to principled eccentricity and scandal; Solange herself was illegitimate. They had seen their mother take a lover, the latest of many, the first to last more than a year, whom she had then enveloped within the bosom of her family, not as surrogate father to her children but in effect, and later by name, as their surrogate sibling. In the meantime, of course, they had grown. Maurice, his mother's favourite, was now twenty-two. He had never liked Chopin, of whom he justifiably felt jealous and increasingly regarded with open contempt. Solange, whose banishment to boarding school had been an accurate index of her mother's affections, had blossomed into a voluptuous if unprepossessing seventeen-year-old with a well-nourished instinct for sexual power. In the summer of 1845 she began to exercise that power to disastrous effect.

If Maurice had cause to be jealous of Chopin, Solange had cause to be jealous of her brother. Their mother, who doted on one while enduring the other, further fanned the embers of Solange's resentment through an act of folly, characteristically generous in impulse, that was to have lasting, and in Chopin's case near-fatal, repercussions on all their lives. She imported into the household and subsequently adopted the nubile young daughter of a disreputable cousin, Augustine Brault. Long abused by her father, who had chosen to market her as a courtesan, she was, unlike Solange, both attractive and intelligent, and Sand now proceeded to lavish on Augustine all the motherly affection she had denied her own daughter and to look on with proud satisfaction as Maurice and Augustine succumbed to mutual desire. With every passing week, Maurice was moving closer to his rightful position, as he saw it, as the master of the house. Chopin and Solange, effectively marginalized, spent more and more time in each other's company, during which periods there seems little doubt that Solange used all her feminine guile on the frail and depressed composer. It would be presumptuous and almost certainly false to suggest that he now fell in love with her, but it seems improbable that there was not a sexual element in their alliance. Nor was the sense of alliance new. From the beginning of their acquaintance, Chopin had felt more drawn to Solange than to her brother, a reflection, in part, of his deep-rooted instinct for siding with the weak against the strong. The lines are already clearly drawn in a letter addressed to Solange by Sand as early as 1841:

> Your brother and I love you, but we have no illusions about certain faults which you must correct and which you will surely try to eradicate: self-love, a craving to dominate others and your mad, stupid jealousy. . . . Good night! Chopin sends you a kiss and is waiting to spoil you, but I will have none of it.

To 'your brother and I', Augustine was now added. Solange lost no opportunity to rub salt in the wounds of her cousin's origins and recent circumstances. Augustine herself, whose personality Chopin seems to have disliked from the start and whose adoption he had strenuously opposed, needed little persuasion to side with Maurice against both of them.

The first casualty of the brewing conflict was Chopin's Polish man-servant. Already unpopular with the kitchen staff as a coarse and abusive foreigner, he was much disliked by Maurice, and Sand herself had threat-ened to douse him with a bucket of water if he could not refrain from ringing the dinner bell each evening for fifteen minutes at a stretch. At Maurice's behest, Chopin was forced to dismiss him and thus lost his only opportunity of speaking in his mother tongue. That loss, at any rate, could be put right the moment he returned to Paris, which he did in September, while Sand and her family remained at Nohant. During this period Sand and he exchanged letters on a daily basis. Nor, despite the mounting tensions of the previous weeks is there yet any sign of an impending rupture. Was Sand only insuring against Chopin's propensity to jealousy when she wrote 'Love me, my beloved angel, my dearest happiness, I love you'? It seems unlikely. But whatever may be said of Sand's conduct or motives, there is no denying that Chopin was some-times easier to love when he was absent. It was something he acknowl-edged himself. 'When I am tired,' he wrote, 'I am anything but cheerful, and I become a wet blanket for everyone.' Long before the ominous tremors of 1846, Sand had complained to a friend:

I have never had, and shall never have, any peace with him. . . . The day before yesterday he spent the entire day without speaking a word to a soul. Was he ill? Has someone annoyed him? Have I said anything to upset him? I shall never know, no more than a million other similar things which he doesn't know himself. . . . But I must not let him think he is the master here – he would be all the more touchy in the future.

Who, then, was the master now? To Maurice, the question was redun-dant. No one was so eager as he to be rid of Chopin. Yet despite much speculation, there is no evidence that his mother was ever party to such a plan. In the spring of 1846 she was even planning to install a central heating system at Nohant, largely with Chopin's comfort in mind. She continued to write warmly to Ludwika, and her solicitude for Chopin's health shows no sign of abating.

In May the little band left Paris for Nohant, where Chopin's delight of the month was the promise of a machine that could manufacture ice cream in twenty minutes. Sand's letters to friends give no hint of impending doom.

We are busy from noon to six o'clock – long summer days during which we are shut up at our work like hermits. We shall think out a way of arranging our work so as not to stifle our dear Chopin. The rest of us make light of everything, but not of him. He is still composing masterpieces, although he claims that nothing he does is worth anything.

The masterpieces in question include the two nocturnes of op. 62, the three mazurkas, op. 63, and most wonderful of all, the strange Polonaise-Fantasie, op. 61, the apotheosis of his lifelong meditations on Poland's most famous dance. It was, after all, with a polonaise that he had made his début as a published composer at the age of seven.

Interlude: Chopin and the Polonaise

There is a pleasing irony in the fact that Poland's most famous and patriotic dance, like her most famous and patriotic composer, bears a French name. The composer, of course, got his from his father; the dance, in its modern manifestation, from its godmothers: three French princesses of the seventeenth century who married successive Polish kings. From that time, the polonaise has been widely accepted as a purely instrumental dance of impeccably aristocratic, if nationally impure lineage. In common with many a latter-day aristocrat, however, it came from humble origins.

Like the mazurka, it spent its earliest youth among the Polish peasantry. Like the mazurka, too, it was originally a sung dance, or rather a whole family of them. Contrary to popular belief, these ancient forebears are not completely buried in the mists of time – many have been preserved and are still in use at various popular ceremonies and festivities, notably at weddings, where their measured and dignified triple metre is deemed particularly appropriate. Another similarity with the elders of the mazurka family is a use of the pentatonic scale.

By the late sixteenth century the polonaise had found its way into neighbouring countries and became particularly popular in Scandinavia, where it sired the polska, destined to become a national folk dance of Sweden. It remained, however, in the realm of folk music and might have continued in relative obscurity for centuries had it not been taken up by the Polish aristocracy, in whose hands it began rapidly to evolve into the distinctive and representative dance we know today. Late in the seventeenth and early in the eighteenth century, the polonaise was increasingly cultivated by the landed gentry, whose lives and, therefore, requirements of the dance were hugely different from that of the peasantry. During this transitional period it continued to be sung, although the words naturally underwent considerable sophistication and its rhythms began to approach those of the courtly polonaises to come. Strictly speaking, the polonaise is not so much a dance as a kind of processional – a *marche dansante*, despite its triple metre. Listeners of exceptional erudition, curiosity or enterprise can find examples

of the polonaise at this stage of its development in the three operas by
Stanislaw Moniuszko, which explore the life of Poland's small, country
aristocracy.

Only when it moved into the palaces of the Polish nobility did the
polonaise acquire its purely instrumental status and assume the stately
splendour that spread its fame throughout the continent of Europe. Its
most outstanding feature was its insistent, rather martial rhythmic
motto ($\frac{3}{4}$♪♫♪♫), and it was this purely musical property rather than
any particular aura of Polishness that recommended it to the likes of
Bach, Mozart and Beethoven. It fell to Chopin alone, however, to infuse
the form with a nationalism which resounds to this day, but until 1835
he too had found in the polonaise little more than a convenient receptacle
for youthful virtuosity and musical experiment. Of these early polonaises, only two, the G minor of 1817 and the B flat minor from 1826,
were published during his lifetime. The rest, despite their opus numbers,
were brought out posthumously and were regarded by Chopin as juvenilia, although they are juvenilia of an altogether exceptional order.

The two polonaises of op. 26 initiate the series of seven in which
Chopin lifted the whole conception of the dance on to a loftier and
more dramatic plane than any previously envisaged for it, even by
himself. The catalyst was undoubtedly the fall of Warsaw in 1831, but
the chrysalis needed time in which to mature. From op. 26 onwards,
however, the polonaise became for Chopin a blazing nationalist tone-
poem, in which the fearsome, the tender and the grandiose combined
to symbolize the splendour of Poland's past, the tragedy of her present
and his hopes for her future. The C sharp minor strikes a challenging
note from the outset, which finds a sombre, even menacing complement
in the following, E flat minor work. Of the next pair, op. 40, the first,
in A, also known as the 'Military', is among the most played and popular
of Chopin's works. Its determined self-confidence speaks for itself. The
first theme of the sombre second polonaise, in C minor, is thought by
many Poles to be a dark, unconscious reminiscence of Karol Kurpinski's
so-called 'Coronation Polonaise' of 1826.

Even these first four of Chopin's 'new-style' polonaises, however,
may be seen as a kind of preparation in view of what follows them.
With the F sharp minor, op. 44, we enter a different realm, larger in
scope and more sophisticated in conception. Chopin himself described
it as more of a fantasy than a polonaise proper. Nominally, it must be
reckoned the most overtly patriotic of them all, since its trio section is
a fully fledged mazurka. In its grandeur and intensity of feeling this
polonaise is a match for the brooding, revolutionary fervour of its E

flat minor predecessor. In the deployment of its dramatic tensions, however, and its peculiarly self-generating construction, it surpasses all Chopin's previous adventures in the genre and poses some intractable challenges to the interpreter, notably in the modulatory repetitions of the episode that leads on to the mazurka.

Of all Chopin's works few have achieved greater or more lasting popularity than the great A flat major Polonaise, op. 53. However, despite its apparently straightforward splendour it would seem to be among his most sinned-against creations. Our witness is Sir Charles Hallé, the founder of the orchestra that still bears his name and a formidable virtuoso pianist himself: 'I remember,' he wrote in his reminiscences, 'how on one occasion, in his gentle way, [Chopin] laid his hand upon my shoulder, saying how unhappy he felt because he had heard his Grand Polonaise in A flat "jouée vite!", thereby destroying all the grandeur, the majesty of this noble inspiration. Poor Chopin must be rolling round and round in his grave nowadays, for this blatant misreading has now unfortunately become the fashion.' A fashion that soon ossified into a tradition. When Chopin himself played the work in Paris, his compatriots and fellow exiles rose to their feet as one and began to sing an old and familiar song: 'Poland has not perished yet, because her sons are living!'

To say that Chopin's next and last essay in the form would arouse no such reaction is hardly to denigrate it. There is widespread agreement amongst serious musicians that the Polonaise-Fantasie, op. 61, is a masterpiece, although by no means an unproblematical one. Indeed, it belongs to that tiny minority of Chopin's works that met with general incomprehension in his lifetime. Astonishingly, even Liszt, himself a prophetic modernist and one of Chopin's most dedicated champions, found the work 'unfathomable' and went so far as to proclaim that such works were basically valueless as art. And although posterity has reversed his judgement, there is no gainsaying that the piece requires familiarity before yielding up its greatest treasures. To be fair, Liszt was not the only one who had problems with it. Chopin himself, while working on the piece, followed his own intuitive genius with a certain uneasy puzzlement. Like many a first-time listener since, he found it hard to identify the work's true character, and the naming of this most complex of his creations caused him more trouble than that of any other. The title he eventually settled on was to the point, and unique. The Polonaise-Fantasie is named like no other because it is made like no other.

In the first fifteen years of his mature life as a composer, Chopin matched his inspiration with an extraordinary originality, manifested principally in the realms of harmony and piano technique. Tradition, never a trustworthy witness, has it that, for all his mastery elsewhere, he was chronically weak in matters of form. True or not, it would seem that from the composition of the B minor Sonata onwards – it was written in 1844 – Chopin's main preoccupations were with structure. The Polonaise-Fantasie shows him advancing on all fronts simultaneously. Its harmonies anticipate Wagner and Richard Strauss, entrusting to the piano sonorities never drawn from it before, and its form, like that of the F sharp minor Polonaise, only more so, is generated throughout from within. While the piece clearly and repeatedly uses the distinctive polonaise rhythm, the emphasis, from the very opening bars, with their luminous harmonic ambiguity, is on the fantasy. Of the several themes that Chopin introduces, three are richly developed and play an important part in the work's intricately woven summation. The clear-cut formal divisions that characterize the earlier polonaises are nowhere to be found.

Of these youthful works, the op. 71 set was published in 1855, and was long assumed to have been written around 1825. The Chopin scholar Arthur Hedley, on the other hand, believed that the first of them, at least, might have been composed as early as 1820. The B flat minor Polonaise that follows is the one written in 1826 for Wilhelm Kolberg after the two friends had heard Rossini's opera *La Gazza Ladra*, hence the reference in the trio to the aria 'Vieni fra queste bracciao' from Act I.

The manuscript of the G flat Polonaise, published in 1870, has long been lost, and its authenticity has been questioned, despite assurances by Ludwika Chopin that the piece is indeed her brother's work. If it is Chopin's, it would appear to have been written in 1829, before he left Warsaw for Vienna. The little G minor Polonaise is authentic beyond doubt. The first of Chopin's works to be published, it was written when he had attained the imposing age of seven. The B flat Polonaise followed a year or so later, while the two remaining works in the form date from 1821 and 1822 respectively.

— 11 —

The Crack-up
1846–1848

Among the most welcome visitors to Nohant that summer was Eugène Delacroix, who had the rare privilege of hearing Chopin play Beethoven: 'He played divinely – which is better by far than a lot of talk about aesthetics.' Chopin returned the compliment, writing to Franchomme that Delacroix was: 'the most admirable artist imaginable. I have had delightful times with him. He adores Mozart – and knows all of his operas by heart.'

By the end of June it began to be evident that the heat of the summer would not be confined to the weather. The growing tension between Chopin and Maurice flared into isolated eruptions of open warfare in which Sand herself could not remain neutral. On one occasion, as she confided to a friend, Mlle de Rozières: 'I quite lost my temper, which gave me the courage to tell him a few home truths, and to threaten to get sick of him.' And threaten to get sick of him. A curious phrase, with its suggestion of wilful decision. Or had the stage of threats already been passed? Sand's own ambivalence is evident in her immediate follow-up: 'Since then he has been sensible, and you know how sweet, excellent and admirable he is when he is not mad.' But the final rumblings had begun.

Chopin's self-protective reflexes seem to have ensured that he was among the last to recognize the fact. Less than a week before the incident just recounted, Sand had begun the serial publication of her latest novel, *Lucrezia Floriani*. Despite her later protestations of innocence, the book is transparently based on her relationship with Chopin, who is depicted as 'a distinguished neurasthenic', the Polish Prince Karol, and it constitutes at the very least a gross intrusion on his private life and a betrayal of shared intimacies. Sand herself, as the eponymous heroine, is portrayed as unfailingly noble, tender and self-sacrificing; Chopin as helpless, jealous, self-pitying and demanding, the ultimate cause of the heroine's untimely demise. Most significantly, Lucrezia is portrayed as the quintessential mother – loving, protective and loyal – whose devotion is tragically corrupted by the emotionally cancerous presence of her sickly and dependent ex-lover.

> No one could even suspect what was going on inside him. The more exasperated he was, the colder was his manner, and one could have an idea of the degree of his rage only by estimating the degree of his icy courteousness. It was at such moments that he was truly unbearable, because he wanted to reason and to subject real life – of which he had never understood anything – to principles that he could not define. Then he would rise to wit, a false and glittering wit, in order to torture those whom he loved.

Across the length and breadth of literary Europe, the book was a gossip's dream come true, eagerly devoured by readers who had never laid eyes on either Sand or Chopin. And those who knew the couple well were in no doubt about its nature. As Pauline Viardot put it many years later,

> Read *Lucrezia Floriani*, in my opinion a literary and psychological masterpiece, and at the same time a cruel action, and you will see, as if you had witnessed it yourself, what little by little, invisibly, fatally, brought about the end of a liaison which was poor Chopin's life, and a slow death for Madame Sand. It is a sad story. I think that in all those love affairs there was no *friendship* – that is a passion which cannot diminish, it is the most beautiful of all.

Yet of an evening in that summer of 1846, Chopin sat elegant and attentive while Sand read the book aloud to the assembled company and showed no sign of recognition or discomfort. Delacroix looked on appalled:

> I was frankly in agony during the reading. . . . The victim and the executioner amazed me equally. Madame Sand seemed completely at ease, and Chopin did not stop making admiring comments about the story.

It is just conceivable that neither of the protagonists recognized what the world outside could see at a glance. In any case, there was no evidence of embarrassment or rancour, but as Chopin withdrew, perhaps uncomprehendingly, into his shell, Sand misread the symptoms. By mid-September she was able to write: 'his nerves have calmed down; he has turned the corner and his character has become calmer and more equable.'

★　　★　　★

The year 1846, for reasons that will soon become clear, was another lean one in terms of quantity – quite exceptionally so. Apart from three mazurkas, it saw the beginning, as the next year saw the completion, of a work that for many musicians stands as the crowning glory of Chopin's entire creative life. In character, the F sharp major Barcarolle stands apart from most of Chopin's other work. Untypically, it invites, even in its title, an allusive, even a programmatic interpretation. A barcarolle is a boating song, widely associated with Venetian gondoliers, and Chopin draws here on actual gondoliers' songs and other scraps of Italian folk music, just as Mendelssohn does in three of his finest 'Songs Without Words'. In the work's very opening gesture one can easily imagine the decisive push of the gondolier's pole and the swish of the water as he launches the boat on its journey. Similar in tone and overall design to the nocturnes, the Barcarolle stands nevertheless in a class of its own. Far more can be learned about it from one of the nineteenth century's greatest pianists, Karl Tausig, than from any number of today's critical 'analysts'. Contemplating this finest flowering of Chopin's *bel canto* style and a piece whose organic form should silence all gossip about his supposed structural inadequacies, he tells us that:

> there are two persons concerned in this affair; it is a love scene in a discrète gondola; let us say this mis-en-scène is the symbol of a lovers' meeting generally. This is expressed in thirds and sixths; the dualism of two notes – two persons – is maintained throughout; all is two-voiced, two-souled. In the modulation to C sharp major – super-scribed *dolce sfogato* [sweet, evanescent] – there are kiss and embrace! This is quite evident! When, after three bars of introduction, the theme, lightly rocking in the bass solo, enters in the fourth, this theme is nevertheless made use of throughout the whole fabric only as an accompaniment, and *on* this the cantilena in two parts is laid; we have thus a continuous, tender dialogue.

Few single works by Chopin have had such far-reaching effects as the Barcarolle. Among the major composers who have fallen profitably under its spell are Brahms (not often cited as a beneficiary of Chopin's genius), Ravel and, most importantly of all perhaps, Debussy, whose 'L'Isle joyeuse' could hardly have been written without it. The ending of Brahms's F sharp minor Sonata, op. 2, too, bears an audible similarity to the end of the Barcarolle. This is no coincidence: Brahms's admiration for the piece is well documented; so is Ravel's. Indeed, much of the essence of Ravel's harmonic vocabulary is prefigured here, especially in bar forty-nine and again in the coda, with its prolonged F sharp pedal point and its extraordinary combination of G minor and B flat major chords in bars 108–110. And there are further Barcarollean echoes, albeit slightly transposed, in the ending of 'Les entretiens de la Belle et de la Bête' from Ravel's *Ma mère l'Oye*.

★   ★   ★

A poignant indication of Chopin's inner state at the time is his sudden and unexpected flowering as a correspondent. Generally a reluctant letter-writer, not least to his own family, he now begins to compose long, rambling accounts of this and that, most of it trivial and much of it suggesting a need to distract himself from too much rumination. Thus his family in Warsaw are informed that

> In London a Mr Faber (a teacher of mathematics), who is interested in mechanics, has exhibited a very entertaining automaton named 'Euphonia', which pronounces quite clearly not merely a word or two but long phrases, and what's more, sings a Haydn aria and *God Save the Queen*, words and all. If they could get hold of a large number of these robots the opera-managers could do without singers for the chorus, who cost a lot and give a great deal of trouble. . . . I wrote to you some time ago about M. Vaucanson's mechanical duck which digested what it ate: Vaucanson has also constructed a robot which plays the flute.

But his bulletins were not confined to trivia:

> You must already have heard about M. Leverrier's new planet [Neptune]. Leverrier, who works at the Paris Observatory, noticed certain irregularities in the planet Uranus and attributed them to another planet, so far undiscovered, whose distance, orbit and mass and everything he described, just as Galle in Berlin and the people in London have been able to observe. What a triumph for science that mathematics could lead to such a discovery!

He persisted in trying to compose, but his efforts were sporadic and his concentration diminished. His most recalcitrant project was a major work for Franchomme, which proceeded by fits and starts, as he reported to his family:

> Sometimes I am satisfied with my cello sonata, sometimes not. I throw it aside and then take it up again. . . . When one is doing something it seems all right, otherwise one wouldn't write anything.

Sand with Liszt – her expression casting doubt on the quality of her cigar.
A caricature by her son Maurice. (*Mary Evans Picture Library*)

Chopin playing at the salon of Prince Radziwill. Note the unusually high position of arms and wrists. (*Mansell Collection*)

Right Extracts from the manuscript of the Cello Sonata in G minor, first movement, with characteristic crossings out. (*Chopin Society*)

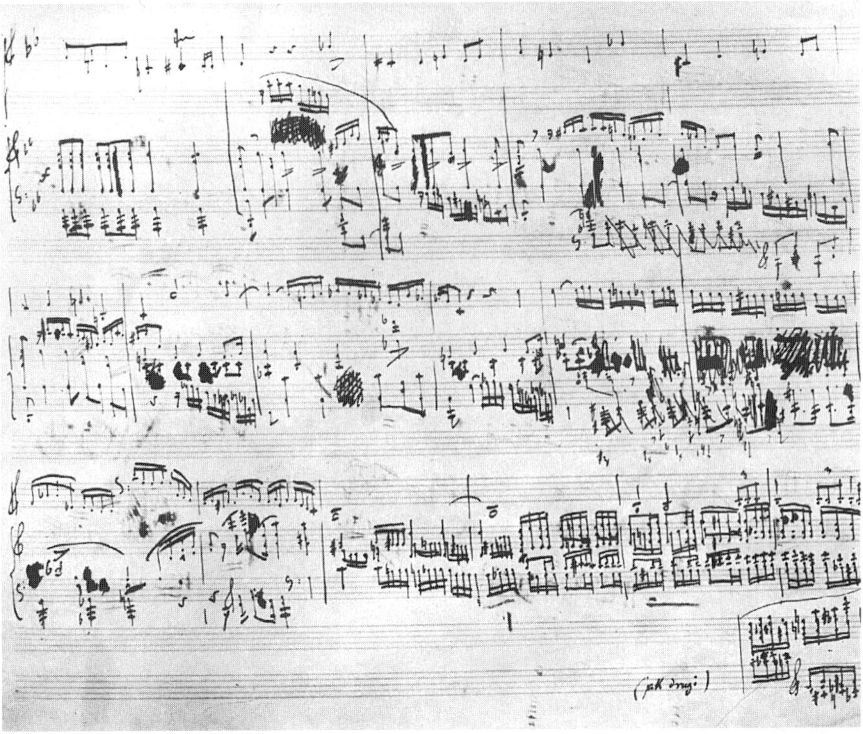

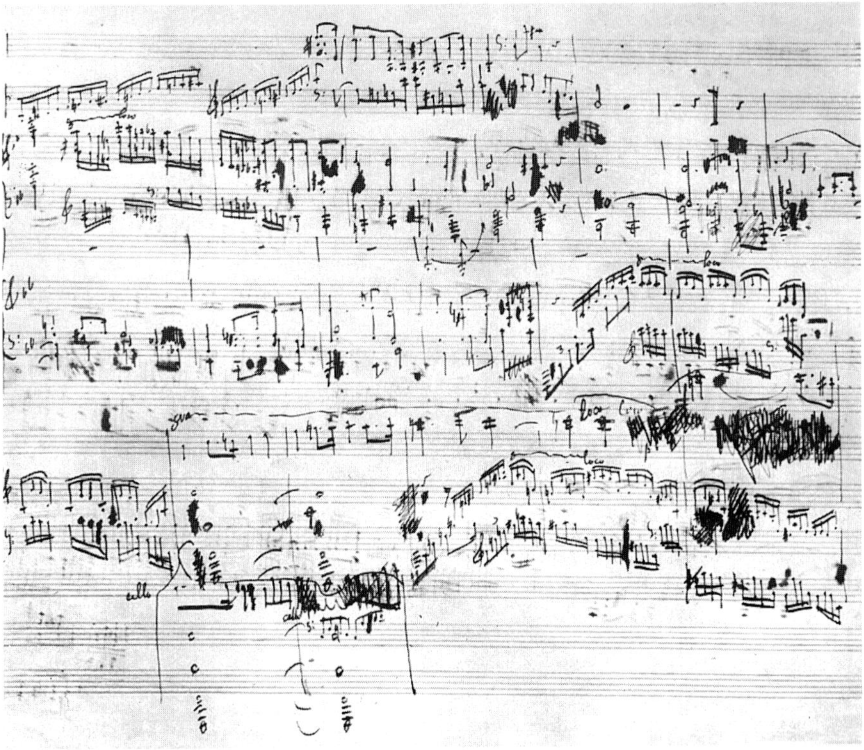
8va
loco
cello

The piano on which Chopin played during the last two years of his life. Seen through the doorway is a portrait by Ary Scheffer, painted in 1847. (*Hulton Deutsch*)

Chopin in his final months, his face swollen with neuralgia. A photograph
(often wrongly described as a daguerrotype) by L. A. Bisson. (*Mansell Collection*)

Above Barricade on the Boulevard Montmartre. An artist's impression of the tumult that brought Chopin's Paris to an end in 1848. (*Hulton Deutsch*)

Left Jane Wilhelmina Stirling. Her near-obsessive devotion to Chopin both before and after his death later earned her the ironical nickname 'Chopin's widow'. (*Chopin Society*)

Above Chopin on his deathbed. Compare this with the profile drawn of him at nineteen. (*Mary Evans Picture Library*)

Death mask of Chopin, made within hours of the composer's death by Auguste Clésinger. (*Mansell Collection*)

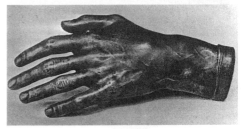

Chopin's left hand, also cast by Auguste Clésinger. (*Mansell Collection*)

The Chopin monument at Monceau Park. (*Mansell Collection*)

It's only later that one reflects carefully, and either keeps a thing or rejects it. Time is the best form of censorship, and patience the finest teacher.

As the summer wore on, the former lay heavily on his hands and the latter was in short supply. In more ways than he could perceive, the ground beneath his feet was shifting. The enforced sacking of his man-servant had initiated a sequence of outwardly minor changes, almost certainly originating with Maurice, which served to undermine his sense of security. Nor did the weather conspire to help him. No one could remember a hotter or more humid summer. It sapped Chopin's energy and subjected him to an indignity that Sand openly ridiculed. She wrote to a friend:

> Chopin is amazed to find himself sweating. He's really upset by it and complains that however much he washes, he still *stinks*! We laugh to the point of tears to see this *ethereal* creature refusing to sweat like everyone else – but don't ever mention it or he'll become quite furi-ous. If the world were to know that he *sweats*, he could scarcely go on living. He only reeks of *Eau de Cologne*, but we go on telling him that he stinks like Bonnin the carpenter, and he goes scurrying back to his room, as though pursued by his own *smell*!

In November, Chopin returned to Paris alone, leaving behind him a simmering cauldron of family tensions, which, when it boiled over, would engulf him and all but extinguish his creative energies. He was never to see Nohant again.

Late that summer, Solange had become engaged to an upstanding and personable young man from the Berry district, Fernand Préaulx. When Sand and her family travelled to Paris in February to settle the details of the forthcoming marriage, they made the acquaintance of the sculptor Auguste Clésinger, who set about flattering the mother while seducing the daughter. Solange now flatly refused to go ahead with the wedding. Distraught, angry and confused, Sand returned to Nohant, taking her rebellious daughter with her. On arrival, she at once began investigating Clésinger's background and was not encouraged by what she found. Dissolute, alcoholic and heavily in debt, he was an ex-cavalry officer and a notorious gambler with a strictly utilitarian view of women, buttressed by eruptions of violence. Yet within a matter of weeks she was apparently giving her blessing to Solange's decision to marry him. In this she stood alone. Her friends and advisers were united in their opposition to the match. Without exception they found the

man as unsavoury as his reputation. If the wedding was arranged with
unseemly haste, it was for the usual reasons. The seventeen-year-old
Solange was apparently pregnant, despite throwing herself into an icy
stream in an attempt to provoke an abortion. Of this, of everything,
Chopin was kept in ignorance. As Sand put it to Maurice in mid-April,
'it is no concern of his; once the Rubicon has been passed, ifs and buts
can only do harm.' Three weeks later, she dispatched a further letter to
her son, now visiting his father.

> Oh come, Maurice, hurry. . . . You must start at once, with or with-
> out Papa, and bring his consent and instructions regarding the draw-
> ing up of the marriage settlement. Our position here is quite
> impossible; hurry. Buy a special marriage licence and have it sent
> on. . . . Oh come; come! Please hurry.

The following day, still greatly distressed, her thoughts turned once
again to Chopin, whose health had taken a sharp turn for the worse.
She wrote to Mlle Rozières:

> I am very frightened. Is it true then that Chopin has been *very*
> ill? Princess Czartoryska wrote and told me yesterday that he is
> out of danger; but how does it come that you don't write? I am
> ill with anxiety and feel quite giddy as I write. I cannot leave my
> family at such a time, when I haven't even Maurice with me
> to save appearances and preserve his sister from all malevolent
> suppositions. I am in great distress, I assure you. . . . Write to
> *me*. Please. I implore you.

And her thoughts on the Rubicon seem to have shifted:

> Tell Chopin what you think best about us. I dare not write myself
> for fear of upsetting him too much; I fear that he will hate the idea
> of Solange's marriage, and that every time I mention it he will suffer
> an unpleasant shock. But I could not keep it from him, and I had to
> act as I have done. I cannot make Chopin the head of my family, and
> its counsellor – my children would not accept such a situation and
> my personal dignity would be lost. . . . His advice in the real business
> of life cannot possibly be considered. He has never looked straight
> at realities, never understood human nature on any point; his soul is
> pure poetry and music, and he cannot tolerate anything that is differ-
> ent from himself. Moreover, his interference in family affairs would
> mean for me the loss of all dignity and love, both towards and from
> my children.

At the same time, there's no evidence that she foresaw a break in their relations, even now, though the image of Lucrezia was never far from her mind. Five days later she wrote to Grzymala, at length as ever:

In a vague and indefinite way I knew he was ill, twenty-four hours before I received the Princess's letter. What I went through during those hours is impossible for me to describe. But no matter what might have happened, I could not have left here. . . . I shall be in Paris for a few days at the end of the month, and if Chopin can be moved I will bring him back here. . . . It is all very difficult and delicate, and I see no means of calming and restoring a sick mind which is exasperated by the very efforts that one makes to cure it. For a long time now the disease which gnaws at the body and soul of this poor creature has been the death of me, and I see him fading away without ever having been able to do him any good, since it is his anxious, jealous and touching affection for me which is the main cause of his misery. For the last seven years I have lived like a virgin with him and other men, but even so, it cost me no sacrifice, for I was so weary of passions and hopeless disillusionments. If ever a woman on this earth should have inspired him with absolute confidence I was that woman – and he has never understood it. I am well aware that plenty of people accuse me of having exhausted him by the violence of my physical passion, others of having driven him to despair by my wild outbursts. I think you know the real state of affairs. He complains that I have killed him by refusing him my consent [to sex?], while I was absolutely certain that I should kill him if I acted otherwise. You see how I am placed in this fatal friendship, in which I have consented to be his slave, whenever I could do so without showing him an impossible and wicked preference over my own children, and when it has been such a delicate and serious matter to preserve the respect it was my duty to inspire in my children and my friends. In that connection I have achieved miracles of patience such as I should not have thought myself capable. It has become a martyrdom to me: but Heaven is implacable towards me, as if I had some great crimes to expiate, since in the midst of all these efforts and sacrifices he whom I love with absolutely chaste and maternal feelings is dying, the victim of the crazy love he bears me. . . . Chopin does not know that I have been informed of his illness and he would want to keep it from me. His noble and generous heart still has a thousand delicate and sensitive feelings which exist side by side with the cruel misconceptions that are killing him. Oh, if Anna

[Princess Czartoryska] could one day speak to him and reach down to the bottom of his heart to cure him! But he seals himself off from his best friends.

Still Sand clings to her belief that Chopin's 'malady' is psychologically induced; if he is indeed mortally ill, it is his 'misconceptions' that are to blame; if Czartoryska could 'reach down to the bottom of his heart' he would then be cured. In sealing himself off from his 'best friends', however, he may have been wiser than he knew. The last place in the world he needed to be at this time was Nohant, where the cauldron was finally boiling over. Relations between Solange and her mother had never been close. The two were best kept apart. Nor did the entry of Clésinger into the family ease matters. Maurice, for his part, had loathed his new brother-in-law from the start, suspecting his motives and provoking his anger at the slightest pretext. In the midst of this explosive soufflé, Augustine Brault, the most blameless of all the Nohant tribe, announced her engagement to Théodore Rousseau, an old friend of Maurice's. Solange, apparently emboldened by the state of matrimony and fuelled by a long pent-up jealousy, now contrived to poison the happiness of her adoptive 'sister' by informing Rousseau that his betrothed had been Maurice's mistress. The ruse was a success, and the prospective groom beat a fearful and hasty retreat. Augustine was reduced to abject misery, and Solange, triumphant, going on to accuse her own mother of having an affair with the journalist Victor Borie, another of Maurice's friends. In July the bounds of propriety gave way to irresistible pressures, and Nohant became the scene of a conflict whose violence secured it a place in Berry folklore for many years to come. As Sand reported to Rozières (and her testimony was supported by several disinterested witnesses),

> There has nearly been murder here. My son-in-law took a hammer and would perhaps have killed Maurice if I hadn't thrown myself between them, punching the former in the face and receiving from him a blow in the chest. If the *curé* who was there, and some friends and a servant hadn't intervened by main force, Maurice, armed with a pistol, would have shot him there and then. And there stood Solange, stirring the flames with icy ferocity, after having caused these dreadful outrages by her tales, lies and incredibly filthy stories. . . . This pair of devils left yesterday. I never want to see them again, and they will never set foot in this house. . . . I had to give Chopin a partial account of all this; I was afraid he might arrive in the midst of a catastrophe and die of grief and shock. Don't tell him the worst of what happened;

we must hide it from him if at all possible. They [the Clésingers] will probably, in their crazy and impudent way, force me to defend Maurice, Augustine and myself against the atrocious slanders they are spreading. I will ask you to do one thing, my dear: be firm and take possession of the keys of my apartment as soon as Chopin is out (if he has not already left), and don't let Clésinger or his wife, or anyone they may send, set foot in it.

It was at this point that Solange took full advantage of Chopin's long-standing partiality to her and her disadvantaged position within the family. From the nearby village in which she and her husband had taken refuge, she wrote to him, representing herself as the hapless victim of her mother's hatred, and seeking his material assistance in making her getaway. Making no mention of her pregnancy (the true cause of her condition), she told him

I am ill, and the journey by stage-coach from Blois will exhaust me. Will you lend me your carriage to return to Paris? Please reply at once. Before I can leave I shall await your reply. I am in a most embarrassing position here. I left Nohant for ever after my mother made the most frightful scenes. Please wait for me before you leave Paris. I simply must see you at once. They positively refused to let me have your carriage; so if you wish me to have the use of it, send me a note giving permission and I will send it to Nohant so as to obtain the carriage.

Chopin, sympathetic as ever, replied at once:

I am most grieved to hear that you are unwell. I hasten to put my carriage at your disposal, and have written to your mother to that effect. Do look after yourself.

Your old friend,
Ch.

The effect of his letter to Sand was catastrophic. Her reply has not survived, but a deeply distressed Chopin showed it to Delacroix, who was much disturbed.

One has to admit that it is horrible. Cruel passions and long pent-up impatience erupt in it, and by a contrast which would be amusing if it did not touch on so tragic a subject, the author often takes over from the woman, and launches into tirades which look as though they were taken straight from a novel or a philosophical homily.

Sand apparently made it a condition of their continuing relationship that Chopin break completely and immediately with 'Clésinger and his wife'. By this time, however, Solange had indicated to Chopin that her mother was eager to prevent him from coming to Nohant so that she might continue her (wholly fictitious) affair with Victor Borie undisturbed. Given his tendency to jealousy, one can imagine the effect of this on Chopin. On 24 July, now aware of Solange's pregnancy, he went to his desk and penned what was to be his last letter to Sand.

I am not called upon to discuss Mr Clésinger with you. His very name did not become familiar in my mind until you gave him your daughter. As for her – I cannot remain indifferent to her. You will remember that I used to intercede with you for both your children, without preference. I did this whenever I had the chance, being certain that it is your destiny to love them *always* – for those are the only affections which are not subject to change. Ill fortune may cast a shadow over them, but cannot alter their nature.

This misfortune must be very powerful today if it can forbid your heart to listen to any mention of your daughter, at the beginning of her life as a woman, at the very moment when her physical condition calls more than ever for a mother's care. When faced with such grave realities involving your most sacred affections, I must pass over in silence that which concerns me personally. Time will do its work. I shall wait – *still the same as ever.*

Yours most devotedly,

Ch.

My regards to Maurice.

Four days later, Sand replied.

I had called for post horses yesterday and I was going to set off in a cab, in this awful weather and very ill myself. I intended to spend a single day in Paris in order to have news of you. Your silence has made me so anxious about your health that I was prepared to go so far. In the meantime, you were taking your own time to reflect, and your reply is very calm.

Very well, my friend, follow now the dictates of your heart and assume that it is the voice of your conscience. I understand perfectly. As for my daughter, her illness gives no more cause for anxiety than last year. Neither my zeal, my attention, my orders, not even my prayers have ever been able to persuade her to behave otherwise than as a person who *enjoys* making herself ill.

It would ill become her to say that she needs her mother's love –

a mother whom she hates and slanders, whose most innocent actions and whose home she blackens by the most frightful calumnies. You choose to listen to it all and maybe believe what she says. I do not propose to wage a war of that kind. I prefer to see you pass over to the enemy rather than defend myself from a foe bred of my flesh and reared on my milk.

Look after her, then, since it is she to whom you think you must devote yourself. I shall not hold it against you, but you will understand that I am going to maintain my right to play the part of the outraged mother, and henceforth nothing will induce me to allow the authority and dignity of my role to be slighted. I have had enough of being a dupe and a victim. I forgive you, and from now on I shall not utter one word of reproach, for you have made a sincere confession. It surprises me, somewhat, but if, having made it, you feel freer and easier in your mind, I shall not suffer from this strange volte-face.

Adieu, my friend. May you soon recover from all your ills: I hope you will *now* (I have my reasons for thinking so); and I shall thank God for this queer end to nine years of exclusive friendship. Let me hear now and then how you are. There is no point in ever discussing the other matters.

Nor did Chopin once try. From this point to the end of his days, he knew only Solange's side of the story and seems to have been her willing pawn. For their part, she and Clésinger lost few opportunities to exploit his generosity and unworldliness, and Chopin was forever obliging.

For no one was the break between Chopin and Sand more distressing than for Pauline Viardot, who continued to hold both in the highest esteem. Like a number of their other friends, she had been shocked by the whole messy episode of Solange's marriage and banishment, and disturbed by the near-paranoid bitterness of Sand's subsequent behaviour. In response to a letter from Sand, which has been lost, she wrote in November:

There is in your letter a passage which I simply cannot pass over in silence – the one in which you say that Chopin belongs to Solange's clique, which makes her out a victim and runs you down. That is absolutely false. I swear it is, at least so far as he is concerned. On the contrary, this dear and excellent friend is filled with, and afflicted by, a single thought – the harm that this wretched affair must have done, and is still doing, to you. I have not found him changed in the slightest degree – he is still as kind, as devoted as ever – adoring you as he always has, rejoicing with your joy, grieving only over your griefs. In Heaven's name, darling, never believe those officious friends who come and tell tales.

To which her husband added this postscript:

To be quite frank I may sum up what he [Chopin] said to us as follows: Solange's marriage is a great misfortune, for herself, her family and her friends. The daughter and mother were both deceived and realized their mistake too late. But since they both shared in the mistake, why should only one bear the blame? The daughter wanted, insisted on, an ill-sorted match; but the mother who consented, has *she* no share in the fault? With her great gifts and experience, should she not have enlightened a girl who was urged on more by mortification than by love? If she deluded herself, one should not be pitiless towards a mistake in which one has a share. 'And I,' he added, 'pitying both from the bottom of my heart, endeavour to give some consolation to the only one of the two that I am allowed to see.' That is all, dear Mme Sand, not a word more – without reproaches or bitterness, but with deep sadness. I feel the breath of evil lips has come between you.

He was right, of course. And Sand was in no doubt about its provenance. Yet no attempt at reconciliation was made by either party. Chopin remained in close touch with Solange, and took what comfort he could from such attention as she chose to give him. Nor did he once show any trace of the animosity towards Clésinger that he had so forcibly expressed before their wedding. From now on, Chopin's life was in decline, and his creative powers effectively extinguished. His mood and general outlook may be gauged by the end of a letter which he penned to Solange on 2 October 1847:

I wish I could have filled [this letter] with all sorts of good news – but I have none to give; and as I lay down my pen I wish you both all possible happiness and thank you from the bottom of my heart for all your kind words.

        My old friendship is yours always, always.

                      Ch.

To no one else was he now writing in these terms. When he next wrote, two months later, his mood was not improved, but at least he had company.

All Paris is ill: the weather here is terrible and you are lucky to be where it is fine. I will try to send you better news of our climate, but for that to happen, this horrible year must come to an end – a year which has now taken away all Grzymala's fortune. He has just lost everything in an unlucky business speculation.

As Christmas loomed, things had not improved.

Now the entire city is coughing. I feel suffocated and am expecting the cholera – Louise [Ludwika] writes to say that it is at the gates of Warsaw, but nobody is afraid. . . . I hardly ever go out now – scarcely even to see Grzymala: and he himself does not go out at all.

Yet on the day after Christmas, Chopin wrote to his family in Warsaw and excused his long silence by reporting that he was 'frightfully busy' and 'up to the neck in work'. Since his composing had virtually ground to a halt, one can only conclude that he refers here to his teaching. He had long since abandoned the *Méthode* proposed by Moscheles and Fétis, and we know that he was a principled opponent of excessive practising. Whatever the reason for his delay in writing, he now made up for it in a letter of considerable length, in which he speaks openly and (*pace* the Viardots) critically of Sand's treatment of Clésinger:

She can't stand him, simply because he has married her daughter – a marriage which I did my best to prevent. She is a strange creature, notwithstanding all her intelligence! She was seized by a kind of madness: she is making a mess of her own life and of her daughter's. Her son too will come to a bad end. I prophesy it and will sign my name to the prophecy. To excuse her behaviour she tried to find some blame to lay on those who wish her well, who believed in her, who have never done her a low-down trick, but whom she cannot bear to see near her, for they are the mirror of her conscience.

He neglects, however, to mention the suggestion, put to him by Solange, that Sand had in fact invited Clésinger to Nohant *for herself*, and that she had been angered and frustrated by his preference for the daughter. As to his own role in Sand's performance as a parent, he speaks only of credit:

I have no regrets for having helped her to bear the eight most crucial years of her life, when her daughter was growing up and her son was tied to his mother. I do not regret all that I put up with. Of me, Mme Sand can have nothing but good memories in her heart if ever she looks back upon the past.

And elsewhere:

Eight years of some kind of order in her life was too much. By God's grace they were the years when her children were growing up; and if it had not been for me they would have gone to their father years ago and would not have stayed with her. . . . I hope you will not worry over this. It happened a long time ago. Time is a great healer – but I have not yet got over it. That is why I haven't written to you. As soon as I begin a letter I burn it. . . . A new novel by Mme Sand is appearing in *Les Débats*. . . . There is talk also of her 'Mémoires', but Mme Sand said that they will consist rather of current reflections on art, literature, etc. and not be memoirs in the ordinary sense of the word. Quite right too! It is too early for memoirs, for dear Mme Sand has still strange paths to tread during her lifetime and many ugly things are still in store for her.

On the evidence available, it would appear that no day went by in Chopin's life now without his thoughts straying at some stage to Nohant. That he had 'not yet got over it' six months after the break is hardly surprising, and in Chopin's case, it is hard to escape the impression that the pain was intensified by his abiding inability to understand what had befallen him. This might explain his otherwise inexplicable devotion to Solange and his readiness to accept her version of events. Nor did she ever fail to play upon his sympathies.

I think there can be few women who, having been brought up like a princess, as I was, would have borne with such severe trials as calmly as I. On the one hand, money worries; on the other, a mother who abandons me to all the saints in Heaven before I have time to know what life is; a father more severe than affectionate, a father without tenderness – such things do not happen every day to girls of nineteen.

It is hardly surprising that Chopin – 'Little Chip-Chip', 'the boy', 'the child', 'my son' – felt a deep empathy for the sentiments expressed by Solange.

More than ever, he now submitted to the casting of himself as patient. His ever-worsening health absolved him of the need for struggle; his posture of helplessness was strangely a part of his charm, not least to the adoring women who made up the bulk of his students. The picture of his life that he painted for his family at the time was not encouraging. 'From time to time,' he wrote, 'I sniff at my homeopathic bottles, I give a lot of lessons at home, and try to keep going as best I can.' Meanwhile, back at Nohant, Sand continued to nurse her grievances. In a letter to Maurice, then visiting Paris, she laid down strict instructions:

> You must avoid any kind of meeting, explanation or exchange of
> words with Clésinger. Do not go back to Rozières, and if you have
> anything to give back to Chopin, leave them with the concierge – it
> will be better not to write anything. If you happen to meet him, say
> 'How do you do?' as if nothing were wrong. That is all, and go your
> way. Unless of course he avoids you – in that case do the same. If
> he asks about me, tell him that I have been ill as a result of my
> worries. Don't mince words, and speak quite sharply.

It didn't come to that, but Chopin got the message, as he informed
Solange, then at Guillery awaiting the birth of her child:

> Maurice is in Paris. He came to visit de Larac without coming upstairs
> to see me. Poor lad, he did no good by giving the people in the house
> something to talk about.

Chopin himself, as it happens, had already given them – and Paris –
something very much bigger to talk about. As he reported to his mother
and sisters on 11 February:

> My friends came in one morning recently and said I must give a
> concert; and that I should have nothing to worry about, merely sit
> down and play. For a week now all the tickets have been sold even
> though they cost 20 francs. The public are putting their names down
> for a second concert which I have no intention of giving. The Court
> has ordered forty tickets and the papers had merely to mention that
> I might give a concert for people to start writing to my publisher
> from Brest and Nantes to reserve seats. This eager rush surprises me
> and I must begin practising for it today, if only for conscience's sake,
> for I feel that I play worse than ever. I shall play (as a novelty) a
> Mozart trio with Franchomme and Alard. There will be no posters
> or complimentary tickets. The hall is comfortably arranged and can
> seat 300. Pleyel always pokes fun at my silliness, and to encourage
> me to give a concert he will have the staircase decorated with flowers.
> I shall feel quite at home and my eyes will alight on practically none
> but familiar faces. I already have here the piano on which I shall play.

For all his well-known dislike of performing in public – something he
had not done since 1842 – Chopin had little practical alternative but to
accept his friends' proposal. His worsening health was threatening to
make serious inroads into his teaching practice and he faced being seriously short of funds. As before, the concert reaped an equal harvest of

honour, praise and money, but predictably left Chopin exhausted. While all the critics vied with one another in their search for appropriate superlatives, perhaps the most eloquent came from the Marquis de Custine, a friend who spoke in many ways for generations yet unborn when he wrote:

> You have gained in suffering and poetry; the melancholy of your compositions penetrates still deeper into one's heart; one is alone with you in the midst of a crowd; it is not a piano that speaks but a soul, and what a soul! Preserve your life for your friends; it is a consolation that one may sometimes listen to you. In the dark days which threaten, Art, as you understand it, is the only thing that can unite mankind divided by the harsh realities of life. One may love and understand one's neighbour through Chopin. You have transformed a public into a circle of friends: and lastly, you are equal to the demands of your own genius – that is all that need be said.

The dark days in question quickly gathered force, preventing a second concert, to which Chopin had reluctantly but realistically agreed. Within a week of his triumph at the Salle Pleyel, the streets of Paris resounded once more to the sound of revolution. Hard on the heels of his break with Sand, the society that had welcomed him into its midst and celebrated him as one of the brightest jewels in its crown was about to collapse. In terms of popular sympathies, the so-called July Monarchy of Louis-Philippe had grown progressively more threadbare, and in the eighteen years since its inception the country had plunged into an upward spiral of inflation, complemented by serious food shortages and mass unemployment. In recent months Paris itself had seen a marked increase in random violence, culminating in the bloody shooting of fifty-two people on the evening of 23 February. Whatever its failings, however, the régime had attached the highest importance to art and cultural affairs and had nurtured an atmosphere in which they could flourish. Such a constellation of artistic vitality and imagination was never to be seen again, in Paris or anywhere else. Chopin, bed-ridden in the aftermath of his concert, saw nothing of the revolution itself, but soon became acquainted with its more immediate consequences. As he reported to his family,

> Paris is quiet now, with the quiet of fear. Everyone has rallied to the cause of order. Everyone has joined the National Guard. The shops are open – but there are no customers. Foreigners, passports in hand, are waiting for the damage to the railways to be repaired. Clubs are

beginning to be formed. But I should never stop if I tried to tell you what is going on here.

In fact, similar disturbances were going on throughout Europe, breeding both fear and hope and rekindling the fires of Polish nationalism. To Fontana, now in New York, Chopin wrote with a new sense of urgency:

If you want to do the right thing, stay quietly where you are and don't come back until something really starts moving in Poland. Our forces are assembling in the Poznan district. Czartoryski was the first to arrive, but God knows what course events must take before Poland may arise again. The papers here publish nothing but lies. No republic has been set up in Cracow, nor has the Austrian Emperor declared himself King of Poland. . . . Nor has the King of Prussia any intention of abandoning the Poznan province. . . . You can see that all this breathes war, but no one knows where it will break out. If it does begin, the whole of Germany will be involved. The Italians have started already – Milan has kicked out the Austrians, but they still hold the provinces and will fight back. France will certainly help for she must take the opportunity to clear out a lot of scum from her territory. The Russians are sure to have trouble on their own hands if they make the slightest move towards Prussia. The Galician peasants have shown the way to those of Volhynia and Podolia, and the whole business will not be settled without frightful happenings. But at the end of it all is Poland, holy, great – in a word, Poland.

So in spite of our impatience let us wait until the cards have been well shuffled. We must not squander our strength which we shall so sorely need at the right moment. That moment draws near, but it is not for today. Perhaps within a month, perhaps within a year. Everyone is convinced our affairs will be in full shape before the autumn.

Well before then, however, the turbulence in Paris had a direct effect on Chopin's life and on his livelihood. With streets torn up and barricaded, communications and supplies were badly disrupted and the cost of living rose dramatically. As a consequence, many of the city's wealthier citizens, including many of his pupils, had taken refuge in the country, and of those who remained, few thought piano lessons worth the risk of being assaulted in the streets. One consequence of which he may not have anticipated was the immediate return to Paris of George Sand, come to lend her energies to the socialist cause (the disturbances were intimately connected with the activities of Louis Blanc,★ soon to take his ill-fated place in the new Provisional Government). For the first time since the break in their relations, the possibility arose that they might accidentally meet. It happened remarkably quickly. On Sunday, 5 March, he reported to Solange, who had now given birth,

I went to see Mme Marliani yesterday, and as I was coming out I ran into your mother at the vestibule door. She was coming in with Lambert. I said good-day to her and my next words were to ask whether she had heard from you lately. 'A week ago,' she replied. 'No news yesterday or the day before?' – 'No' – 'Then allow me to inform you that you are a grandmother. Solange has a little girl, and I am very glad to be the first to give you the news.' I raised my hat and went downstairs. Combes, from Abyssinia (he had arrived from Morocco and had fallen straight into the revolution), was with me, and as I had forgotten to say that you were well – a very important point, especially for a mother – I asked Combes to go back upstairs and say that you and the child were both doing well. I couldn't climb those stairs again myself. I was waiting below for the Abyssinian when your mother came down with him and showed great interest in asking me about your health. . . . She asked how I was – I said I was well, and then I called for the concierge to open the door. I raised my hat and walked back home to the Square d'Orléans, accompanied by the Abyssinian.

A Foreign Sojourn and an Early Grave
1848–1849

Edmond Combes, a Frenchman, in fact, not an Abyssinian, noted an immediate and profound change in Chopin's demeanour and later reported: 'I brought him home very sad, very depressed.' With few and slight exceptions this was to describe Chopin's mood for the rest of his life. Certainly Paris did little to lift his spirits. Returning to the city after an absence of some months, Berlioz, that vivid chronicler and sometime friend, was appalled by what he saw:

> What a sight! What hideous ruins! . . . the fallen trees, the crumbling houses, the squares, the streets, the quays, seem still quivering with the murderous struggle! . . . Fancy thinking of Art at such a period of wild folly and bloody orgies! . . . All the theatres are closed, all the artists are ruined; all the teachers are idle . . . poor pianists play sonatas in the squares; historical painters sweep the streets; architects are mixing mortar on the public works. . . . The Assembly has just voted fairly considerable sums towards the opening of the theatres, and in addition has granted some slight relief to the more unfortunate among the artists. But how inadequate to meet the wants especially of musicians! Some of the first violins at the Opéra only had 36 pounds a year and were hard put to it to live even by giving lessons as well.

As a consequence, many musicians had followed the example of Louis-Philippe and many lesser aristocrats and fled the country. Chopin, daily more wraith-like, had thus lost not only the bulk of his livelihood but much of the society that had been at the centre of his Parisian life for the best part of two decades. The proceeds from his last concert were nearing exhaustion when rescue arrived in the person of Jane Stirling, a well-to-do Scottish pupil who idolized her teacher and was almost certainly in love with him, although her British reserve precluded her giving any outward sign of this. With her sister Mrs Erskine, from whom she appeared to be inseparable, she proposed to Chopin that he should come with them to London, where he could have all the students he wanted, a guaranteed welcome into the ranks of English high society, and potentially limitless opportunities to give and to attend concerts. Already there were Berlioz, Liszt, Moscheles, Kalkbrenner, Thalberg, the renowned Swedish soprano Jenny Lind and, most importantly for Chopin, Pauline Viardot, whose regard for him had never wavered. There, too, he could meet such non-musical luminaries as Dickens, Carlyle and Emerson, and play before the young Queen Victoria, reputedly an avid music lover. Even had he wanted to, he was in no position to refuse. Thoroughly wearied by the journey, he arrived in London on the evening of 20 April and was deeply touched by the arrangements that had been made for him.

> My good Mrs Erskine and her sister have thought of everything, even of my special drinking chocolate – and not merely of rooms. I shall be changing these, however, for better ones which have just become available in their street. I've only just noticed that this paper I'm writing on has my monogram, and I've met with many similar delicate attentions.

Marginally restored by a single night's sleep, he was then cast into the maelstrom of British high society with an enthusiasm and disregard for his health which left him more exhausted than ever. A further strain was his own lack of English; strangely for so gifted a mimic, he was a poor linguist. Even his French was highly flawed. His letters from this period all tell a similar story. To Franchomme on May Day:

> After ten days I am just settling down. At last I have a room – a nice large one – in which I can breathe and play, and here comes the sun to see me today, for the first time. I feel less suffocated this morning, but all last week I was good for nothing. I've done nothing so far – just tiresome visits. I am wasting my time on trifles.

To his pupil Gutmann, a week later:

> I have at last managed to get a foothold in this abyss. . . . I now have three pianos at my disposal, but what's the use when I have no time to play them? I have countless calls to make and receive – my days pass like lightning. . . . All the same, I shall have to play here. . . . When I've played before the Queen I shall then have to give a musical matinée for a limited audience at some private house . . . but at the moment all these things are merely plans, nothing more.

To Grzymala on 13 May:

> I am wasting my time. I cannot get up before eight. My Italian valet,
> who thinks only of himself, wastes the first part of the morning for
> me, and after ten begin all sorts of tribulations which don't bring in
> any money. . . . It's only the day after tomorrow that the Duchess
> of Sutherland is to present me to the Queen. If the Queen and Prince
> Albert are pleased with me – they already know about me – all will
> be well: I shall be starting from the top.

The occasion came and went. The Queen failed even to register his
name, writing in her diary that evening: 'There was some pretty music,
good Lablache, Mario and Tamburini singing, and some pianists playing.' So much for starting at the top.† And well down the social ladder,
Utopia still looked a long way off:

> At last I have good lodgings; but no sooner have I settled in than my
> landlord now wants to make me pay twice as much, or else accept
> another room (I'm already paying twenty-six guineas a month). It's
> true that I have a large and splendid drawing-room and can give my
> lessons there, but so far I have only five pupils. I don't know what
> I shall do. . . . Since coming here, I've heard the grimmest news of
> what's happening in the Grand Duchy of Poznan: I learnt of it from
> Stanislav Kozmian . . . Oh how dreadful! It makes my heart sink. I
> feel quite despairing.

Nor was it easy to get away from reminders of Sand, for even the
English papers printed bits of gossip about her. His letters to Grzymala
on the subject are seasoned with an unmistakable bitterness: 'I know
that Mme Sand has written to Mme Viardot and has inquired most
sympathetically about me!!! How she must be playing the part of the
honest and upright mother over there!' And later in the same letter: 'I
cannot finish this. My nerves are all to pieces: I am depressed by a stupid
feeling of melancholy, and with all my resignation I am worried and
don't know what to do with myself.' Nor did London offer much in
the way of compensation.

> I am not yet used to this London air, and this endless round of visits,
> dinners and soirées is very hard on me. I have been spitting blood
> these last few days, and have had nothing but ices and lemonade,
> which seems to have done me some good. I am now acquainted

† Curiously, a rumour started doing the rounds in Paris that the Queen had come
to Chopin *incognito* for piano lessons!

somewhat with London society – a host of *Ladies* whom I have been
introduced to and whose names go in one ear and out the other as
soon as they are mentioned. . . . The weather has been horrible and
that does me no good at all. Besides, I have had to stay out late every
evening at fashionable gatherings. I really haven't the strength for
such a life. . . . If I were younger and if I were not up to the neck in
social obligations – then I might start my life all over again. . . . As
a result of my outlay on lodgings and carriages I have not yet been
able to save a penny. . . . And the distances here! When I have been
jolted up and down in a carriage for three or four hours I feel as
though I had travelled from Paris to Boulogne. I feel more dead than
alive. . . . The upper classes here are proud, but educated and fair –
when they deign to take notice of anything. But their attention is
frittered away so much on a thousand different trifles, they are so
hemmed in by tiresome conventions, that it's all the same to them
whether music is good or bad, for they are compelled to listen to it
from morning till night. There is music at every flower-show, music
at every dinner, every sale is accompanied by music. And the street
musicians – Czechs and my pianist colleagues are as numerous as
dogs – and all mixed up together [*sic*].

In London, Chopin found himself, for the first time in his life, in a
society which commonly regarded musicians as just another brand of
hired help, useful for dishing out background music while the regular
domestics served the food. Gone were the Parisian salons where he was
an honoured and much sought-after guest. Yet it would be quite wrong
to suggest that England was a land in which musicians *per se* were
without honour. The constellation of artists then in its midst was evidence enough of that. Indeed Mendelssohn, not resident but a frequent
visitor, was an object of widespread veneration and, by sad contrast
with Chopin's recent experience, much favoured at court. But then
Mendelssohn, an intimate of such luminaries as Goethe while still a
child, was a consummate though wholly honourable politician, reaping
the benefits of a privileged and sophisticated upbringing in Berlin, a
great city hardly to be mentioned in the same breath as Warsaw. It is
inconceivable that he would ever have created the blunder which
Chopin, not normally a blunderer, committed within a fortnight of his
arrival in London. Invited to play a concerto with the orchestra of the
London Philharmonic Society, an honour withheld that season even
from such well-established virtuosi as Kalkbrenner and Hallé, he
declined on the spot. Despite the offence, for which in some circles he

remained unforgiven, it was entirely a just decision. In his weakened state he could not have hoped to penetrate the massed sonorities of a symphony orchestra, a problem even at the height of his career, nor had he the stamina required for so long a continuous exertion. Add to these very pertinent objections an orchestra whose quality was in no way commensurate with its reputation and which allowed only one rehearsal for each performance, and Chopin's position seems unassailable. In earlier days he would doubtless have handled the whole thing with impeccable polish and grace. Now, tired, depressed and aware that his career was effectively over, he probably could not be bothered. As his compatriot Stanislav Kozmian put it:

> His visit to England was an event in the musical world, and his sojourn a continuous succession of triumphs. But Chopin no longer took any interest in his success. He was sad and dejected. It was difficult to drag him to the piano, unless he had to play. Most often he selected a funeral march [presumably the famous centrepiece of his B flat minor Sonata]. He talked only about Poland.

If Chopin no longer took any interest in his success as a performer, he can hardly have been indifferent to the reception of his music. And here again the widespread and uncritical adulation of Mendelssohn worked against him. The oft-aired claim that Chopin's music was basically unknown in England, however, is simply inaccurate. Many of his works had been both published and performed in London for some time, albeit under often fanciful titles which he abhorred, but they had by no means achieved the near-universal celebrity accorded them in France and Germany. Not since the early assaults of Rellstab in Berlin had his music been so roundly attacked as in London's *The Musical World*, a staunch Mendelssohn supporter, in 1848: 'The entire works of Chopin,' it trumpeted, 'present a motley surface of ranting hyperbole and excruciating cacophony.' No amount of success inoculates a creative artist against the hurt of such remarks. But if the critics were out with their crossbows, the streets at least were safe enough. Politically, as Chopin observed in a letter to Grzymala, the place was blessedly a little dull.

> Things are very quiet here. No one seems much frightened of Irish or Chartist troubles, these things don't appear so enormous as from a distance, and people are more concerned, on the whole, with the state of affairs in Paris, Italy or Poland. As far as Poland is concerned, *The Times* publishes such fantastic nonsense that even the English are struck by its hostility.

. . . They are not afraid of any disturbances here, and if your papers say they are there's no truth in it. Everyone who owns the smallest property is signing on as a special constable. And there are plenty of Chartists among them who are all against the idea of violence.

Meanwhile, in France, things were going from bad to worse. In June, three days of rioting had delivered an unmistakable verdict on Louis Blanc's so-called National Workshops and left the propertied classes in control of a government that rapidly shed most of its original, radical characteristics. On balance, Chopin was better off where he was.

On 23 June, under mounting financial pressure, he gave his first English concert, at the home of Mrs Sartoris, the wife of a wealthy industrialist and also a retired singer of considerable repute, who as Adelaide Kemble had years before earned Chopin's very great respect when both were freshly arrived in Paris. The concert was very much a high society event, with ticket-holders including William Makepeace Thackeray, Jenny Lind and Mrs Jane Carlyle, who echoed the Marquis de Custine when she wrote

I prefer his [Chopin's] music to all others', for it is not a specimen of art offered to the general admiration – which is the effect that most music has upon me. It is rather the reflection of part of his soul, and a fragment of his life lavished on those who have ears to hear and a heart to understand. I think that each of his compositions must have taken away from the number of days allotted to him.

His programme on that occasion reflected his current frailty in its avoidance of anything particularly strenuous. When he made his second London appearance two weeks later, this time at the home of Lord Falmouth, he was feeling more robust and included such substantial works as the B flat minor Scherzo. Like everyone else present, the critic for the *Daily News* was powerfully impressed by what he heard:

M. Chopin performed an *Andante sostenuto* and a Scherzo from his Op.31 [*sic*], a selection from his celebrated Studies, a Nocturne and a *Berceuse* and several of his own Preludes, Mazurkas and Waltzes. In these various pieces he showed very strikingly his original genius as a composer and his transcendental powers as a performer. His music is as strongly marked with individual character as that of any master who has ever lived. It is highly finished, new in its harmonies, full of contrapuntal skill and ingenious contrivance; and yet we have never heard music which has so much the air of unpremeditated effusion. The performer seems to abandon himself to the impulses of his fancy and feeling, to indulge in a reverie and to pour out unconsciously, as it were, the thoughts and emotions that pass through his mind.

He accomplishes enormous difficulties, but so quietly, so smoothly and with such constant delicacy and refinement that the listener is not sensible of their real magnitude. It is the exquisite delicacy, with the liquid mellowness of his tone, and the pearly roundness of his passages of rapid articulation which are the peculiar features of his execution, while his music is characterized by freedom of thought, varied expression and a kind of romantic melancholy which seems the natural mood of the artist's mind.

Chopin can hardly have been disappointed by such a response, but on the whole he found the English perplexing. While there was much that he admired, he felt alienated by more than language.

It is difficult to do things well here – there are so many rules to be observed. . . . There is such confusion here in everything. . . . They are awful liars here: as soon as they don't want anything they clear off to the country. One of my lady-pupils has already left for the country, leaving nine lessons unpaid. Others, who are down for two lessons a week, usually miss a week, thus pretending to have more lessons than they really do. . . . Whatever is not boring here is not English. . . . If only London were not so black and the people not so heavy and dull, and if only there were no sooty smell or fogs, I might already have learnt English. But these English are so different from the French, whom I have become attached to just as if they were my own people. They consider everything in terms of money; they love art because it is a *luxury*. They are good and kind souls, but so eccentric that I quite understand that if I stayed here I myself could become petrified or turned into a machine.

In his letters from England there is a steadily increasing streak of misanthropy and morbidity alike:

My Scots ladies are dear and kind, but they sometimes bore me to distraction. . . . My health is passable at times, but often in the morning I think I am going to cough myself to death. I am miserable at heart but I try to deaden my feelings. I even avoid being alone, so as not to be left to my own thoughts, for one can't be long ill here and I don't want to risk developing some fever.

On an otherwise empty page in his diary for July, he drew a sketch of the gateway to a cemetery. There are several graves with small crosses – and a single, imposing sepulchre marked with a large cross.

With the end of the 'season' in July, the fashionable of London dispersed variously into the countryside, many of them headed for Scotland. The indefatigable sisters Stirling and Erskine saw to it that Chopin did likewise. On 6 August he was installed at Calder House, near Edinburgh, and, despite his mood, could not remain unmoved by its romantic grandeur.

It is an old manor-house surrounded by a vast park with hundred-year-old trees. One sees nothing but lawns, trees, mountains and sky. The walls are eight feet thick; galleries everywhere and dark corridors with countless portraits of ancestors, of all different colours and with various costumes – some in kilts, some in armour, and ladies in farthingales – everything to feed the imagination. The room I occupy has the most splendid view imaginable.

In Scotland, the hospitality and dedication of his 'dear Scottish ladies' attained new heights. Their foresight and solicitude admitted to no limits:

I no sooner have time to wish for something than it is ready to hand – they even bring me the Paris newspapers every day. I have quiet, peace and comfort. . . . My room is well away from the others', so that I can play and do as I please. I am completely free; for the chief consideration with these people is that a guest should not be restricted in any way. In my room I found a Broadwood, and in the drawing-room there is a Pleyel which Miss Stirling brought with her. Country house life in England [sic] is most pleasant. The houses are most elegantly fitted up: libraries, horses, carriages to order, plenty of servants etc. Although everyone in high society, especially the ladies, speaks French, the general conversation is in English, and then I regret that I can't follow it; but I have neither the time nor the desire to learn the language. Anyhow, I understand everyday conversation. I don't allow myself to be cheated and I shouldn't starve to death, but that is not enough.

The fact is that Chopin was now largely beyond the reach of those most eager to help him – something that he acknowledged himself, but powerlessly:

It's horrible. I am unwell and depressed, and my hosts simply weary me with their excessive attentions. I can neither breathe nor work. Although I am surrounded by people, I feel alone, alone, alone. All those with whom I was in most intimate harmony have died or left me.† All that remains to me is a long nose and a fourth finger out of practice. I can feel neither grief nor joy – my emotions are completely exhausted – I am just vegetating and waiting for it all to end quickly. I haven't a decent musical idea in my head – I am out of my rut – like a donkey at a fancy-dress ball – a violin E string on a double-bass – amazed, bewildered, as drowsy as if I were listening to Baudiot playing. I am vegetating, patiently waiting for the winter, dreaming now of home, now of Rome. I can scarcely breathe. I am just about ready to give up the ghost.

But not his sharp, caricaturist's powers of observation:

If I were in a more cheerful mood, I would describe one of these Scotswomen, said to be the thirteenth cousin of Mary Stuart (*sic*! her husband, whose name is different from his wife's, told me so in all seriousness!). They're all cousins here, male and female, belonging to great families with great names which no one on the continent has ever heard of. The whole conversation is conducted along genealogical lines: it's just like the Gospel – such a one begat so-and-so, and he begat another who begat still others – and so on for two pages, up to Jesus Christ.

Depression, clinical, not circumstantial, is a distorting mirror that robs the mind of its perspective. Positive memories are either obliterated or dismissed as unrealistic fantasies. In such a state one often loses the capacity either to recall or to anticipate the condition of happiness and self-belief. Distraction can be a powerfully, even insidiously curative device, and twice in this Scottish August it came to Chopin's aid. On the first occasion it nearly cost him his life:

I was travelling in a coupé, with a very handsome pair of young thoroughbred English horses. One horse began to rear; he caught his foot and then started to bolt, taking the other horse with him. As they were tearing down a slope in the park, the reins snapped and the coachman was thrown from his seat (he received a very nasty bruising). The carriage was smashed to bits as it was flung against tree after tree: we should have been thrown over a precipice if the vehicle had not been stopped at length by a tree. One of the horses tore itself free and bolted madly, but the other fell with the carriage on top of it. The windows were smashed by branches. Luckily I was

† This seems a little hard on his mother, his sisters, Grzymala, Fontana, Franchomme and others, all of whom were very much alive and continuously devoted to him.

unhurt, apart from having my legs bruised from the jolting I had received. My manservant had jumped out smartly, and only the carriage was demolished and the horses wounded. People who saw it all from a distance cried out that two men were killed when they saw one thrown out and the other lying on the ground. . . . None of those who saw what had happened, or we ourselves, could understand how we had escaped being smashed to pieces. I confess that I was calm as I saw my last hour approaching, but the thought of broken legs and hands appals me. To be a cripple would put the finishing touch to me.

The second occasion was less dramatic but equally effective. Now badly in need of any money he could honestly lay his hands on, he accepted at short notice an engagement to play at one of the 'Gentlemen's Concerts' in Manchester. It was a long time since he had faced an audience of 1,200 people, but as usual the majority were mesmerized, just as many observed, too, that his sound was inadequate to the size of the venue. The critic of the *Manchester Guardian* observed:

Chopin appears to be about thirty years of age. He is very spare in frame and there is an almost painful air of feebleness in his appearance and gait. This vanishes when he seats himself at the instrument, in which he seems for the time perfectly absorbed. Chopin's music and his style of performance partake of the same leading characteristics – refinement rather than vigour, subtle elaboration rather than simple comprehensiveness in composition, an elegant, rapid touch rather than a firm nervous grasp of the instrument. But his compositions and his playing appeared to be the perfection of chamber music – fit to be associated with the most refined instrumental quartets and quartet-playing – but wanting breadth and obviousness of design and executive power to be effective in a large concert hall.

Another critic, in a generally enthusiastic review, missed 'the astonishing power of Leopold de Meyer (the self-styled "Lion of Poland", reputed to be the loudest pianist in history), the vigour of Thalberg, the dash of Herz'. Chopin, of course, had heard it all before. But the concert had contained one novelty, which both puzzled the audience and unsettled the pianist. Roughly halfway through his performance of the 'Funeral March' Sonata, he had suddenly arisen from his chair and left the platform. Almost immediately he returned, picking up where he'd left off and carrying the concert through to its conclusion. The explanation of this curious episode is to be found in a letter to Solange, written some days after the concert.

> A strange adventure befell me while I was playing my Sonata in B flat minor before some English friends. I had played the Allegro and the Scherzo more or less correctly. I was about to attack the March when suddenly I saw arising from the body of my piano those cursed creatures which had appeared to me one lugubrious night at the Chartreuse [Majorca]. I had to leave for one instant to pull myself together, after which I continued without saying anything.

After the concert, he escaped from the clutches of his Scottish hosts to visit a Polish family, lately settled near Edinburgh, and exulted in the chance to speak and hear his own language. The high point of a low period, however, was marked by the arrival in Scotland, soon afterwards, of his friends the Czartoryskis. This unexpected double dose of contact with his compatriots did more for his spirits than any number of doctors and helped him to get through another concert, this time in Glasgow. No sooner had his Polish friends departed, however, than he fell back, more deeply than ever, into despondency.

> Nowadays I am not fit for anything during the whole morning, until two o'clock (lunch) – and after that, when I have dressed, everything irritates me and I go on gasping until dinner-time. Dinner over, I have to remain at the table with the menfolk, watching them talk and listening to them drinking. Bored to death (thinking of quite different things from them, in spite of all their politeness and explanatory remarks in French around the table), I must call up all my strength of mind, for they are by that time curious to hear me. Afterwards my good Daniel carries me upstairs to my bedroom, helps me to undress, puts me to bed, leaves a candle, and then I am free to gasp and dream until morning, when it starts all over again. As soon as I have got somewhat used to being in one place I have to go off somewhere else; for my Scots ladies give me no peace. They either turn up to fetch me or cart me around to their families. They will suffocate me out of kindness and I, out of politeness, will not refuse to let them do it. Wherever I may choose to go, they come running after me. Perhaps that is what has given someone the idea that I am going to be married. But there must be some sort of physical attraction; and the unmarried one is far too much like me. How can one kiss one's self?
> Supposing that I could fall in love with someone who loved me in

return, and as I would wish to be loved, even then I would not marry, for we should have nothing to eat and nowhere to live. But a rich woman looks for a rich husband – and if she does choose a poor man he must not be a feeble creature, but young and vigorous. A man on his own can struggle along, but when there are two, poverty is the greatest misfortune. I may give up the ghost in an institution, but at least I won't leave a wife to starve. In any case, I'm nearer to a coffin than to a bridal bed. . . . But what has become of my art? And where have I squandered my heart? I can scarcely remember what they sing at home. This world seems to slip from me, I forget things. I have no strength. I no sooner recover a little than I sink back lower still.

Rather to his surprise, he roused himself sufficiently to give a second Edinburgh concert, to which he attached little importance – 'a little success, a little money'. By now the summer was over. The London rich had returned to the capital, Paris was in semi-chaos, and Chopin remained adrift in Scotland, counting the minutes between periods of sleep, dreading the onset of winter and unable to make any but the most immediately practical decisions. Beyond the aimless social engagements in his diary, most of them arranged by his hosts and self-appointed guardians, his life had lost all semblance of structure or purpose. Nor did prolonged exposure unlock for him the secrets of the British psyche.

By 'art' they mean here painting, sculpture and architecture. Music is not an art, and is not called by that name. Music here is a *profession*. Of course musicians have only themselves to blame, but just you try and alter things! They play the most fantastic pieces, supposing them to be beautiful, but it's absurd to even try and teach them decent things. Lady Something-or-other, one of the most important ladies here, is said to be both a *grande dame* and a musician. Well, after I had played and other Scottish ladies had sung various songs, they brought out a sort of accordion [a concertina] and she, with the utmost gravity, began to play the most dreadful tunes on it. Another lady, showing me her album, said 'I stood beside the Queen while she looked at it'. Another, not to be outdone in originality, accompanies herself *standing* at the piano. The Duchess of Parma told me that one of them actually *whistled* for her, with guitar accompaniment! But what can you expect? It seems to me that every one of these creatures has a screw loose.

On the last day of October Chopin returned to London, very much the worse for wear. For three weeks he remained indoors, 'more dead than alive', to use an expression that was becoming a kind of byword with him. Despite the desperate state of his health, he did venture out on 16 November to play at a charity ball for Polish refugees. The concert preceding the ball took place in a side room at the Guildhall. Chopin was only one of several performers, and had at his disposal nothing more than an inferior upright. There is no record of what he played, but it left him exhausted.

> As soon as I had finished I came home, but could not sleep all night. I had an awful headache, in addition to my cough and choking spasms. I had already been ill for two and a half weeks. I regularly see Szulczewski, Broadwood and Mrs Erskine, who is here with Miss Stirling. They followed me here, just as I said they would. But I see most of all Prince Alexander [Czartoryski] and his wife. Princess Marcellina is so kind that she visits me practically every day, just as though I were in hospital. . . . I really have no heart for anything. Everything is so unbearable for me. I have never cursed anyone, but I should feel easier if I could curse Lucrezia [clearly Sand's message had finally penetrated, and lay at the heart of his prolonged apathy]. Why doesn't God just finish me off straightaway, instead of killing me by inches with this fever of indecision? . . . My Scots ladies are getting me down more than ever. Mrs Erskine, who is a very devout Protestant, bless her, would seem to want to make a Protestant out of *me*. She brings me her Bible, speaks of my soul and marks psalms for me to read. She is devout and kind, but she is much concerned about my soul – she's forever going on about the next world being better than this one. I know it all by heart, and answer her by quoting Holy Scripture.

By the third week in November he had resolved to return to Paris before the winter made him a prisoner in London. Prior to his departure, he wrote to Grzymala, explaining his current state and specifying his needs:

> By midday on Friday I shall at last be in Paris! One more day here and I should not die but go MAD – my Scottish ladies are so tiresome! May the hand of God protect them! They have got their grip on me and I cannot tear them off. Princess Marcellina is the only one who keeps me alive – she and her family and dear Szulczewski. Besides my usual troubles I have neuralgia and my face is all swollen. Please get them to air the bedclothes and pillows. See that they buy plenty of fir-cones so that I can get warmed right through as soon as I arrive. . . . On Friday get them to buy a bunch of violets to scent my drawing-room – let me find a little poetry when I come, just for

a moment, as I go through on my way to the bedroom where I know I am going to lie for a long, long time.

The next day, he wrote to Solange:

> Tomorrow I return to Paris – scarcely able to crawl, and weaker than you have ever seen me. The London doctors urge me to go. I can neither breathe nor sleep. The climate here is inconceivable for people in my state. So I am going back to lie whimpering at the Place d'Orléans while hoping for better times.

Accompanied by his friend Leonard Niedzwiedszki, Chopin took his leave of England early in the afternoon of 23 November 1848. Niedzwiedszki has left his own account of the journey, in the course of which Chopin collapsed, causing both men to believe he was dying. To their joint relief, he soon recovered, though he had to be helped on to the train and into his seat, and the forlorn little party reached Paris, as planned, at midday on the following day.

Once returned, Chopin showed encouraging signs of recovery. Not only was he back in France, he had finally escaped the clutches of his determined Scottish guardians. Life began to look better at once. At last he was restored to the company of people whose language he spoke and understood fluently; he could breathe again without struggle, and above all he was again among old and devoted friends, although not so many as he had expected. A number of aristocratic families who, like him, had fled the city after the troubles of the spring, had not felt emboldened to return. Among them were many of his pupils, who had always provided the bulk of his income. Now too weak to contemplate performing, he was more than ever dependent on teaching if he was to escape the jaws of poverty. With failing health, he had hardly lost his taste for luxury. But hope strengthened him. While having, inevitably, to rest and avoid undue exertion, he soon found that he could get out and about a little and by the end of the year he was even able to resume teaching, though without his former energy. He now restricted himself to pupils whose requirements were least taxing and who were least discomfited by frequent and sudden cancellations. The winter kept him inside most of the time, and his friends did their best to keep him occupied and cheerful, but it was becoming increasingly obvious that he was doomed. The death of his favourite doctor had come as a great blow to him, and he was none too sanguine about the replacements, as he made clear to Solange in a letter written at the end of January 1849.

I've been too ill these last few days to write and tell you that I've seen your husband. He came to see me on Friday and I found him well. We're having real March weather here, and I have to lie down ten times a day. Molin had the art of pulling me together. Since he died I have had Mr Louis, Dr Roth – for two months – and now Mr Simon, who has a great reputation as a homeopathic doctor. But they try their different remedies without bringing me any relief. They all agree about climate – quiet – rest. Rest! I shall have that one day without their help. . . . Paris hasn't been disturbed for a moment recently, although some disorder was expected as a result of the controls placed on the Mobile Guards or the Ministry's plan for closing political clubs. Soldiers and guns were to be seen everywhere yesterday and this firm attitude has obviously made an impression on the political troublemakers. Now even I am writing about politics, instead of sending you amusing news. But I am becoming stupider than ever, for which I blame the cocoa I drink every morning instead of coffee. Never drink cocoa! And stop your friends from doing so, especially if you correspond with them. I shall try and arrange for my next letter to be written after some 'sulphate of wit' which Mr Simon may give me to sniff.

Meanwhile, at Nohant, Sand could not keep Chopin out of her thoughts. Of Viardot she enquired in February,

Do you ever see Chopin? Do tell me about his health. I am unable to repay his furor and hate. I think of him often as a sick child, embittered and lost.

And where was the evidence of his 'furor and hate'? Perhaps only in the minds and the mouths of herself and her daughter. Viardot was insistent on the subject:

You ask for news about Chopin. Here it is: his health is slowly declining, with passable days during which he can ride out in his carriage and other days during which he spits blood and has fits of coughing which choke him. He no longer goes out at night. However, he can still give lessons and on his good days he can still be quite cheerful. That is the exact truth. Anyway, I haven't seen him for some time. He called on me three times without finding me. He talks of you with the greatest respect. I persist in affirming that he has *never* spoken of you in any other way.

*   *   *

He put a brave face on it, but Chopin's situation was growing daily more critical. His teaching dwindled to practically nothing. The will to compose seemed to have left him altogether. And the keys of his piano began to gather dust. Only now did all his father's homilies on the wisdom of thrift and saving come home to roost. He now faced living entirely on the charity of his friends, and for a man of his pride this was the bitterest of pills. Once again, Jane Stirling came to his rescue. On 8 March she sent him, anonymously, a parcel containing 25,000 francs in bank notes. By some strange quirk of character and fate, the concierge to whom the packet was delivered took it and hid it in her room, where it remained undiscovered for almost six months, when it was found after consultations with a clairvoyant. In the meantime he received a gift of 1,000 francs from the Rothschilds and accepted 'loans' from other friends, who had neither the expectation nor the desire that they should be reimbursed. In the spring his doctors recommended that he move out to Chaillot, then a relatively rural area, in bucolic surroundings and with plenty of fresh air. This, too, was managed by a friend, the Princess Obreskoff, who paid half the rent without Chopin's knowledge. That summer the Czartoryskis sent a servant to look after him while they arranged with the Russian authorities for his sister Ludwika and her family to obtain passports for Paris. No one by this time was in any doubt as to the urgency of the mission. In June Chopin wrote to her from his new lodgings:

> I gasp and cough as usual. I haven't even tried to play, and I cannot compose. God knows what sort of fodder I shall have to live on before long. Everybody is leaving town again – some for fear of the cholera, others for fear of revolution. But the weather is lovely today. I'm in my sitting-room, admiring the view all over Paris. From my five windows, with nothing but gardens in between, I can see the Tour Saint-Jacques, the Tuileries, the Chamber of Deputies, the Church of St Germain-l'Auxerrois, St-Etienne-du-Mont, Notre Dame, the Panthéon, St Sulpice, the Val-de-Grâce and the Invalides. You will see it all when you come.

News of Chopin's decline spread throughout fashionable Paris. In July an admirer of no very close acquaintance addressed a letter to George Sand, apprising her of the situation and entreating her to act.

> Madame,
>   I am venturing to take a step which may strike you as very strange, and for which I beg your forgiveness. You have probably

forgotten my name, Madame, but a mutual acquaintance [Mlle de Rozières] had brought me to your notice, and I possess two books of yours, which you yourself presented to me.

I will not describe the feelings which your admirable talent has aroused in me, or say how natural it was that my lively interest should have given me the desire to know more of you. All of which brings me to say that, knowing your long friendship for the illustrious person now cruelly struck down by illness, I feel that I am not mistaken when I say that he grievously misses you. And as he is, Madame, nearing the last stage of his long sufferings, if you, through ignorance, did not give him the consolation of receiving some mark of remembrance, *you* would lament it and *he* might die in despair. I make so bold as to send this note, Madame, and beg to assure you that no one in the world shall know of this approach.

I venture to express the wish that I may not incur your censure, and I also implore you not to mention this warning of mine to a soul.

In answer, Sand wrote a characteristically lengthy apologia, outlining the background to the break-up as it appeared to her:

Nohant, 19 July 1849

Madame,

I appreciate the kind feeling which dictated the step you have taken. But what can I do, Madame, for the moral relief of the unhappy friend to whom you refer? I am compelled to live where I am, and even supposing that the connection between us had not been voluntarily and mutually broken, circumstances would inevitably have separated us.

An extreme partiality on his side for one of my children had estranged the other, and in my view the latter was in no way wrong. Things had reached the point where I had to choose between my son and my friend. . . . That is the fundamental truth. But sooner or later, and indeed before long, lack of financial resources would have put an end to my residing in Paris, while lack of strength would similarly have put an end to my friend's visits to the country. It was in fear and trembling that I kept him so distant from the attentions of celebrated doctors while leading a life which he found disagreeable in itself: he did not hide this from us, for he used to leave us with the first days of autumn, only to return as late as possible with the beginning of summer.

The best doctor, who was also the best friend he had in this part

of the world, had long advised me to loosen the bonds of this friendship until they ceased to be bonds. I had long worked to achieve that,
and it was no fault of mine that it was not smoothly accomplished.
But with a nervous constitution like his, with a character so strange
and unhappy (albeit a noble one), it proved to be impossible; and I
myself often lost patience when confronted with inexplicable and
unjust reproaches. . . .

Most wrongs in this world are the result of inescapable destiny,
itself created by the outside world. . . . Had I sought your judgement
at the time of the breach, and had you seen things as they really were,
you would have said 'You must part without bitterness and without
breaking the bond of affection.' I repeat, it did not depend on him
or me, but on *others*. For it is others who have come between us.
There was not even a cooling-off in the friendship between the two
of us. But, you will say, even when it was over, there was still time
for us to come to an understanding and to console each other with
tender words and lasting pledges of esteem. I asked for nothing better.
I have met him since then, and offered him my hand. . . . One would
have said he hastened to avoid me; I sent someone after him, and he
came back unwillingly, to speak neither of himself nor of me, but to
show in his attitude and looks anger and indeed almost hatred.

Since then he has unburdened himself of bitter confidences and
frightful accusations levelled at me. I have taken it all, as I was bound
to, for mere raving; and I swear I have forgiven him everything, and
from the bottom of my heart.

Had he but called me to him during my brief visits to Paris, I
should have gone. Had he but written himself, or got someone to
write some affectionate note, I should have replied. But *now*, does
he really wish to have from me a word of friendship, of pardon, or
any sign of interest? If so, I am ready. . . . But were I to write, I
should fear to provoke an emotional reaction more harmful than
salutary. . . . Go and see him? That is absolutely out of the question
at this moment and would, I believe, only make matters worse. . . .
But I have the inward conviction that he does not wish it. His affection
has long been dead, and if he is tormented by the memory of me it
is because he feels in his own heart a pang of self-reproach. . . .
This is all a long and painful family story, and my friends have well
understood the suffering it has caused me.

Sand remained at Nohant. In Paris, on 8 August, Ludwika, accompanied
by her husband and daughter, arrived to nurse her brother through his

final decline. In early September she unexpectedly received a letter from George Sand:

Nohant, 1 September

Dear Louise,

I hear you are in Paris. I did not know this. At last I shall obtain through you some real news of Frédéric. Some people write that he is much worse than usual, others that he is only weak and fretful as I have always known him. I venture to ask you to send me word, for one can be misunderstood and abandoned by one's children without ceasing to love them. . . . Your memories of me must have been spoilt in your heart, but I do not think I have deserved all that I have suffered.

Yours from the bottom of my heart,

George

The letter was never answered, nor did Sand make any further enquiries. Rumours of Chopin's imminent death spread rapidly, and a long sequence of friends prepared to take their leave of him. Among them was the Polish poet Cyprian Norwid.

I found him dressed, but reclining on his bed, with swollen legs; this could be perceived at once, although he wore stockings and shoes. The artist's sister was sitting next to him, strangely resembling him in profile. . . . He was in the shadow of the deep bed with curtains, leaning on his pillows and wrapped in a shawl, and he was very beautiful, and as always there was something perfect, something classical, in his most casual gestures. . . . In a voice broken by his coughing and choking, he began to reproach me for not having come to him for such a long time. After that he spoke jokingly and wanted to tease me about my mystical tendencies, and since it gave him pleasure, I let him do it. He had fits of coughing, and then the moment came when he had to be alone. I said farewell to him, and he, pressing my hand, threw his hair back from his forehead, and said 'I am going . . .' and then began to cough. Upon hearing this I kissed him on the arm and, knowing that he was pleased when sharply contradicted, I said, in a tone that one uses with a strong and courageous person, 'You have been going, in this way, every year, and yet, thank God, we still find you alive!' To this, Chopin, finishing the sentence that was interrupted by the coughing, said 'I am going to leave this apartment and move to the Place Vendôme.'

This he did, towards the end of September, on the recommendation of his doctors, who felt he should return to Paris well before the onset of winter. Accordingly, he was installed in a large, sunny apartment at 12 Place Vendôme, and as always he took a keen interest in its furnishing and decoration. Despite his pitiable state, he was clearly not ready to give up the ghost. Within a mere fortnight of the move, however, his condition worsened rapidly. On the evening of 12 October his doctor, Cruveillher, feared that Chopin would not last the night and summoned a priest to administer the final sacraments. Chopin protested at first, but relented, saying to the sacristan afterwards: 'Without you, my friend, I would have died like a pig.' But he did not die as expected. For four days he hung on, suffering bouts of extreme pain with a strength and courage both moving and terrible to those who witnessed it. As Grzymala wrote to a friend: 'I have never in my life seen such a tenacious vitality.' Among his last requests was that all his unfinished manuscripts should be destroyed and that only complete pieces should ever be published. The last of his friends to arrive at his bedside was Delfina Potocka, who had travelled from Nice to be with him. Chopin was deeply touched and asked her to sing to him. His piano was rolled into his bedroom and Delfina sang, first Alessandro Stradella's 'Hymn to the Virgin' and then a psalm setting by Benedetto Marcello, which was at one stage interrupted by an appalling fit of coughing. The next day he was often in an agony of pain and was slipping in and out of consciousness. He begged for death, but would not die. He asked for music. Franchomme and Princess Marcelina played some Mozart. He asked to hear his own G minor Cello Sonata, but it was not far advanced when he began to choke and the music stopped. As Charles Gavard reported:

> The whole evening of the 16th was spent reciting litanies; we gave the responses, but Chopin remained silent. Only by his strained breathing could one tell that he was still alive. That evening two doctors examined him. One of them, Cruveillher, took a candle, and holding it before Chopin's face, which had become quite dark with suffocation, remarked to us that his senses had ceased to function. But when he asked Chopin whether he was still in pain, we quite distinctly heard the answer: 'No more.' These were the last words heard from his lips.

When he died, around two o'clock in the morning of 17 October, he was surrounded by his sister Ludwika, Princess Marcelina Czartoryska, his pupil Gutmann, Thomas Albrecht – and Solange, who sat with him, his hand in hers.† Suddenly he suffered a frightening convulsion. Solange cried out to Gutmann, who gathered his teacher in his arms. 'We wanted to give him a drink,' Solange recalled, 'but death prevented us. He passed away with his gaze fixed on me. He was hideous. I could see the tarnishing eyes go dark. I knew then that his soul had died too.' He was thirty-nine years of age.

Almost immediately, Ludwika took a pen and addressed a brief note to her husband, who had now returned to Poland:

> Oh my darling, he has gone – little Louise and I are both well. I embrace you tenderly. Remember Mother and Isabella. Adieu.

To which Princess Marcelina added a lengthier postscript:

> Our poor friend's life is over. He suffered very much before the final moment came, but he suffered with patience and angelic resignation. The way your wife nursed him was exemplary. God gives her immense physical and moral strength. . . . I am too exhausted to write any more, but I can say from the bottom of my heart that I will fulfil conscientiously the promise I made to you and to our dying friend and will look after your wife as though she were my own sister.
>
> Marcelina Czartoryska (née Radziwill)

Later that morning Clésinger arrived to make a death mask and took casts of Chopin's hands, the sight of which has bewitched and tantalized pianists ever since. Slender, strong and mysteriously supple, even in deathly immobility, they almost eerily complement the essence of Chopin's style as a composer and the descriptions of his playing bequeathed to us by those who heard him. But the memorials were not to stop there. At his own request, Chopin's heart was cut out and sent in an urn to Warsaw, where it rests to this day in the church of the Holy Cross.

The death mask and the drawings made by Kwiatkowski that same morning combine with the famous portrait by Delacroix and the pain-racked, slightly bewildered expression in the daguerreotype of 1849 to give a clear impression of Chopin's physical appearance. Not handsome by conventional standards but strangely beautiful in its chiselled

---

† There is no truth in the once popular story that George Sand came to be with him in his final hours but was not admitted. That she remained prominent in Chopin's thoughts is confirmed by the discovery in his date book for 1849 of a small silken envelope containing a lock of her hair and embroidered with the initials G.F. (George–Frédéric).

refinement, the face in life, by all accounts, was as supple and expressive as the music, whether deliberately contorted in feats of caricature or quietly reflective and observant, as in the Kwiatkowski painting, with its intelligent eyes, its sensitive, rather supercilious mouth and its suggestion of a defensive pride.

When Chopin's funeral took place on 30 October, more than 3,000 people, each admitted by special invitation, crowded the great Church of the Madeleine, while many hundreds more gathered in the streets outside, bringing that part of the capital to a standstill.

The funeral itself was of extraordinary splendour. At Chopin's request, the Mozart Requiem, unheard in Paris since 1840, was performed with a stellar cast of soloists, including Pauline Viardot and the great bass Luigi Lablache, who had sung, in the same work, at Beethoven's funeral in 1827 and at Bellini's in 1835. As the coffin was borne up the aisle to the catafalque, draped like the portals of the church itself in black velvet with the initials F.C. embroidered on it in silver, the orchestra played an arrangement of the Funeral March from the B flat minor Sonata, and during the Offertory of the Mass itself, the organist played the fourth and sixth of Chopin's preludes. The enormous expenses were met in part by a donation from Jane Stirling of 5,000 francs. The pallbearers included Meyerbeer, Franchomme and Delacroix, with Prince Adam Czartoryski at their head. The procession of thousands walked the three miles (5 kilometres) from church to cemetery with scarcely a word spoken. A similar silence marked the burial itself. Contrary to custom, no speech was made. After the interment, the crowd dispersed into small groups and the streets gradually returned to normal. One year later to the day, a Chopin monument, carved by Clésinger, was unveiled at the composer's grave and the contents of a small box of Polish earth, brought to Paris expressly for this final act of mourning, was sprinkled on the composer's grave.

Interlude: Chopin and the Mazurka

No composer's career has been more appropriately framed than Chopin's, which began with a polonaise and ended with a mazurka, the desolately yearning F minor, published, after his death, as op. 63, no. 2. Nor has any musical genre been more consistently, more deeply or more tragically steeped in the bittersweet pain of nostalgia than the mazurka in the hands of Chopin. He didn't invent it, of course, any more than he invented the concert polonaise, nor could he, or would he, have claimed to have introduced it into the world of western European art music. It was he alone, however, who made it a household name in musical circles all over the world, by the not so simple expedient of lifting it, repeatedly, into the realm of highest art. So much has been made of Chopin the émigré, the Parisian Pole, the passionate patriot, that one easily forgets the fact that, unlike his equally patriotic contemporary Liszt, he spent the whole of his childhood and youth in the land of his birth. In the Polish countryside he heard the indigenous music of his countrymen as naturally as he spoke their language. Native to the district of Mazowse were two dances derived from folk-songs: the *mazur* or *mazurek*, named after the people of the plains, and the *obertas* or *oberek*. Closely related to these was another dance, the *kujawiak*, eponymously named for the neighbouring district of Kujawy where it originated. Unbeknown to most of the people who used it, the word *mazurka* was a portmanteau term embracing all three dances. While they differ in matters of tempo, the *obertas* being generally faster than the other two, they have in common a triple metre with a strong accent on the second or third beat of the bar, and are constructed of two or four parts of eight or very often six bars, each part being repeated.

Originally a sung dance, which may explain why Chopin took no exception to hearing his mazurkas appropriated by Pauline Viardot, the earliest examples of this type, which goes back to the sixteenth century, were accompanied on the bagpipes, or *dudy*, a fact plainly reflected in several of Chopin's mazurkas. Indeed in the earliest version of the A minor Mazurka, op. 7, no. 2, there is an introduction over which Chopin actually wrote the word *duda*.

Despite their rather square structure, mazurkas lend themselves to a wide variety of feelings, including the enigmatic and inconclusive: some, which have miraculously resisted the effects of urban sprawl, have no definite endings and are repeated or not, in whatever cross-section, as the spirit of the moment dictates. The absence of any clear cadence in Chopin's last mazurka, the F minor, op. 68, no. 4 – his last composition of any kind – is perhaps less indicative of his deathly weariness, therefore, than romantic legend has it, although his weakness at that point was beyond argument, and more deeply Polish than any outsider could be expected to guess.

By the end of the seventeenth century the mazurka had spread from the plains of Mazowse to the whole of Poland, and in the early eighteenth century it was introduced into the royal courts of Germany by Augustus II, Elector of Saxony. From there it was a short hop to Paris, where the dance was much cultivated by the aristocracy, besotted with Rousseau's image of 'the noble savage', and by 1750 the English too had taken it up. This trend in the life of the mazurka, which might now be diagnosed as 'upward social mobility', was marginally less steep than many people supposed. Far from reflecting only the illiterate traditions of the Polish peasantry, the mazurka, in common with many another folk-song type, enshrines one or other of the old ecclesiastical modes, most notably the Lydian, with its sharpened fourth (white-note scale from F on the piano) and another, consisting of six notes only, which used widely to be known as 'the Polish mode'. Its cultivation among the literati of Europe may in one sense at least, therefore, have been as much a return as an arrival.

In the studiedly pastoral diversions of eighteenth-century aristocrats, the mazurka retained much of its original, folk-like character. In the fashionable Parisian salons graced by Chopin a century or so later and in many humbler homes ever since, it retained very little. The conclusion that Chopin had only the most tenuous acquaintance with the authentic mazurkas of the peasantry, however, although drawn by no less an ethnomusicological authority than Bartók, will not stand up to scrutiny. It is perfectly true that the mazurkas he heard in Warsaw had been through the urban refiner's fire, with not always happy results, but no one understood that better than Chopin himself. Hence his determination in Szafarnia to collect as many examples as possible of the real thing. By 1830, when he left Poland for good, he had become a genuine connoisseur of his country's music and was roused to displays of real anger by attempts to dress it up for popular consumption. If Bartók believed, on the basis of the mazurkas, that Chopin himself was guilty of doing precisely that, albeit at the highest artistic level, he was seriously mistaken.

Unlike Bartók, many of whose piano works consist of actual folk-song settings, arranged with a view to preserving the character and enhancing the spirit of the originals, Chopin took the authentic mazurkas and, perhaps just as importantly, the memories and visions they kindled in him as a point of departure: a source of inspiration and a spur to the imagination, out of which he could fashion a new and highly sophisticated kind of music, whose salient features were nevertheless quintessentially Polish and whose spiritual character enshrined in a supra-national art what he deeply felt to be the collective voice of his own people. To this end he abjured, in general, the direct quotation of recognizable folk tunes, and with very few exceptions – the *poco più vivo* of op. 68, no. 3, being one of them – his sixty-odd mazurkas are composed of entirely original material.

Among the characteristics whose innate Polishness transcends the limits of specific tunes are the frequent repetition of short thematic figures, which Chopin develops, despite the ostensibly 'miniature' framework of the mazurka, with a resourcefulness aptly described by several writers as 'symphonic' (witness, for example, op. 41, no. 1, op. 59, no. 3, and op. 63, no. 1); a tendency to hover around a single note (op. 50, no. 3); the decorative use of triplets at significant points (op. 7, no. 5); the tell-tale accenting of traditionally weak beats, and the ending of phrases on the second beat. Sometimes too, as in op. 33, no. 4, there is a mixture of duplet and triplet rhythms, a procedure that musicians in the late nineteenth and early twentieth centuries took for granted but that in the mid-1830s was startlingly modern.

This, then, is the expressive vocabulary that gives Chopin's mazurkas their identifiably Polish character; and if this were their most notable feature they could take their place in that sea of pianistic flotsam from the nineteenth century whose picture-postcard 'nationalism' provided a welcome distraction from the artistic bankruptcy that so often lay behind it. What raises Chopin's mazurkas to the level of the subtlest poetry is the unmistakable stamp of his creative genius, which by its nature transcended the merely national. If the peasants of Mazowse had chanced to hear a group of these extraordinary transformations they would probably have made no connection whatever between Chopin's music and their own. Nor might they even today, when ears long accustomed to post-Wagnerian chromaticism can still find the prophetic harmonies of something like op. 56, no. 3, as startling as they were in 1843. In their unique combination of the primitive and the learned – the counterpoint at the end of op. 63, no. 3, should satisfy even the stuffiest pedant – the cerebral and the sensual, the robust and the frail, the ingratiating and the aristocratic, many of these miraculous creations were regarded in the last century, and by some of Chopin's most passionate admirers too, as the enigmatic aberrations of a fevered brain. Yet here, more than anywhere else, we find the most complete musical portrait of Chopin the man. Written from his fifteenth year onwards, his many essays in the form can be interpreted as a kind of lifelong diary of his innermost spirit. This is not to suggest that his mazurkas are all masterworks of emotional profundity, on the model of, say, Beethoven's Bagatelles. Some, like the B flat, op. 7, no. 1, and the D major, op. 33, no. 2, are of a definitely playful character, some merely wistful or ingratiating. But it is in his mazurkas above all that we find him at his subtlest, at his richest, at his most daringly original and dangerous.

— 13 —

Chopin and Posterity

Strangely for a man so afflicted by illness, Chopin never made a will. In any case, at his death he had little to leave: had his friends not been so generously minded he might indeed have left nothing but debts. Among the personal effects found in his apartment was a pocketbook containing a lock of George Sand's hair and a carefully wrapped parcel containing all of her letters to him. By a tortuous route these were eventually returned to Sand, who promptly consigned them to the flames. Even had she wanted to, it would have been too late to mete out similar treatment to his life's work. That had already become part of the heritage of the world. As it is today, Chopin's name was known to many who had only the slightest interest in music, and as noted earlier, one of his melodies in particular was widely known among people who had never even heard his name: the famous Funeral March, which quickly achieved the near folkloric status it enjoys today.

If people knew anything about Chopin other than his name it was almost certainly the fact that he was a Pole. It was he, perhaps more than any figure before Paderewski,* who had put Poland on the map – not only of the world but of people's consciousness, irrespective of their interest in either politics or art. To a certain extent this was inevitable and just, but labels of any kind tend to limit as much as they define. The degree of Chopin's Polishness is still a matter of heated debate, because the issue of national sovereignty has not even now been finally resolved.

In an age beset by political turmoil and international tension, self-conscious nationalism quickly became a central feature of the whole Romantic ethos. In Poland itself Chopin was prized above all as an essentially national composer, to the virtual exclusion of those more 'abstract' products of his genius that could not be readily perceived as

Polish.† More, perhaps, than any other figure, artistic or political, Chopin was enshrined as a symbol of the nation, and more importantly still, the aspirations of a subject nation. This was particularly true in the decades following his death. During his lifetime, surprisingly, he was only the fifth most played composer in Warsaw,‡ whereas after his death he topped the bill for the next hundred years. A contributory element here was the fact that no pianist, of whatever provenance, could hope to succeed in Poland without playing Chopin's music. At the same time, most of his later works remained unknown to the average musical Pole until the advent of the twentieth century. The standard Chopin repertory played in Poland consisted almost entirely of early pieces. It was not until 1866, more than twenty years after its composition, that the B minor Sonata was given its first complete performance in Poland, while many other late works were badly neglected well into the twentieth century. And of those works that *did* enter the central repertory, many were commonly played in arrangements for voice or melody instrument, especially the violin, with piano accompaniment.

If Chopin was represented as an essentially feminine 'composer of sentiment', to quote one critic, this is not in fact a misrepresentation of his more robust and virile works, but a feature of their more or less wholesale neglect. In an age rocked by pestilence, revolution and chauvinistic sloganism, an age, moreover, in which the overwhelming majority of amateur pianists were women, it is hardly surprising that a cult of innocence and intimacy, of 'feeling', of 'the voice of the heart', should have arisen. For much of the nineteenth century, Chopin was viewed almost entirely as a lyricist. Symptomatic of this image is the enormous number of his more obviously 'melodic' works to be arranged, however inappropriately, as songs and accompanied instrumental solos – a trend that lasted well into the twentieth century, witness such popular hits as 'I'm Always Chasing Rainbows' (a hijacking of the middle section of the Fantasie-Impromptu) and the adaptation of certain nocturnes as violin encores.

Whenever his concertos were played, their most talked about features were the poetic reveries of the slow movements and the 'exotic' nationalism of their finales. A quick trawl of critical writing by nineteenth-century commentators results in an interesting harvest of adjectives.

---

† At the same time, great ingenuity was applied to the ascribing of Polish characteristics to almost everything he wrote, including such un-national works as the Études.
‡ Chopin ranked below Rossini, Donizetti, Bellini and Charles Auguste de Bériot, a popular Belgian violinist-composer now almost completely forgotten.

Again and again Chopin is described as 'sweet', 'poetic', 'tender', 'refined', 'melancholy', 'fanciful' and 'original' (that, at least, the critics recognized).† With only slight variation, this was also the prevailing nineteenth-century view of Mozart. It is not an entirely 'wrong' view, of course, but it is an incomplete one, which seriously misrepresents the essence of Chopin's musical personality. And again as with Mozart, there were many who recognized the novelty of Chopin's music while failing to understand its most prophetic aspects. That, perhaps unsurprisingly, was left largely to composers.

Of all the undercover revolutionaries in the history of the arts, none, with the possible exception of Mozart, has betrayed so little or portended so much. It says a lot about Chopin that the 'guns' perceived by Schumann were so skilfully buried beneath the flowers of his outer style that the musical public at large had no inkling of their presence. This is not to say, of course, that all of Chopin's music is either revolutionary or prophetic, and a significant number of those works now regarded as his greatest achievements – the F minor Ballade, the Polonaise-Fantasie, even the Barcarolle – were slow even to approach the popularity accorded to the waltzes, the earlier nocturnes, the B flat minor Scherzo, the A flat Ballade and the bewitching Berceuse.

In the realm of harmony alone, Chopin anticipated many of the 'innovations' credited to such different composers as Liszt, Wagner, Tchaikovsky, Brahms, Debussy, Mahler, Scriabin, Szymanowski, Rachmaninov and Ravel. Among the most prophetic of Chopin's harmonic procedures is the phenomenon of the unresolved dissonance – a clear case in point being the final chord of the F major Prelude, whose hovering E flat appears to transform the tonic into a dominant harmony – leading to a vastly widened harmonic vocabulary, no longer dependent on the tyranny of enforced resolution. On the face of it, it might seem difficult to find two more uncongenial musicians than Chopin and Wagner, yet the debt of the latter to the former is immense. Both in his much vaunted concept of 'endless melody' and in the longing

---

† Before the sexual revolutions of the twentieth century, ostensibly 'feminine' characteristics in a male were regarded as negative attributes. There were always critics, throughout the nineteenth century, who disparaged Chopin's works as 'unmanly' and 'weak', one going so far as to deplore his 'hermaphrodite nature'. Some ventured further still, seeing Chopin as a dangerous and emasculating influence: Oscar Bie, a much respected figure, cautioned his readers against Chopin's 'mental sickness', citing among other symptoms 'sorrowful chords, *which do not occur to healthy, normal persons*', and declaring that it has become a '*very bad habit to place this poet in the hands of our youth*' (author's italics).

chromaticism on which it largely depends, Wagner's musical language has clear precedents in Chopin. Indeed in the heartbreaking final mazurka, op. 68, no. 4, Chopin anticipates Wagner's famous *Tristan* harmony with eerie prescience (especially in bar fourteen); and there are similarly 'Wagnerian' touches in the C sharp minor Mazurka of op. 63.

In Poland itself, until the emergence of Karol Szymanowski in the twentieth century, Chopin's work was more imitated than understood, and it is at the door of Chopin's imitators, Polish and otherwise, that the charge of misrepresentation can most deservedly be laid. The carefully bound 'Young Lady Albums', which proliferated on both sides of the Atlantic in the nineteenth century, contain a depressing amount of quasi-Chopinesque dross, perpetuating, if only in name, the genres that he had made famous – the polonaise, the mazurka, the nocturne, the waltz and even, though less frequently, the scherzo and the ballade. It is here, far more than in the music of Chopin himself, that we find the image of the languid artist, poetically coughing his life away beneath a halo of romantic melancholy. In the twentieth century, greatly aided by the advent of recording and the decline of 'Young Ladies', that image has been largely replaced by a leaner, more sinewy, more 'classical' approach, in keeping with the composer's own oft-proclaimed affinities.†

Among those substantial composers whose development was fundamentally influenced by Chopin's pioneering imagination and who have not thus far been mentioned are Rimsky-Korsakov, Fauré, Balakirev, Busoni, Grieg and Smetana. His most far-reaching influence, however, as has already been intimated, was on Debussy, still cited in many books as 'the father of modern music'. Debussy's immersion in Chopin's music was at times almost obsessive, and, as we have seen, he once went so far as to declare that: 'Chopin is the greatest of us all, for he discovered everything through the piano alone.' Behind the characteristic hyperbole, Debussy was almost certainly thinking of Chopin's unprecedented liberation of harmonic movement, and its concomitant increase of chromaticism and decrease of tonal stability; of his subtle use of texture as an agent of musical architecture; and of his rhythmic daring, starting with such avant-garde procedures as the combined metres in his original version of the C sharp minor Nocturne of 1830. To these one might also add an originality in the treatment of folk music which had far-reaching effects, not least for the emergent nationalists in Russia, and a colouristic palette of almost infinite range and subtlety. Considering the popularity

† For further treatment of this subject see Appendix 1.

enjoyed by Chopin from boyhood to the brink of middle age, it comes as something of a shock to find a number of his last works effectively rejected by some of his deepest admirers, including Liszt, as the disordered thoughts of a mind worn down by debilitating illness. The fact is, however, that Chopin had already done what Liszt later and quite fairly claimed for himself, namely 'to hurl [his] lance into the indefinite reaches of the future'. Ironically, it took longest to land (to pursue the metaphor) in the very country where Chopin was most conspicuously revered. Of all European nations, Poland was among the last to recognize the true, prophetic stature of its favourite musical son.

It is not only as a composer, however, that Chopin left a lasting imprint on the European, now worldwide, musical tradition. Through the testimony and example of his pupils and those who heard him play, and more reliably, perhaps, through the careful study of his music, we know a great deal about his approach to piano-playing. Much has been made of the fact that, to quote Liszt, 'Chopin was unlucky in his pupils'. That is to say that, unlike Liszt's, there were no great pianists among them, with the exception of Karl Filtsch, who unfortunately died at the age of fifteen. In terms of the establishment of an authentic and reliable tradition, however, he may well have been luckier than Liszt. Great pianists, perhaps especially great nineteenth-century pianists, tend to have powerful personalities of their own and are therefore less, rather than more likely to distort what they inherit than a string of devoted and accomplished aristocratic pupils. In any case, it is the job of great teachers to release the hitherto untapped resources of their pupils' individual personalities, not to establish a race of clones. The pupils of the great Leschetizky* were in many respects as unlike one another as the proverbial chalk and cheese, and precisely *because* they included such powerful but dissimilar pianists as Ignaz Friedman and Mieczyslaw Horszowski, or Schnabel, Paderewski and Moiseiwitsch, it would be next to impossible to divine much through their example about Leschetizky's own playing.

The ideal passed on by Chopin is centred on the utmost refinement of time and tone, translucency of texture, a soaring cantilena complemented by the subtlest harmonic nuance and a virtuosity free from struggle, although not from the greatest of difficulties, but invariably subordinated to musical and expressive ends. The emphasis will always be on suppleness and rhetorical restraint, if one even admits rhetoric to the canon of Chopin's expressive vocabulary. While his work contains many examples of undeniable power, Chopin is not basically one of music's declaimers. Nowhere does he indulge in the pictorialism so common in Liszt – the use of *tremolandi* to simulate certain orchestral effects, for example – partly because it would have risked the blemishing of a sound world that was comprehensively based on euphony (aural, if not harmonic) and partly because of his lifelong aversion to programme music, which, incidentally, played no part in the Polish tradition with which he grew up. In this last regard, Chopin has proved, albeit posthumously, uncommonly accident-prone. Few commentators have seen fit to encumber the works of Brahms, for instance, with such elaborate programmatic interpretations, yet Chopin, well into the twentieth century, has been all but suffocated by them.

First into the field, among the great interpreters, was the pianist and conductor Hans von Bülow, who, in the tradition of Chopin's English publisher Wessel, began by giving a title to each of the op. 28 preludes. Once launched, he appended to each a programme all its own. Readers familiar with the works but not with Bülow's enhancements might like to try and identify this one:

> Here Chopin has the conviction that he has lost his power of expression. With the determination to discover whether his brain can still originate ideas, he strikes his head with a hammer (here the semiquavers and demisemiquavers are to be carried out [*sic*] in strict time, denoting a double stroke of the hammer). In the third and fourth bars one can hear the blood trickling (trills in left hand). He is desperate at finding no inspiration (fifth bar); he strikes again with the hammer and with greater force (demisemiquavers twice in succession during the crescendo). In the key of A flat he finds his powers again. Appeased, he seeks his former key and closes contentedly.

Thus Bülow on Prelude no. 9 in E major, which he understatedly entitles merely 'Vision'. And if great musicians have lent themselves to such effusions, how much more have the well-intentioned also-rans. In England one Wilkinson took pen to paper on behalf of Chopin's so-called 'Raindrop' Prelude in an entertaining trilogy, *Well-Known Piano Solos: How to Play Them with Understanding, Expression and Effect*, clearly aimed at the ivory-tinkling Victorian maiden. Mindful of more delicate sensibilities than those addressed by Bülow, the author bids us hark unto the water dripping

> perhaps from the eaves above his open window. It is not difficult to conjure up in the memory the impressions of such a wet day, and we may well feel surprise that under depressing circumstances Chopin's music should sing into his ear sweet melody. In the middle section,

the deep voices of the brethren are heard chanting in two parts in the cloisters. As they approach the composer's window, their breath might almost be felt, and as they retire behind the pillars their voices become subdued. Make your two parts sing like a double file of monks. At the *ff*, where they are close on the composer one can almost see one peep curiously from his book toward the open window. Then they go round again, to return once more.

And there were many more such midwives, foremost among whom is the Chopin biographer James Huneker, a capable if fanciful American pianist and critic, who waxed equally lyrical in the early 1900s, and whose book *Chopin: The Man and his Music* shaped the outlook of a generation. Since then, the pendulum has swung away from such subjective raptures and it has become fashionable to sneer at the Hunekers of this world. Indeed, with the inevitable standardization brought about by the electronics revolution and the widespread substitution of musicology for imagination, the pendulum has almost ceased to swing at all. The process that Artur Rubinstein claimed, implicitly, to have initiated is now complete.

I heard quite a bit of Chopin during my childhood in Poland. . . . All of it was played interminably, and most of it badly. Why badly? In those days both musicians and the public believed in the Chopin myth. . . . The myth was a destructive one. Chopin the man was seen as weak and ineffectual; Chopin the artist as an irrepressible romantic – effeminate if appealing, dipping his pen in moonlight to compose nocturnes for sentimental young women. Pianists whose heads were filled with such nonsense had to play Chopin badly. . . . At my next recital (about 1902) I included Chopin and presented him nobly, I hoped, without sentimentality (sentiment, yes!), without affectation, without the swan dive into the keyboard with which pianists customarily alerted the audience to the fact that they were listening to the music of Chopin. What was the result of what I considered conscientious work? My interpretation was adjudged 'dry'. The audience and critics preferred the 'good old Chopin' they knew from before. When I went to America four years later, I was chastened, as had also happened in Europe, for my 'severe' interpretations of Chopin. Stubbornly, I continued programming Chopin in my concerts. And stubbornly the critics continued to criticize. It was admitted subsequently that I could play Spanish music, and I certainly could play Ravel and Debussy. But Chopin? No. Only very much later was the validity of my interpretation granted.

In fact Rubinstein was not alone – his slightly younger compatriot Mieczyslaw Horszowski, for one, played a similarly 'classical' Chopin, quite untainted by sentimental excess – but the overall picture painted by Rubinstein was more or less accurate. By the early 1950s the self-indulgent mannerisms of earlier generations had been largely replaced by a more stringently objective approach which resulted, in its turn, in a widespread anonymity, rendering one pianist much like another.†
Rather than heaving a collective sigh of relief, many music-lovers succumbed to a wave of nostalgia. In each decade of the mid-to-late twentieth century, one pianist after another has been billed as 'the last of the great Romantics', just as one biography after another has been promoted as 'rescuing Chopin the man from Chopin the myth' or 'returning Chopin to his rightful place'. His rightful place has nothing to do with history or the calendar. It is in the hearts of those who love his music, for whatever reason or from whatever vantage point, and in the minds and fingers of those who are fortunate enough to play it.

★   ★   ★

There is no single factor that can account for Chopin's unabating popularity. Like Mozart, he seems infinitely adaptable to every age's image of itself, each claiming to have revealed the 'real' Chopin, yet in the final analysis he remains inimitable. The main features of his style are easily copied, but none of his imitators have come anywhere near to achieving genuine popularity (not even Schumann succeeded in catching his true likeness in that movement of *Carnaval* which he specifically entitles 'Chopin'). In any case, Chopin's effect on composers has been both profound and highly sophisticated. One must look elsewhere to explain his effect on the ordinary music-lover.

The most obvious aspect of his style is his melody. He had the kind of instinct for a good tune that many envy but no one acquires. Hardly less seductive are his harmonies and the wave-like contours of his accompaniments, which are usually a primary rather than a secondary element of Chopin's textural weave. And while his reputation as a 'miniaturist' (common to most of the nineteenth century and much of the twentieth) does him much less than full justice, the brevity of many of his pieces renders them particularly attractive to that vast majority of listeners whose attention span is relatively slight. Closely allied to this is the

---

† There are great and individual pianists in every generation; I refer here only to the generality of performers.

relative speed of mood and textural changes. Then, too, there is the sheer, sensuous beauty of sound which he conjured up almost as a matter of course. Combine these characteristics with the richly physical rhythms of the many dance forms he explored (polonaise, mazurka, waltz, écossaise, bourée, bolero, tarantella, galop), stir in the requisite servings of genius, and you may at least come close to an explanation for his perennial popularity.

Appendix 1: A Discographical Survey of Chopin in Performance

A number of pianists have set out to record the complete works for piano solo, of whom only two, Vladimir Ashkenazy and Idil Biret, have stayed the course, with Nikita Magaloff coming in a close third. Each of these cycles has much to recommend it, just as each is predictably uneven in quality, and Biret's is the only one to include the orchestral works as well. The ideal Chopin collection must therefore be selective and fulfil a number of different criteria. It will reflect the outlook not only of one individual or generation but of several. It will embrace the composer's entire output. It will contain at least two contrasting versions of every important work, in acknowledgement of the fact that any performance, however great, represents only a cross-section of the almost infinite possibilities afforded by any work. It will serve not only to confirm one's natural prejudice but, equally, to challenge it. It will emphasize in character and scope the universality of Chopin's appeal and his greatness, which are by no means necessarily the same. It will both nourish the spirit and stimulate the mind. And it will be personal to a degree that all but guarantees its uniqueness.

The following selection and commentary inevitably reflects one man's tastes and judgements, but it also includes all those recordings that are generally conceded to be among the greatest Chopin performances ever set down: Rachmaninov's of the B flat minor Sonata, for instance, Ignaz Friedman's of the late E flat Nocturne and Lipatti's of the B minor Sonata. By way of perspective, however, it proceeds chronologically rather than generically, in the hope that the continuous evolution of a Chopin 'tradition' will emerge.

Vladimir de Pachmann (1848–1933)
Considered by some as the foremost Chopin player of his day after Paderewski and Cortot, Pachmann was essentially a miniaturist who made almost a fetish of playing *pianissimo*. Today his recorded legacy seems more notable for its sophisticated pianism than for its interpretative insight, but it affords an interesting glimpse of the way in which Chopin was regarded during the last phase of the romantic era (*c*. 1880–1920). **OPAL CD 9840**

Raoul Pugno (1852–1914)
Deeply admired for his eloquence, power and originality, Pugno was a pupil of Chopin's pupil Georges Mathias. His few Chopin recordings, of the Nocturne, op. 15, no. 2, the Funeral March from op. 35, the A flat Waltz, op. 34, the A flat Impromptu and the Berceuse, were made as early as 1903 and in unfavourable

circumstances, but they reveal an artist whose classical restraint, subtle colouring and spacious tempi accord well with what we know of Chopin's teaching.
OPAL CD 9836

Ignacy Jan Paderewski (1860–1941)
No pianist has been more widely associated with Chopin than Paderewski –
virtuoso, composer and statesman, who served for a time as the first Prime
Minister of modern Poland – nor has any been so misrepresented by his recordings, many of which were made when he was well past his prime, and most
of which have been transferred to LP or CD. The mannered rubato and the
intentional de-synchronization of the hands were not peculiar to Paderewski
but reflected the prevailing style of the time. Behind them lie a deep-rooted
artistry and aristocratic poise perfectly suited to Chopin's music. In his 1911
recording of the F sharp major Nocturne, op. 15, no. 2, and his 1912 version
of its F major companion, as in the 1925 account of the A flat Mazurka, op. 59,
no. 2, music and musician become one. There has been no more naturally
persuasive Chopin playing from anyone. **PEARL: GEMM CD 9323 and 9397**

Moritz Rosenthal (1862–1946)
A formidable virtuoso in his prime, the force of his own personality should,
on the face of it, have rendered him unfit to become an ideal Chopin player,
yet the subtlety, restraint and delicate shadings of his playing, especially in the
mazurkas, are beautifully idiomatic: rhythmically supple yet buoyant, articu-
lated with meticulous attention to detail, and marked by an extraordinary control of *pianissimo*, which may have been close to Chopin's own. **PEARL: GEMM
CD 9963**

Sergei Rachmaninov (1873–1943)
His 1930 recording of the B flat minor Sonata is the most famous ever made,
characterized by unsurpassed technical mastery and a freshness of insight that
has stood the test of more than half a century. The only negative property may
be to have eclipsed unfairly his other Chopin recordings, which are hardly less
stimulating or enjoyable. This is the playing, however, of a strong-minded,
unambiguously Romantic composer with a will of his own and listeners hoping
to discover here something of Chopin's own style should be warned off. Fortunately, Rachmaninov's entire recorded output has been reissued on CD and
with any luck should remain in the catalogue for ever.

Alfred Cortot (1877–1962)
For many musicians, Cortot remains unequalled as a Chopin player. Forget
the anecdotes about his memory lapses, his wrong notes and his retouchings –
this was a player of luminous intelligence and an incomparably sophisticated
technique, whose playing in many ways is probably as close as we will ever
get to knowing how Chopin himself played. In its balance and poise, its improvisatory spontaneity, its sensuous beauty and its depth of feeling, Cortot's
playing remains a seemingly inexhaustible source of deepening insight into the
composer's art and very soul. He recorded most of Chopin's output, much of
it several times, and virtually all of his recordings have been well transferred
to CD. His 1933 account of the 24 preludes is generally acknowledged to be

among the greatest records ever made, with the waltzes (1934), études (1942), F minor Fantasy (1934) and the C sharp minor Nocturne, op. 27, no. 1, running it a close second. **EMI CZS 767359-2 (6 CDs); BIDDULPH LHW 001**

Ignaz Friedman (1882–1948)

A pianist of extraordinary elegance and virtuosity, his recordings of Chopin mazurkas are unique and inimitable, often quirky, and for some tastes dangerously 'creative'. His greatest Chopin recording is undoubtedly of the E flat Nocturne, op. 55, no. 2, in which he combines in perfect balance all the qualities necessary to an ideal Chopin interpreter: crystalline textures, rhythmic flexibility combined with a large-scale metrical discipline, a kaleidoscopic tonal palette, the most arching *bel canto* melodic inflections, harmonically illuminating pedalling, nobility of spirit, urbanity of manner and a technique so finely honed to the requirements of the music that one is scarcely aware of the discipline that lay behind it. All of Friedman's Chopin recordings have been reissued on CD and give a vivid picture of the transition from high-ground romanticism to mid-century musicological rigour. **PEARL: IF 2000 (4 CDs)**

Raoul Koczalski (1885–1948)

A pupil of Chopin's disciple Mikuli, Koczalski was a pianist of great stylishness and refinement whose most important bequest to the archives of recording is an account of the E flat Nocturne, op. 9, no. 2, incorporating the coloratura-style elaborations pencilled into Mikuli's copy of the music by Chopin himself. Accounts of Chopin's playing suggest that he often introduced embellishments and variations into his own performances, and this hand-written example is a tantalizing glimpse of his improvisatory style. **PEARL: GEMM CD 9472**

Artur Rubinstein (1887–1982)

Still regarded by many as the pre-eminent Chopin player of the twentieth century, Rubinstein was among the most influential prophets of the new classicism, dispensing with the once almost obligatory Romantic liberties of his elder contemporaries. Criticized well into his long career for the 'severity' of his Chopin performances (see Chapter 13), he recorded all the major works with the substantial and regrettable exception of the études. The 78s he made in the 1930s (reissued on CD by EMI) are perhaps characterized by a greater sense of spontaneity and adventure than the more careful studio recordings of the LP era (transferred to CD by RCA/BMG), but both are treasurable collections. Rich in tone, authoritative and buoyant in rhythm and consistently virile in character, they are entirely free of mannerism or narcissistic 'eloquence', and they reveal the sheer stature of the music to a degree matched by very few. Especially memorable are his interpretations of the G minor Ballade, the B minor Scherzo and the A flat Polonaise, which became something like his personal signature tune. From a late twentieth-century vantage point, his playing sounds far from severe and there is no sense of musicological wing-clipping. The quality of his playing is singularly hard to describe, being entirely free from mannerisms or period quirks, but its directness and emotional richness are unassailable. **RCA VICTOR RED SEAL: GD 60822 (11 CDs)**

Mieczyslaw Horszowski (1892–1993)

Horszowski's career spanned almost a century. When he retired in his hundredth year, he had been before the public for ninety-five years. Sadly, he was almost entirely ignored by record companies until his ninth decade. Earlier recordings, notably of the four Impromptus and the E minor Concerto, convey the nobility and unforced simplicity of his playing, but only the later, nonagenarian ones capture the very essence of his art, the nocturnes in particular being among the richest and most eloquent Chopin recordings ever made. Horszowski was a classicist, whose playing, unmarred by the slightest trace of mannerism, has a timeless quality that will never date. In spirit if not in every detail of style, it brings us probably as close to Chopin's own playing as we can hope to get. ELEKTRA/NONESUCH 7559-79261-2 (3 CDs)

Claudio Arrau (1903–91)

No pianist ever gave more considered attention to the music he played than Arrau, but his penetrating and aristocratic mind proved a mixed blessing, often resulting in a mannered, didactic approach, viable, perhaps, in the concert hall but ill-suited to the unnatural eternity of recording. Among the greatest of his Chopin recordings is his magisterial and deeply poignant account of the nocturnes, which is unlikely ever to be surpassed. PHILIPS 432 303-2 (6 CDs)

Vlado Perlemuter (b. 1904)

Of the great twentieth-century Chopin players, Perlemuter is among the lesser known, partly, perhaps, because his notoriously accident-prone memory (an offshoot of platform nerves) made him a highly erratic concert performer. In the recording studio, too, his playing could be unreliable, suffering from bouts of rhythmic stasis, which distracted from the immense sophistication of his readings. He was never a remotely flamboyant artist, but he was a very considerable virtuoso, with an extraordinarily wide and deftly deployed colouristic palette, which he never displayed for its own sake. His Chopin playing, which often had about it something of the directness and simplicity of Edwin Fischer's Bach playing, was particularly well suited to the spiritual nobility of the music. His discriminating intellect combined with a multi-layered command of the keyboard to produce playing of a quite exceptional wholeness: rich, complex and with such a sense of naturalness that at the moment of hearing it one could scarcely imagine the music going any other way. Perlemuter's Chopin playing only improves on repeated hearings, each encounter revealing some new beauty or pregnant insight. NIMBUS NIM5064, 5209; BBC REB 153

Vladimir Horowitz (1904–90)

When the distinguished English critic Neville Cardus described Horowitz as 'the greatest pianist alive or dead', he had Chopin in the forefront of his mind, and particularly the mazurkas, whose elusive rhythms and intricate textures tended to bring out the best in this uniquely fascinating artist. The knife-edge tension and cataclysmic power, which led Rudolf Serkin to describe Horowitz's G minor Ballade as being 'like a fireball exploding', worked both for and against him. His machine-gun-like, *martellato* virtuosity introduced an element of twentieth-century angularity into the history of Chopin-playing, which proved predictably controversial and exerted a largely negative influence on his less gifted imitators. And while it seems a little harsh to assert, as one critic has, that Horowitz took Chopin's music 'as a medium with which to express his own neuroticism', there are many who would broadly back that view. The world of music would be a poorer place, however, without his formidably disciplined and intense account of the B flat minor Sonata from 1962, his 1964 recording of the B minor Scherzo, the Polonaise-Fantasie of 1966 or, indeed, any number of mazurkas, études and waltzes in a recording career that lasted for the best part of six decades. There is no way to objectify an approach as intensely personal as that of Horowitz, nor is there any analytical tool by which to explain the sheer magic of a great many Horowitz performances, as remarkable for their delicacy, poise and extreme intimacy as for their coruscating virtuosity. In Horowitz the spirits of Chopin, Liszt and Paganini were all rolled up in one. **SONY SK 53457, 5345761, 53465**

Dinu Lipatti (1917–50)
Before cancer claimed him, Lipatti had recorded only a little of Chopin's output, but his playing of almost every note was a model of spiritual and stylistic purity. His powerful, superbly integrated account of the B minor Sonata (1947) is one of the greatest performances on record, while those of the D flat Nocturne (1947), the Barcarolle (1948) and the waltzes (1949) are of comparable quality. The studio recording of the waltzes is by common consent superior to that made at his final recital, when he was in pain and close to death. For many it remains the most completely satisfying version on disc. In Lipatti's playing is to be found all the best features of the mid-twentieth-century ideal of emotion filtered through the disciplines of the intellect. His sovereign technique is put entirely at the service of the music, and the trappings of romanticism are left way behind. Of the great pianists of the past, none was so stringently or eloquently classical in outlook. From that point of view it might fairly be said that Lipatti was the first truly modern interpreter of Chopin. **EMI CDH 769802-2, CZS 767163 (5 CDs)**

Vladimir Ashkenazy (b. 1937)
Ashkenazy's affinity with Chopin has been evident from his childhood. Very much a mid-century classicist, he brings to his Chopin playing an exceptionally effortless technique and an intense concentration, which is focused entirely on the music. Like most of his contemporaries he sometimes lacks something of the richness and range of tone colours so characteristic of earlier generations, and his rhythmic inflection is sometimes distractingly metrical (and indeed over*symmetrical*, which is not the same thing, by any means), but his recorded traversal, for Decca, of the complete works for solo piano is as remarkable for its quality as for its quantity. Of his youthful, pre-Decca recordings, his dazzling Saga disc of the op. 10 and op. 25 études, dating from the early 1960s, must surely take pride of place, exceeding in quality even his very fine re-recording for Decca in the mid-1970s.

Martha Argerich (b. 1941)
In some ways, Argerich is a throwback to an earlier generation, her playing characterized by an intensely personal stamp and a degree of spontaneity seldom

encountered in the electronicized age of the CD. She has the confidence to act on the spur of the moment. As a re-creator of the composer's thoughts she is one of the world's great improvisers. Indeed she often seems, in the best possible sense, to be the very embodiment of Artur Schnabel's jubilant motto 'Safety last!' That sense of living dangerously is one of the hallmarks of Argerich's Chopin performances, yet seldom if ever is she reckless. Her detractors are all but unanimous in their claims that she is indiscriminately electrifying; that she injects a high voltage level of excitement and tension into music that neither requires nor benefits from such attributes. One pianist, possibly nursing a certain jealousy, described her prize-winning performance of the Chopin E minor Concerto at the 1965 Chopin Competition in Warsaw as 'hell on wheels'. Her Chopin recordings are sadly few, but they include one of the truly great performances of the A flat Polonaise, a superb account of the op. 59 mazurkas, and a traversal of the op. 28 preludes, which mysteriously imparts to the set a uniquely integrated sense of wholeness and deserves to be in the collection of everyone seriously interested in Chopin playing.

Maurizio Pollini (b. 1942)
Like his elder compatriot Michelangeli, Pollini's technical command is near-legendary. The authority and strength of his playing are altogether exceptional and his meticulous attention to every detail of the composer's text often results in the nearest thing to an aural photograph of the printed page. His virtuosity is untainted by any sense of ego, indeed there are many musicians who find his playing cold and impersonal. While by no means ascetic, there is a sometimes forbidding element in his performances, placing him at the opposite extreme from such interpretative, 'romantic' players as Pachmann, Paderewski or Cortot. Among the greatest of his Chopin recordings are those of the E minor Concerto, recorded by EMI as long ago as 1960, when Pollini was 18, and the 1972 DG release of the op. 10 and op. 25 études, although all of them are of a very high distinction indeed.

Murray Perahia (b. 1947)
The great English pianist Sir Clifford Curzon once confessed that he had waited a lifetime to hear playing that wholly complemented the hauntingly beautiful strength and grace of Chopin's hands, as cast in plaster by Auguste Clésinger. On hearing Murray Perahia he announced that the wait was over. In its particular combination of suppleness, textural clarity, penetrating analytical insight and command of colour, Perahia's playing combines the disparate virtues of all the greatest Chopin players in a synthesis whose natural eloquence is in no way imitative of those who came before him. Allowing for subjective differences of opinion, he may well be the most faithfully Chopinesque player now before the public.

Krystian Zimerman (b. 1956)
Zimerman's affinity with Chopin is no secret. He brings to his playing a breadth of technique equal to anything Chopin has to offer, an incisive intelligence matched by a stylistic instinct second to none, and an imagination sometimes sufficiently idiosyncratic to recall an earlier, more 'romantic' generation. For

some tastes, his magnificent account of the four ballades may seem a little wayward in its temporal flexibility, but the controlled intensity and unforced eloquence of his interpretations are compelling in the extreme. This playing is both vibrantly alive and deeply reflective. His keyboard approach is on the classical side, avoiding dynamic extremes, on the whole, and complemented by a very discreet use of the sustaining pedal, which he uses to wonderful colouristic effect. Although his playing is profoundly poetic, he's not a dreamy, 'moonlight' poet, but one in whom tenderness mingles with a powerfully dramatic, sometimes even tragic vision.

Evgeny Kissin (b. 1972)

From early childhood, Kissin has been a Chopin player to the manner born. With a tonal palette as economical as it is rich, a continuous suppleness of phrase, a keen ear for rhythmic nuance, a technique that can embrace anything with apparent ease, a singing tone and a profound instinct for harmonic rhythm, he has all the makings of an ideal Chopin player. Add to these virtues a capacity for melodic inflection, which emulates the subtlety and continuity of the human voice, an ear for Chopin's 'hidden' polyphony, a deep understanding of the pedals and a classical sense of proportion, and you have a Chopin player who is perhaps already unsurpassed.

Appendix 2: Chopin and the Interpreter

A conversational symposium arising out of individual discussions with Vladimir Ashkenazy, Emanuel Ax, Alfred Brendel, Mitsuko Uchida, Michael Roll, Carl Schachter, Howard Shelley, Melvyn Tan and Tamas Vasary – distinguished Chopin-players all, though Schachter, who has never sought a performing career, is better known as one of the most penetrating and illuminating musical analysts of our day, and Brendel no longer plays Chopin in public.

JS: Is it possible to generalize about the kind and range of technical challenges encountered in Chopin? Failing that, can you cite specific examples of technical hurdles to be overcome – that's to say, pianistic rather than interpretative, although of course I realize that in many respects the two are one?

Vladimir Ashkenazy: Well technical problems are very individual, of course. Each pianist has his own technical problems, relating to the size or shape of the hand, and the motoric connections to the brain. And each great pianist-composer composed the way his hand *felt*. And you can see this in Chopin. There are certain chords which were obviously easy for him but are very difficult for me, certain things which I just can't reach – like in the end of the coda to the First Ballade. My hand just doesn't lie like that, yet something like the étude in double-thirds has never given me any problems.

Tamas Vasary: I have to say that for me Chopin is technically the most difficult of all composers to play well. Among the greatest challenges is the sheer amount of notes and the stretches that you have to play in a very short time *combined* with textures that leave the player almost as exposed as in Mozart. The speed and quantity of notes which you find in Liszt and Rachmaninov may sometimes be even more, but you can also get away with more. Chopin's textures are so clear, so linear, on the whole, and his notes are so carefully chosen that every note, every detail counts. He gives you nowhere to hide. With Chopin you can often feel quite naked!

Emanuel Ax: One musical effect of this is to make virtually every running passage into a significant melodic element. You can actually do an interesting and revealing experiment. You can play almost any running passage of Chopin in a slow tempo and it'll make some kind of beautiful music.

Carl Schachter: And the degree of concentration needed to play the Chopin études or some of the more technically demanding preludes is something quite extraordinary, because you have such intricate detail and at the same time such a large sweep that will carry you over every part of the keyboard. Rubinstein used to say that he was more tired out after a two-minute Chopin étude than after a big piece of Liszt.

Michael Roll: I do believe there are specific technical challenges, notably in the stretch between the fingers. This isn't something, perhaps, that you can see in the cast of his hands, but it's very much there in the writing. The power often required, say, to enunciate sixths, thirds and octaves while retaining this great sort of fluidity and elasticity, and the ability to cope with very rapid changes of hand positions – more than with almost any other composer, you really are expected to pull the hand in and out at the most dramatic speeds, and all while maintaining the greatest fluidity and beauty of sound – and very often, of course, with great power as well. And another thing is the independence of the two hands, which are almost always doing very different things, and also the tremendous flexibility demanded of the thumb, for instance. There's hardly a place where you don't either have to have it curled under the hand or stretching out way beyond what's comfortable or even possible for some hands. And it's not just a question of a large hand, but of a certain *shape* of hand. And from that point of view, I'm really not a natural Chopin player. There are many passages combining white and black keys with a big reach between the thumb and forefinger, far more so than most composers. And this combines with a particular *musical* challenge, because very often the phrases are very long, and you have to work very hard to get to the peak of the phrase and back again with the minimum of lumps and bumps. With Chopin I almost always feel that the musical impulse has come first and that the technical challenges are an offshoot of the strictly musical gesture, and never mind how difficult it is in a purely pianistic sense. He's not thinking primarily about how the pianist is going to get round it, whereas I think Liszt does. I really don't think Chopin makes any allowance whatever for sheer pianistic difficulties.

Ax: And he uses the hands in a way that virtually no other composer does. He demands an extraordinary amount of flexibility. This kind of constant opening and closing of the hand is quite unique to him, I think – and of course everything has to be done somehow in a melodic way.

Schachter: I think Chopin's writing is really completely opposed to the ideal of two right hands, as it were, two hands of exactly equal capacities and properties. His left hand is just as hard as his right hand, but it's very, very different; you really need two different techniques for your right hand and your left. This combination of the need for relaxation, suppleness and flexibility with this very extreme concentration is really quite extraordinarily difficult, and in many ways reminiscent of Bach.

Ax: For me, the basic *musical* problem is to achieve the same sense of proportion that you need in Mozart without giving short shrift to any sense of freedom.

JS: And so far we've just been discussing the hands. What about the feet? What are the main characteristics and purposes of pedalling in Chopin, both specified and unspecified?

Roll: Well, it's not always straightforward. The evolution of the piano as we know it has affected the way we need to interpret pedalling, but there are also a lot of very dubious editions, and they all have a lot of different notations, and while the pedal indications on the whole are in agreement, I'd be very nervous of giving them a wholesale bill of health. But it's clear that Chopin was often concerned with the beauty of the harmonic line, as it were, and he was certainly not afraid of really big harmonic climaxes – think of the G minor Ballade, for instance – and this is often dependent on the use of the pedals. There's a kind of continuous harmonic rocking, if you like. Chopin was an intensely harmonic composer. But of course there are clear cases where the pedal has to be used with great caution, if at all. Chopin's use of *rests* is very important – again, look at the G minor Ballade – and here he seems often to be seeking a much sparer, leaner, more plaintive response (and, of course, the rests are just as important rhythmically as the notes). And so much of Chopin was inspired by the human voice. The rests are often 'breathing' points. And along with his love of harmonic colour and movement you also get the need for polyphonic clarity, and *that* demands a very careful use – and, indeed, an equally careful *non*-use – of the pedal.

Ax: What strikes me more than Chopin's pedal markings as such is the unique spread of the left hand, which of course necessitates the *use* of the pedal. This unbelievably wide-ranging bass really starts with Chopin – this low bass supporting everything, almost like an organ pedal-point, but at the same time having the function of an Alberti bass, so here in a way you get both Bachian and Mozartian features. This is something that Liszt took from Chopin, if you look at the Consolations, for example, most of that aspect comes straight from the Chopin Nocturne in D flat.

Schachter: Chopin's very individual sound world is the result, I think, of a uniquely complicated amalgam of things, very definite polyphonic textures being one of them, even in things like those very left-hand accompaniments. The sense of part-writing that one finds there is really totally different from outwardly similar passages in Liszt. You can feel strands of almost chorale-like, linear writing, you can feel a sort of texture of four parts (sometimes even more) in these spun-out sort of arpeggios. But I also feel that the polyphony is very often not there on the surface, the edges of it are very much softened, so that it's seen through a kind of shimmer, and of course that shimmer is to a very large extent *provided* by the pedal. He indicated more differentiated and more complicated pedalling than anyone before him, and of course it's quite obvious that there are many many places where one uses the pedal where he *doesn't* mark them. But where he does mark it, one absolutely must follow it. When there are important sustained basses, for example, that he wants to sound *through* the transient changes above, here cowardly people will be changing pedal all the time. I strongly suspect that Chopin used the pedal at different depths. Some of the very long pedals, certainly on the modern piano, have to be done with a kind of 'half-pedal' so that you don't get the full resonance. I think a lot of pianists tend too much to change pedals all the time, that is to have a little bit of pedal throughout.

On the other hand, it's also possible to over-articulate the polyphony at the expense of the whole. Many of the most characteristic and beautiful examples of Chopin's polyphony are at least a little bit in the background, though it's always there – with something like the development section in the first movement of the B minor Sonata it's maybe not possible to resolve this problem, it sounds, perhaps, a little bit too learned, almost pedantic. I have to admit that after all these years I still can't say I really understand this section.

Another source of Chopin's sound world, of course, is the human voice, and the influence of the whole *bel canto* tradition, and I think they go very deep into the composition itself, and not just the manner of performance. The climactic notes, the high notes of his melodic line have a very very vocal quality, even in virtuoso, rapid pieces which don't sound vocal at all on the surface. And that's yet another component of this complicated amalgam.

JS: As a man, Chopin was compounded of paradox. Do you find this in any way reflected in his music? Given that a large part of the interpreter's role is the control of ambiguity, are there particular types of ambiguity which require clarification by the performer, one way or the other? Are there instances where that ambiguity needs to be deliberately enhanced, where it requires emphasis rather than solution?

Roll: I do find definite *harmonic* ambiguities: suspensions, for instance, that don't quite resolve, and I think you can find elements of this in almost all of Chopin's mature works – the Barcarolle comes to mind particularly in that regard. And when it comes to *rhythmic* ambiguities, in the mazurkas, say, a lot of this, surely, comes from that specifically Polish lilt, which is so hard to catch. There's something indefinably nationalistic about so much of Chopin's writing, and if you think about the really great Chopin players, they are often people whose background is steeped in Polish traditions – Rubinstein, of course, springs to mind; and Zimerman, among a younger generation. They seem to have a very special feel for the rhythmic *flexibility* of Chopin's music. But of course you don't *have* to be Polish to play his music wonderfully; look at Lipatti, for instance, whose playing had a particular cleanness and classicism about it, in terms of his use of light and shade, and his very spare use of rubato, but nevertheless it remained very plastic, very pliable, very beautiful – and very *romantic*. And the other very great non-Polish Chopin player, for me, is Cortot. His playing of the preludes is really one of the great, great performances: full of tremendous colour and variation and subtlety. But in the end, all of these players are really deeply romantic. As of course was Chopin – perhaps the most innately, the most profoundly, the most fundamentally romantic composer there is – and the one from whose romanticism it's least possible to escape. Chopin created a whole new world, a very romantic world, and anyone trying to get away from that, I think, is really missing the point.

Mitsuko Uchida: I'm sorry, but I must disagree. Chopin was *not* a romantic composer. *Schumann* was a romantic composer, yes. But for me, Chopin is *absolutely* a *classical* composer. His examples were Bach and Mozart and that is the world where he belongs. Bach's influence can be heard in his most beautiful voice-leading [part-writing]. Of course he doesn't write counterpoint or fugue as obviously as Bach, and yet there's a clear-cut and very beautiful polyphony going on throughout very much of his music, and he has complete control of that. And this is something, obviously, that the performer must make clear. There is also in his music a very Mozartian reserve and a love of proportion and finesse. Like Mozart, he disliked being too obvious. And he must be played in that way. And another reason why I consider Chopin to be a classical and not a romantic composer is his use of ornamentation. If anything, he's even more rigorously classical here than Mozart, where there are several possibilities – of the accentuation and placement, for instance, of appoggiaturas and turns. In Chopin, most of these are really spot-on the bass note, and the accent is almost always on the beginning note of the embellishment – and this is a really classical gesture. And you know, there is a very important passage in which Chopin, drawing a distinction between his own music and Liszt's, remarked 'You play Liszt as a declamation. *My* music is *never* declamatory!'

Schachter: There are so many difficult balances to maintain in Chopin's music. One is between a certain tendency, compositionally, to sectionalize things, very often to go in quite regular four-bar groups, and then at the same time to subvert those groups by all sorts of overlapping and links from one to the other. And the performer really has to be aware of both those tendencies. It's actually a very difficult thing to do, and many many people come to grief in one way or another in trying to do that. Another problem is to be able to accommodate both Chopin's considerable violence, say in the B minor Scherzo, and a kind of sensuous beauty. One also needs to be able to feel the emotion, the depth of feeling, in a way that is commensurate with the music, but to control those feelings so that one doesn't ever rant. I think that one should never be outspokenly rhetorical in Chopin, or melodramatic. There's a fastidiousness in the writing that forbids that. And that's also very hard. I tend to think that the 'roughness' or violence in Chopin's music must always be stylized. For instance, there should always be a kind of beauty of sound. I think there should always be a kind of legato 'ideal', even in passages which aren't themselves legato. There's something singing in all of Chopin's music. It never shouts. And in that way I think the difficulty of playing Chopin is very similar to the difficulties of playing Mozart. If you take something like the B minor Scherzo, I don't think I've ever heard a performance of that which was completely satisfying, except perhaps from Rubinstein. Wildness can be there, of course, but never ugliness.

Roll: I can certainly agree about that. But never rhetorical or declaiming? What about the A flat Polonaise? If that isn't 'declaiming' I don't know what is. And there are times, and not only in the obviously nationalistic works, where he comes close to bombast – the last movement of the B minor Sonata, for instance. No, I think Chopin was very *much* capable of rhetorical gestures.

Not that *all* his big gestures are rhetorical, of course: even the biggest, most powerfully projected of the preludes, it seems to me, are quite free of rhetoric.

JS: Are there particular kinds of rhythmic challenges in Chopin's music – particularly, but not exclusively, where his expressly Polish works are concerned?

Schachter: The national, the Polish, the folkloric element is extremely important. This is particularly obvious in the mazurkas, of course, where there's the necessity sometimes of lengthening certain beats, of playing with agogic accents. One of the things which makes the mazurkas so elusive, especially for non-Polish players, is the sheer variety of types. Instead of having a situation, as in a waltz, for example, where a certain rhythmic pattern tends to perpetuate itself and where the accentuation remains fairly uniform, in the mazurkas the accentuation will often change from bar to bar. And just to deal with those in a way that doesn't sound choppy is a major difficulty. And then the phrase-rhythm tends to be extremely free, despite the regular four-bar regularities, because the placement of stable harmonies will often be on the [metrically] weaker bars. Being able to project these kinds of thing, and *yet* have it sound like a dance, with a kind of swing and a kind of underlying symmetry, is very very hard to do. And then the tonal language is often very strange, and so chromatic, that it's hard to make a really beautiful, euphonious sound out of what are sometimes very discordant elements. And here again, even when Chopin is drawing most obviously on the peasant element in all this, I think the edges need to be a little bit refined.

Ax: One of the rhythmic problems in the mazurkas, for me, is the particular pattern of accentuation. In most of the faster ones the accent comes fairly regularly on the third beat, and yet I'm often tempted to put an accent on the second beat, even though the second note in a lot of bars is a long note, even when there's *not* a long note, he wants an accent on the third beat. I find a real difficulty with this, in making the dance work properly, because, is it a Viennese waltz in some bars? Often I really don't know, and I've kind of cheated on it when I've played them, because I do go ahead and accent the second beat quite often. I think you have to decide at some point that there is perhaps more than one strong beat, that there's more than one possibility for a strong beat. It's really not a clear-cut thing. Now in the slower mazurkas, you have the added problem of making these very elegiac kind of songs that he writes into a dance. Sometimes that's true in a waltz too, the A minor for example. How do you marry these two qualities? How do you combine the two? And that's also a question of how you choose the tempo as well. It's quite easy to make the A minor Waltz sound like a nocturne. And I think *that* kind of rhythmic ambiguity is present all the time. Things like the F major Ballade are a tremendous problem from that point of view, too – this marrying together of opposites.

JS: And what about the polyrhythms, the combining of two different rates of triplets, for instance, or the very asymmetrical character of the many *bel canto* style fioriture and other coloratura-like embellishments?

Schachter: Chopin's fioriture are very often variations of underlying patterns which often occur in their simpler forms earlier in the piece, so that one has to relate the later to the earlier ones. Let's say if you have twenty-three notes against four notes, one takes as one's point of departure that if it were twenty-four notes against four, you would have six against each one of those, and then one can see where one might take a little bit more time. In other words, you start with a mathematical approximation, but then you soften that by trying to give special emphasis to what seems to be the really crucial, climactic notes, or the most expressive notes, or the like. There's also the question of what goes before and what comes after. If the coloratura passage is going right into a long note, you might accelerate at the end of it. But if you ask me whether it's useful to try and count up exactly how many notes and how many fractions of a note, then I would have to say no.

Howard Shelley: I agree. And in playing the kind of arabesques that you find especially in the nocturnes, I think it's important to understand and *feel* the melodic shapes *within* them, and to relate *those*, rather than the note-to-note correspondences of the elaborations themselves, to the continuity and development of the left-hand accompaniment.

JS: How do you approach the question of rubato in Chopin? Do you subscribe to his very Mozartian pronouncement that temporal liberties should be confined to the melody, the accompaniment to be kept strictly in tempo?

Ax: Well, I've tried to put Chopin's rule into practice and frankly I've found it quite impossible. It's a nice thing to aspire to and it's actually possible, perhaps, if you take it as a broad concept rather than as a rigidly metronomic instruction – in other words, if you can feel a single pulse arising from the basic underlying movement and play your rubato off that pulse, that's certainly possible. I don't believe either Chopin or Mozart wanted every note of the left hand to be an exact mathematical measurement. As long as you treat Chopin as a composer who is as great as Bach, Mozart, Haydn, Beethoven, Brahms, I think you'll find a way.

Schachter: I think Chopin made a distinction between true rubato, which I think *was* a kind of free melodic declamation against a steady beat, and other kinds of liberties with time. If you look in the F minor Concerto you find that in several places he actually *writes* 'rubato' into the piano part – in the last movement, the A flat section, and when he does that, the orchestra has nothing, but when he writes 'rallentando', or even 'stretto' in the piano part, it's also written in the orchestral parts. I don't think Chopin ever intends that everything should be metronomic in his performances. Descriptions of his own playing suggest that he played with very great rhythmic freedom, but never at the expense of a kind of underlying rhythmic structure, that there was a kind of interplay between them.

Uchida: Well this is very interesting. If you take Beethoven, his music pulls and pushes without any clear-cut sense of *having* to keep in time, but Mozart *must* be kept in time, and so must Chopin. Because he *is* a *classical* composer.

And I hate it when people play Chopin's music as if it were rubber, particularly at the end of a beautiful phrase, where they wait forever until the final resolution comes. As to Chopin's *definition* of rubato, this is really quite straightforward. I myself have never found it difficult to put into practice. Never. I believe in that, as he did. And therefore I play the first movement of the E minor Concerto, for instance, exactly in one tempo. Everybody else has about five tempi. I try always to keep it in one. In fact I think that Chopin's rubato is, if anything, even stricter than Mozart's, especially where you have one 'singing' line with an accompaniment. And the main *reason* for having a rubato in the first place derives from the harmony, and is used to help certain harmonic turnings and resolutions work. This is exactly what Cortot does, with all his amazing rubati. Once you understand what he's doing, it no longer disturbs you – it *used* to disturb *me* very much. Another thing which Chopin shares with Mozart and which has a clear-cut bearing on rubato, is the enormous, refined skill with which he manipulates chromaticism against a diatonic background.

Roll: For me, judging the *feel* of the rubato in Chopin is the most difficult challenge of all – more than with any other romantic composer. And it's often got to do with the speeding up of the second beat – take the finale of the F minor Concerto – if you play that strictly according to the metronome it's going to sound very dull. The rhythm needs almost to 'float' through the second beat, as it were. I find that the timing of the second beat is so often vital in Chopin, I think straightaway of the first ballade, and not only the timing of the entry but the actual length allotted to the second beat is often crucial, it seems often to demand the kind of treatment which tends to be taken for granted with the *third* beat. Very rarely in Chopin can you play, or rather *should* you play, the three beats (or the four or the six beats) equally. The rhythmic flexibility in Chopin is usually so extraordinarily subtle, and therefore extraordinarily difficult to master and to feel absolutely comfortable with. For me, Rubinstein was the absolute master of this element. Like nobody else, he somehow managed to get the feel of the rubato exactly right. But again, he had Poland as his background. This particular combination of yearning lyricism and delicacy with a kind of heroic determination seems to me peculiarly Polish. You don't get quite that mix anywhere else. And then, too, there are the incredibly vast and abrupt changes of mood, almost frightening sometimes.

The natural delayed placing of sixteenths after eighths, as in the A flat Polonaise, after dotted notes the shorter ones must be delayed and therefore shortened. The willingness to 'toss off' rhythms in this way is an important ingredient in Chopin playing. And Chopin's dramatic use of rests is another vital feature of his rhythm, a source of great power.

I don't actually see Chopin's rubato as being like Mozart's. Chopin's 'accompaniments' require a great flexibility of a very significant kind, a real sense of lilt against the background of a clearly defined pulse, but it needs a much greater degree of rhythmic flexibility than, say, a Mozartian Alberti bass.

Ashkenazy: I'm distrustful of the word rubato altogether. I think the most helpful thing here is to remember the very important fact that Chopin loved Italian opera, that he loved the human voice. When we play something like the second movement of the F minor Concerto, and the E minor Concerto too, we must think 'how would a great singer do this?' and play it like that. The natural use of the human voice is something other than rubato, it's something one can't help. It's natural, it's organic, the voice is the most natural instrument in the world. That's what I usually am directed by. In the early Chopin, and some of the middle Chopin too; but late Chopin is different. There isn't so much of this *bel canto*, fioritura style any more. His genius developed to heights where these fioriture and so on were no longer of much use to him. His late nocturnes, the F minor Ballade, the Fantasy, the Polonaise-Fantasie, have very little of that. But there is no recipe for how to do a musical phrase. In the end you have to *feel* it.

JS: Where structure is concerned, is Chopin problematical for the performer?

Schachter: No more than any other great composer, I think. The main difficulty lies in reconciling the big, overall design of a piece with its detail, giving each detail as much as it needs but not to the point where one can't perceive the larger background structure. In Chopin I think that some of the solution is to hear in very long phrases, that is, not to hear each four-bar group as a phrase in itself but hearing it more like a single bar in some much larger phrase. Obviously this is hardest of all in the big pieces, where you sometimes have even sixteen-bars, or even more, that have to be heard as one thing. And if you can do that, then that will at least give you a large rhythmic framework within which to deal with whatever freedom one feels one needs in order to accommodate the details.

I think that understanding the music harmonically and contrapuntally can help, for instance if one realizes that one is in the middle of some kind of extended, prolonged harmony, then even if there is the end of a phrase, or a cadence or something, one will do not as much to make it sound like a definitive ending, as if the music itself tells you that a really important phrase has come to its conclusion, and something else is starting. I also think that often with Chopin there are, especially in some of the dance pieces which are quite sectionalized, a piece in A–B–A form, that there will almost always be elements at the end of one section that will somehow project over into the next. I can't offer any foolproof solution to this kind of thing, but I do believe that if interpreters are aware of these things, they'll find a way to deal with it.

Ax: I find Chopin's structures immensely strong, in fact. The F minor Ballade, for instance, is certainly as large a piece as many Beethoven sonatas, and just because it takes only eleven minutes to play is no reason not to recognize it as a large form.

Ashkenazy: Chopin's structures are so right for his musical materials, so organic, that the fact that there's no recapitulation of the first subject in the first movement of the B flat minor Sonata, for instance, doesn't bother me at all. Do things like this really matter in a work of such genius? It's the subject matter that's the most important thing, and a genius finds the suitable form for that. For us to question that is almost to imply that we are on the same level, which we are not.

Uchida: Structure is really not a problem in Chopin – unlike with Schumann. Chopin's structures tend to go easily into either ABA or ABACA or whatever. More often than not, Chopin's structure is basically an enlargement of a mazurka. Chopin is *not* a Germanic thinker, of course; he doesn't write sonata forms as such – specifically as structures – the way Beethoven does, for instance, but I really don't think one need make a point of Chopin's structures, as so many people do. For me that question simply doesn't arise.

JS: Now you're the only pianist I've ever heard who incorporates the introductory bars into the exposition repeat of the B flat minor Sonata; what's your thinking there?

Uchida: Well, I discovered that what I once assumed to be the first manuscript of the B flat minor Sonata turns out actually to have been the very first copy (he had a copyist who wrote very much like himself) and in that the repeat markings after the introduction don't exist. It is all of a piece, it's part of the structure, so I play it. It does make sense to me.

JS: Has the period instrument revival offered anything useful to the Chopin interpreter?

Uchida: Well I've played Chopin on both Erards and Pleyels of his time and I have to say that it's hardly affected my approach on the modern concert grand at all. Whereas the difference between Mozart's pianos and our own is enormous, the only basic difference between Chopin's and our own is that they're very much easier to play. But even in the case of Mozart, I don't think period instruments have much to offer either. In Chopin I really can't think of a single revelation in this connection, even though I've actually played on the Broadwood which he used when he was in London.

Melvyn Tan: Strangely enough, I agree here, on the whole, although I've been playing nothing *but* period instruments for the last seventeen years. You certainly get a greater degree of clarity, but even though the touch *is* very much lighter, and the keys narrower, the technical difficulties are really not dramatically reduced by any means.

Shelley: *I've* found that playing on a period instrument *is* instructive, particularly from the point of view of sonority and pedalling, which in many ways seem to me to make more sense than even the best-intentioned player can do on a modern piano. On any of those earlier pianos there's a certain bite, even a metallic quality and a particular kind of clarity in the treble which cuts through the effects of the sustaining pedal and is really quite different from the warm, plummy sonorities of a modern grand. You really have to be careful, I think, when pedalling on a modern instrument, not to obscure too much of the detail, which Chopin obviously intended us to hear. Particularly in something as polyphonically complicated as the B minor Sonata I think you have to restrict somewhat the modern piano's sonority; I think clarity of texture is of absolutely paramount importance in Chopin.

JS: Clarity of texture, clarity of phrasing, clarity of rhythm – these, of course, are only starting points – and hardly the only ones – for any really successful Chopin performance. But all the things which make the difference between a competent and a great interpretation, these are, and will always remain, of a subtlety that defies even the most eloquent and articulate verbal definition. And if the quality of the music will in almost every case transcend the quality of the performance, this should deter no one. Among the greatest joys and excitements of the musician's experience is the stimulus of infinite discovery. And great music is robust and eternal. It isn't diminished by our own limitations. Of course we should aim at the highest possible standard, but we should also exult in the wisdom of G. K. Chesterton's mischievous but heartening reminder that 'if a thing's worth doing, it's worth doing badly!'

Yet there are great musicians who have chosen *not* to perform Chopin. And that decision needn't imply a slight on Chopin's genius. It can be a matter of practical priorities. I leave the last word here to perhaps the greatest *non*-Chopin player of the present age.

Alfred Brendel: To sum up my thoughts about Chopin, I would have to say that he is the only 'true' composer for the piano because he derives his inspiration primarily from the sound of this instrument. Other important composers of piano music have entrusted to the piano sounds encompassing all musical possibilities – orchestral, vocal, specifically instrumental in other timbres, solo, tutti and so on (which means that the piano should only be a vehicle, constantly being turned into something else). All other great composers for the piano have composed for other media as well. The young Schumann may have written some predominantly 'pianistic' works in his early years, but even here there is a clear attempt, in the *Symphonic Études*, to turn the piano into an orchestra, something that has been done with great determination by the young Liszt, who transcribed [Berlioz's] *Symphonie Fantastique* aged twenty-one. In this way, Chopin is a kind of bird of paradise among composers. He seems to need specialization more than any other, or at least this has been the case in the older generation of players.

Appendix 3: A Calendar of Chopin's Life and Times

Year	Age	Life	Arts	World events
1810		Chopin born at Zelazowa Wola; his family moves to Warsaw	Robert Schumann born; Scott's *The Lady of the Lake*; Beethoven's *Egmont*; Rossini's *Cambiale*	Napoleon at the height of his career; first canning of food
1811	1		Franz Liszt born; William Makepeace Thackeray born; Beethoven's *Emperor Concerto*; Jane Austen's *Sense and Sensibility*	Napoleon annexes Oldenburg; George III of England pronounced insane; Regency begins; Luddites sabotage machinery in Britain
1812	2		Beethoven's Symphonies 7 and 8; Grimms' *Fairy Tales* published; Charles Dickens and Robert Browning born	Rout of Napoleon's army in Russia
1813	3		London Philharmonic Society founded; Verdi and Wagner born; Turner's *Frosty Morning* painted; waltz craze throughout Europe	Wellington's victory at Vittoria; Prussia declares war on France; Napoleon defeated at Leipzig
1814	4		Beethoven's *Fidelio* (final version); Schubert's *Erlking*; Byron's *Corsair*; Scott's *Waverley*; Maelzel invents metronome	Napoleon banished to Elba; Louis XVIII assumes French throne; Westminster, London, becomes first district to have gas lighting
1815	5		Anthony Trollope born; advent of Biedermeier style in Vienna; Goya etchings, *Tauromaquia*	Napoleon's return to France; Louis XVIII flees; '100 Days'; Wellington's victory at Waterloo; Louis XVIII returns; Napoleon banished to St Helena

Year	Age	Life	Arts	World events
1816	6	First piano lessons with his mother	Rossini's *Barber of Seville*, Austen's *Emma*; Coleridge's *Kubla Khan*; Byron's *Manfred*	Metternich opens German Diet at Frankfurt; Argentina declares independence; stethoscope invented
1817	7	Lessons with Zywny; first polonaise	Rossini's *La Gazza Ladra* and *La Cenerentola*; Clementi's *Gradus ad Parnassum*	Riots in Britain against low wages; Erie Canal begun in USA
1818	8	Plays at charity concert in Warsaw; his cultivation by the aristocracy; presents Empress with two polonaises	Gounod born; Keats writes *Endymion*; Mary Shelley's *Frankenstein* published	Chile declares independence; first professional horse racing in USA; Karl Marx born
1819	9		Beethoven loses hearing; Offenbach and Clara Wieck born	Florida bought from Spain by USA; Queen Victoria born
1820	10	Catalani presents him with gold watch; he plays for the Grand Duke Constantine	Pushkin's *Ruslan and Ludmilla*; Keats's 'Ode to a Nightingale'; Henri Vieuxtemps born; metal frames introduced into pianos	Platinum discovered in Russia; revolutions in Spain and Portugal; assassination of Duc de Berry in France
1821	11	Dedicates polonaise to Zywny	Beethoven's opp. 110 and 111 piano sonatas; Weber's *Der Freischütz*; Constable paints *The Hay Wain*	Abdication of Victor Emmanuel in Italy; Napoleon dies; first steps in sound reproduction; Elsner founds Warsaw Conservatory
1822	12	First lessons with Elsner; writes G sharp minor Polonaise	Liszt (11) makes début in Vienna; Royal Academy of Music founded in Britain; Schubert's 'Unfinished' Symphony	Greek–Turkish war intensifies; first iron railroad bridge; gaslight comes to Boston, Massachusetts, USA
1823	13	Enrols at Warsaw Lyceum; first studies of harmony	Beethoven completes *Missa Solemnis*; Erard builds 'double-escapement' piano; Weber's *Euryanthe*	Death penalty for over 100 crimes abolished in England; Mexico becomes a republic; Monroe Doctrine, USA; Babbage attempts to build a calculating machine
1824	14	Wins first-year prize at Lyceum; edits *Szafarnia Courier*	Beethoven's 'Choral' Symphony; Byron dies; Bruckner, Smetana and Cornelius born	Simon Bolivar proclaimed Emperor of Peru; RSPCA founded in London

Year	Age	Life	Arts	World events
1825	15	Performs for the Tsar, who gives him a diamond ring; Rondo, op. 1 published	Johann Strauss II born; Pushkin's *Boris Godunov*; Jean Paul Richter dies	First Baseball Club organized at Rochester, N.Y.; sacrilege becomes capital offence in French law; horse-drawn buses introduced in London; first passenger railway inaugurated
1826	16	Composes B flat minor Polonaise; visit to Bad Reinertz; gives two concerts; enters Warsaw Conservatory	Mendelssohn (17) composes *Midsummer Night's Dream* Overture; Weber (40) dies; Fennimore Cooper's *The Last of the Mohicans*	Russia declares war on Persia; Thomas Jefferson dies in USA; first railway tunnel in Britain; Munich University founded
1827	17	His sister Emilia (14) dies; he composes 'Là ci darem' Variations and C minor Sonata	Beethoven (56) and William Blake (50) die; Schubert composes *Die Winterreise*; Liszt settles in Paris	Battle of Navarino: destruction of Turkish and Egyptian fleets; Russia defeats Persia; first sulphur friction matches introduced
1828	18	Visits Berlin; meets Hummel; composes Fantasia on Polish Airs, *Krakowiak* Rondo and Rondo à la mazur	Schubert composes last three piano sonatas and C major Quintet and dies (31); Tolstoy and Jules Verne born; Goya dies	Wellington becomes prime minister in Britain; Russia declares war on Turkey; first passenger-and-freight railway built in the USA
1829	19	Paganini visits Warsaw; Chopin graduates from Conservatory and travels to Vienna where he gives two concerts; visits to Prague, Teplitz and Dresden; reveals love for Constantia Gladkowska	Rossini's *Guillaume Tell*; Mendelssohn gives first performance of Bach's *St Matthew Passion* for 100 years; Bellini's *La Straniera*	Slavery abolished in Mexico; suttee abolished in British India; first typewriter patented in the USA
1830	20	Plays F minor Concerto at his first public concert in Warsaw; later plays E minor at his third; leaves Poland for Austria, France and Italy	Auber's *Fra Diavolo*; Bellini's *I Capuleti ed i Montecchi*; Donizetti's *Anna Bolena*; Hans von Bülow born; Stendhal's *Le Rouge et le Noir*	France captures Algeria; July Revolution in Paris; Charles X abdicates; Louis Philippe, the 'Citizen King', crowned in France; stiff collars become part of men's dress; steam cars appear for the first time in the streets of London; hemlines rise, sleeves billow, hats expand, topped by flowers and ribbons
1831	21	Depressed in Vienna; in Stuttgart he hears of Warsaw's defeat by Russian forces; proceeds to Paris, where he meets Kalkbrenner and Liszt	Bellini's *La Sonnambula* and *Norma*; Meyerbeer's *Robert le Diable*	Polish Diet declares independence of Poland; collapse of Polish revolt; slave revolt in Virginia led by Nat Turner; first horse-drawn buses appear in New York; Charles Darwin sails to South America, New Zealand and Australia; uprisings in Lyon, France; mass demonstrations in Switzerland

Year	Age	Life	Arts	World events
1832	22	First Paris concert; friendships with Berlioz (29) and Mendelssohn (23); opp. 6–7 published; begins his lucrative teaching career	Berlioz's *Symphonie Fantastique*; Clementi dies; Constable paints *Waterloo Bridge*; Goethe and Sir Walter Scott die; Manet born	Mass demonstrations in Germany; the First Reform Act passed by House of Lords; Britain occupies Falkland Islands; the word 'socialism' gains currency
1833	23	Plays with Liszt (22) at benefit; opp. 8–12 published; friendship with Bellini; gives several private concerts	Mendelssohn's 'Italian' Symphony; Turner's Venetian pictures; Balzac's *Eugénie Grandet*; George Sand's *Lélia*; Schlegel completes German translation of Shakespeare	William IV grants new liberal constitution to Hannover; abolition of slavery in British Empire; Whig Party established in USA; General Trades Union formed in New York
1834	24	Visits Germany where he renews friendship with Mendelssohn; his music savaged by Ludwig Rellstab	Berlioz's *Harold in Italy*; Borodin born; Ingres's *Martyrdom of St Symphorian*; Balzac's *Père Goriot*	Palmerston effects alliance of Britain with France, Spain and Portugal; Spanish Inquisition officially ended after 500 years; Sixth Kaffir War in South Africa; Abraham Lincoln enters politics in USA
1835	25	Reunion with parents at Carlsbad; falls in love with Maria Wodzinska	Donizetti's *Lucia di Lamermoor*; Bellini dies (34); Saint-Saëns and Mark Twain born	Sam Colt takes out patent for his single-barrelled pistol and rifle; Charles Chubb patents burglar-proof safe; Texas moves to secede from Mexico; Second Seminole War in Florida; Melbourne, Australia, founded
1836	26	Proposes marriage to Maria at Marienbad; meets George Sand; opp. 21–3, 26 and 27 published	Glinka's *A Life for the Tsar*; Mendelssohn's *St Paul*; Charles Dicken's publishes *Pickwick Papers*	The People's Charter initiates national working-class movement in Britain; Texas becomes a republic; Boer farmers launch 'The Great Trek' away from British rule; Davy Crockett killed at the Alamo
1837	27	Marital hopes dashed, he visits London; opp. 25 and 29–32 published	Berlioz's *Grande Messe des Morts*; Balakirev born; Field and Hummel die; Constable dies; Pushkin killed in duel	Victoria becomes Queen; Ernst Augustus succeeds William IV as King of Hannover; constitutional revolts in Canada; Isaac Pitman publishes *Stenographic Soundhand*
1838	28	Plays for Louis Philippe; liaison with Sand begins; their disastrous winter in Majorca; op. 28 finished	Berlioz's *Benvenuto Cellini*; Bizet and Bruch born; Dickens's *Oliver Twist* and *Nicholas Nickleby*; Schumann dedicates *Kreisleriana* to Chopin	Victoria's coronation; Boers defeat Zulus in Natal; British–Afghan war; Talleyrand dies; Bessel makes first parallax measurement for a fixed star

Year	Age	Life	Arts	World events
1839	29	Falls seriously ill in Majorca; returns to France; summer at Nohant; op. 28 preludes completed; opp. 35 published	Berlioz's *Roméo et Juliette*; Mendelssohn conducts first performance of Schubert's Ninth Symphony	First British–Chinese Opium War; Uruguay declares war on Argentina; Boers found Republic of Natal in Africa; first bicycle constructed; transatlantic shipping line started by Samuel Cunard
1840	30	Spends whole year in Paris, teaching and composing; opp. 35–42 published	Schumann writes over 100 songs; first Harmonium made; Renoir, Rodin and Tchaikovsky born	End of transportation of British criminals to New South Wales; moves to limit hours of child labour in New England
1841	31	Gives brilliant concert in Paris; summer spent at Nohant; music-making with Pauline Viardot; opp. 43–9 published	Rossini's *Stabat Mater*, saxophone invented; Dvorak and Chabrier born; Schumann's 'Spring' Symphony	Britain proclaims sovereignty over Hong Kong; New Zealand becomes British colony; Lajos Kossuth becomes nationalist leader in Hungary
1842	32	Gives concert with Viardot and Franchomme; friendship with Delacroix at Nohant; death of Jan Matuszynski; op. 50 published	Glinka's *Ruslan and Ludmilla*; Wagner's *Rienzi*; New York Philharmonic founded; Gogol's *Dead Souls*; Sullivan and Massenet born; Cherubini dies; polka craze grips Europe	Riots and strikes in north of England; Boers establish Orange Free State; Treaty of Nanking ends Opium War, first use of ether for surgical anaesthesia
1843	33	Withdraws for 5 years from public performance; opp. 51–4 published	Wagner's *Flying Dutchman*; Mendelssohn's music for *A Midsummer Night's Dream*; Donizetti's *Don Pasquale*; Grieg born	Military revolt in Spain; Maori revolt against Britain in New Zealand; Morse builds first telegraph system; first propeller-driven crossing of the Atlantic; the world's first nightclub, *Le Bal des Anglais*, opens in Paris
1844	34	Nicholas Chopin dies; Chopin visited by his sister Ludwika; opp. 55–6 published	Mendelssohn's Violin Concerto in E minor; Verdi's *Ernani*; Rimsky-Korsakov born; Turner's *Rain, Steam and Speed*; Verlaine born	Treaty of Tangier ends French war in Morocco; military revolts in Mexico; weavers' revolt in Silesia; Marx meets Engels in Paris; Nietzsche born; US–Chinese peace treaty
1845	35	His health declines; family tensions mount at Nohant; opp. 57–8 published	Wagner's *Tannhäuser*, Mérimée's *Carmen*; Fauré and Widor born; first photo portraits	Maori uprising against British; Anglo-Sikh War; Swiss Sonderbund formed; first submarine cable across English Channel; power loom invented in USA
1846	36	Rift with Sand deepens; publication of *Lucrezia Floriani*; opp. 59–61 published	Berlioz's *Damnation de Faust*; Mendelssohn's *Elijah*; Edward Lear's *Book of Nonsense*; Balzac's *Cousin Bette*	Revolts in Poland; Austrian and Russian troops invade Cracow; USA declares war on Mexico; Sikh defeat by East India Company; first sewing machine patented; Irish famine

Year	Age	Life	Arts	World events
1847	37	Sides with Sand's daughter Solange, provoking final break; opp. 63-5 published	Verdi's *Macbeth*; Flotow's *Martha*; Charlotte Brontë's *Jane Eyre*; Emily Brontë's *Wuthering Heights*; Thackeray's *Vanity Fair*	US forces capture Mexico City; Sonderbund War breaks out in Switzerland; British Factory Act restricts working day for women and children to 10 hours; discovery of evaporated milk
1848	38	Gives last concert in Paris; visits England and Scotland; his health declines alarmingly; gives his last concert; returns to Paris	Donizetti dies; Parry born; Dumas *fils'* *La Dame aux Camélias*	Revolts in Paris, Vienna, Berlin, Milan, Venice, Rome, Parma and Prague; Second Sikh War begins; Sardinia declares war on Austria; serfdom abolished in Austria; first settlers arrive in New Zealand; Californian Gold Rush begins
1849	39	Grows too weak to teach; financial support from friends; Ludwika comes to nurse him through his final illness; he dies in Paris	Liszt's *Tasso*; Meyerbeer's *La Prophète*; Nicolai's *The Merry Wives of Windsor*; Schumann's *Manfred*; J. Strauss I dies; Dickens's *David Copperfield*; Dostoevsky sentenced to death; sentence commuted	British defeat Sikhs in India; Venice surrenders to Austria; Hungary defeated by Austria; Britain annexes Punjab; A. Fizeau measures speed of light; Livingstone crosses Kalahari, discovers Lake Ngami; Amelia Bloomer sets out to reform US women's dress

Appendix 4: Personalia

Alkan, Charles Henri Valentin (1813–88). French composer and virtuoso pianist who wrote many études and other works of colossal difficulty. He was greatly liked and admired by Chopin.

Baillot, Pierre (1771–1842). Highly esteemed French violinist, once a member of Napoleon's private orchestra. A composition student of Cherubini★ and Reicha,★ he wrote many violin and chamber works.

Blanc, Louis (1811–82). French historian and socialist politician. His *Organisation de travail* (1840) denounces the principle of competitive industry and proposes the establishment of co-operative workshops, subsidized by the state.

Catalani, Angelica (1780–1849). Famous Italian operatic soprano who in 1813 became manager of the Italian Opera in Paris.

Cherubini, Maria Luigi (1760–1842). Italian composer known for his exceptional mastery of counterpoint. He settled in Paris in 1778 and in 1822 became director of the Paris Conservatoire. He was greatly admired by Beethoven and his *Treatise on Counterpoint and Fugue* was avidly studied by Chopin. Renowned for his crusty conservatism, he was amusingly (and unfairly) pilloried by Berlioz in his highly readable and equally suspect *Memoirs*.

Clementi, Muzio (1752–1832). Italian composer and virtuoso pianist, he pioneered a truly idiomatic piano style when the instrument was only just beginning to oust the harpsichord in public favour. A teacher of both Cramer and Field, he composed a celebrated book of pianistic studies, *Gradus ad Parnassum*.

Copernicus, Nicolas (1473–1543). A native Pole and the founder of modern astronomy, he was also a lawyer, physician, clergyman, classical scholar and Latin translator, bailiff, military governor, judge, tax collector and reformer of coinage.

Coxe, William (1747–1828). English historian and clergyman, and the author of many books on history and travel; after twenty years abroad he became a prebendary of Salisbury and archdeacon of Wiltshire.

Cramer, Johann Baptist (1771–1858). German pianist and composer. A pupil of Clementi,★ he too produced many studies for the piano, a number of which are still in use today and have considerable artistic merit.

Czerny, Karl (1791–1857). Austrian pianist and composer, a pupil of Hummel, Clementi and Beethoven and the teacher of Liszt. Astoundingly prolific, he had several writing desks in his study, each supporting a different work in progress. While the ink dried on one, he moved on to the next, thus becoming music's first one-man assembly line. His many studies have driven countless piano students to distraction.

Delacroix, Eugène (1798–1863). French romantic painter and perhaps the greatest figure in nineteenth-century French art, whose loose style of drawing and brilliant use of colour shocked the classically minded establishment of the day even more than the prominence of violence and the macabre among his chosen subjects.

Fétis, François Joseph (1784–1871). French composer, musicologist and critic. A professor at the Paris Conservatoire from 1821, he became its librarian in 1827. His *Biographie universelle des musiciens* was an important forerunner of *Grove's Dictionary of Music and Musicians*, and his *Histoire générale de la musique* is still a valuable reference book for scholars.

Field, John (1782–1837). Irish-born pianist and composer. A pupil of Clementi, he produced many studies for the piano, a number of which are still in use today.

Franchomme, Auguste (1808–84). Minor composer and major cellist, he played in the orchestras of the Paris Opéra and Théâtre Italien, and was cellist of the Alard Quartet. A close and much admired friend of Chopin's.

Goethe, Johann Wolfgang von (1749–1832). German poet, dramatist, scientist and courtier. The most renowned of all German writers, his works had an incalculable effect on the birth and early development of the Romantic movement.

Gutmann, Adolf (1819–82). German pianist and composer. He was a pupil of Chopin who won the composer's affection and was present at his death.

Gyrowetz, Adalbert (1763–1850). Prolific Bohemian composer in many genres. Among the most admired musicians of his day, his name is hardly known at all today.

Heine, Heinrich (1797–1856). German poet, essayist, journalist, politician and lawyer, he chose to live as a self-styled exile in Paris. His poetry has found musical immortality in the songs of Robert Schumann.

Herz, Henri (1806–88). German piano virtuoso and composer of much *saloniste* confectionery, he was a minor darling of Parisian high society and later made a great reputation for himself in America.

Hiller, Ferdinand (1811–85). German pianist and minor composer, he studied with Hummel, settled in Paris in 1828 and enjoyed the friendship of Mendelssohn, Chopin and Liszt.

Hummel, Johann Nepomuk (1778–1837). German-Hungarian pianist and composer, he studied with Mozart and Clementi, taught Czerny and Thalberg, and was ranked in his day only just below Mozart and Beethoven. His music had a pronounced effect on Chopin's own.

Kalkbrenner, Friedrich (1788–1849). Immensely accomplished German pianist and very minor composer, he spent much of his life in Paris, where he was more admired by the public than by his peers.

Kosciuszko, Tadeusz (1746–1817). Polish soldier and patriot. In 1794, after the Second Partition, he headed the national movement in Crakow, of which he was appointed dictator and commander-in-chief. He died when his horse fell over a precipice.

Kurpinski, Karol Kasimir (1785–1857). Polish composer, conductor and violinist. He was a prolific and popular opera composer.

Malibran, Maria (1808–36). Franco-Spanish soprano, who was perhaps the most famous female singer of her time and was the sister of Pauline Viardot.*

Mickiewicz, Adam (1798–1855). Great Polish poet and patriot, he was banished to Russia between 1824 and 1829. His epic *Pan Tadeusz* was published in 1834 and has been acknowledged ever since as his greatest work.

Moriuszko, Stanislaw (1819–72). Polish composer and conductor. Ranked in

Poland second only to Chopin among nineteenth-century nationalists.

Moscheles, Ignaz (1794–1870). Bohemian composer and pianist of distinction, he was among the first peripatetic concert virtuosos, and settled, respectively, in Paris and London.

Paderewski, Ignace Jan (1860–1941). Polish pianist and composer. The most popular pianist of his day, he served as the first Prime Minister of modern Poland.

Paër, Ferdinando (1771–1839). Italian composer who served as Napoleon's music director. He composed more than forty operas.

Pashkievitch, Ivan (1782–1856). Brilliant Russian soldier. He took part in successful campaigns against the French, the Turks and the Hungarians and was pronounced Prince of Warsaw after his crushing of the Polish revolt in 1831.

Pixis, Johann Peter (1788–1874). German pianist and composer, equally noted for the size of his nose and his libido.

Reicha, Antonin (1770–1836). Bohemian composer and teacher. He was among the first to experiment with polytonality.

Rellstab, Heinrich (1799–1860). German music critic. He was among Chopin's fiercest detractors before undergoing a late and fashionable conversion. It was he who saddled Beethoven's C sharp minor Sonata with the nickname 'Moonlight'.

Smith, Adam (1723–90). Scottish economist and philosopher. His most famous book, *The Wealth of Nations*, examines the consequences of economic freedom and attacks the lingering medieval monopolies and the theories of the French physiocrats.

Staszyk, Stanislaw (1755–1826). Polish philosopher, scientist, classical scholar and politician of great learning and influence. A disciple of the physiocrats, he was the first Pole to free the serfs and grant them land in communal tenure.

Thalberg, Sigismond (1812–71). Swiss-German pianist and composer. A pupil of Hummel, he was one of the most famous virtuosos of the day and specialized in a style of keyboard composition designed to give the illusion of three hands.

Viardot, Pauline (1821–1910). One of the greatest mezzo-sopranos of the nineteenth century, she was also an accomplished pianist and a fluent composer of operettas and songs. Sister of Maria Malibran.★

Wieck, Clara (1819–96). One of the foremost pianists of her day, and a gifted composer, she was the first in Germany to champion Chopin's music in performance, winning his wholehearted approval. Married Robert Schumann in 1840.

Sources

The main sources consulted were drawn upon in one form or another for Chapters
1–12 and are as follows:

Hedley, A. (ed. and trans.), *Selected Correspondence of Fryderyk Chopin*, London,
    1962
Kobylanska, Krystyna, *Chopin in His Own Land*, Warsaw, 1955
Kobylanska, Krystyna, (ed.), *Korespondencja Fryderyka Chopina z Rodzina*,
    Warsaw, 1972
Opienski, Henryk (ed.), *Chopin's Letters*, trans. Ethel Voynich, New York 1931,
    rev. 1971
——, ——, *Listy Fryderyka Chopina*, Warsaw, 1937
Samson, Jim (ed.), *The Cambridge Companion to Chopin*, Cambridge, 1992
Sydow, B. E. (ed.), *Correspondance de Frédéric Chopin*, Paris, 1960
——, ——, *Korespondencja Fryderyka Chopina*, Warsaw, 1955

Further sources are listed under the appropriate chapter headings:

1   PROPHETIC BEGINNINGS

Carlyle, Thomas, *Frederick the Great*, London, 1865
Coxe, The Rev. William, *Travels in Poland*, London, 1802
Heine, Heinrich, quoted in Niecks: *Frederick Chopin as a Man and Musician*,
    London, 1888, p.61
Niecks, Frederick, *Frederick Chopin as a Man and Musician*, London, 1888

2   TOWN AND COUNTRY

Niecks, Frederick, *Frederick Chopin as a Man and Musician*, London, 1888
Skrodzki, Eugeniusz, quoted in A. Czartowski and Z. Jezewska, *Fryderyk Chopin*,
    Warsaw, 1970

3   CELEBRITY AND SECRET LOVE

Kurier Warszawski, 23 December, 1829

4   PATRIOTS, PLEASURES, PAIN AND PROFITS

Heine, Heinrich, *Musikalische Berichte aus Paris*, ed. F. Strich, Munich, 1925
Revue Musicale, Paris, 3 March 1832
Sand, George, *Historie de ma vie*, Paris, 1855
Sandeau, Jules, quoted in Curtis Cate, *George Sand*, New York, 1975

5 THE DANDY AND THE DILETTANTES

Eigeldinger, Jean-Jacques, *Chopin vu par ses élèves*, Neuchâtel, Switzerland, 1970
Lenz, Wilhelm von, *The Great Piano Virtuosos of Our Time*, trans. M. R. Baker, New York, 1899
Mikuli, Karol, *Chopin's Pianoforte-Werk*, Leipzig, 1880
Sand, George, *Histoire de ma vie*, Paris, 1855

6 PRIMING THE PUMP

Delacroix, Eugène, *The Journal of Eugène Delacroix*, trans. L. Norton, London, 1951
Hallé, Charles E. and Marie, *Life and Letters of Sir Charles Hallé*, London, 1896
Heine, Heinrich, *Lutèce: Lettres sur la vie politique, artistique et sociale de la France*, Paris, 1855
Krasinski, Zygmunt, *Listy do Delfiny Potockiej*, Warsaw, 1965
Kurier Warszawski, 8 January, 1836
Lenz, Wilhelm von, *The Great Piano Virtuosos of Our Time*, trans. M. R. Baker, New York, 1899
Mendelssohn-Bartholdy, Felix, *Letters*, ed. G. Selden-Goth, London, 1946
Mirska, Maria and Hordynski, Wladyslaw, *Chopin na Obczyznie*, Krakow, 1965 (Hiller quotations)
Sand, George, *Historie de ma vie*, Paris, 1855

7 MAJORCA, MISERY AND THE MUSE

Balzac, Honoré de, *Correspondance*, Paris, 1966
Heine, Heinrich, *Lutèce: Lettres sur la vie politique, artistique et sociale de la France*, Paris, 1855
Sand George, *Correspondance*, ed. Georges Lubin, Paris, 1964
——, ——, *Historie de ma vie*, Paris, 1855
——, ——, *Les Majorcains*, Paris, 1843
——, ——, *Winter in Majorca*, trans. Robert Graves, Palma, 1956

8 RURAL RETREAT

Hiller, Ferdinand, *Erinnerungsblätter*, Cologne, 1884

9 SINFONIA DOMESTICA

Delacroix, Eugène, *The Journal of Eugène Delacroix*, trans. L. Norton, London, 1951
France Musicale, Paris, 2 May 1841
Revue Musicale, Paris, 2 May 1841

10 FAME, FEAR AND FAMILY

Delacroix, Eugène, *The Journal of Eugène Delacroix*, trans. L. Norton, London, 1951
Rozengardt, Zofia, letter to her brothers, 24 December 1843, Jagiellonian Library, Krakow, Ms. 9292

II   THE CRACK-UP

Delacroix, Eugène, *The Journal of Eugène Delacroix*, trans. L. Norton, London,
     1951
Sand George, *Correspondance*, ed. Georges Lubin, Paris, 1964
——, ——, *Lucrezia Floriani*, Paris, 1846

12   A FOREIGN SOJOURN AND AN EARLY GRAVE

Berlioz, Hector, *Mémoires*, Paris, 1870
Daily News, London, 10 July 1848
Gavard, Charles, quoted in Niecks: *Frederick Chopin as a Man and Musician*,
     London, 1888
Hiller, Ferdinand, *Erinnerungsblätter*, Cologne, 1884
Manchester Guardian, 30 August 1848

13   CHOPIN AND POSTERITY

Bülow, Hans von, quoted in Schonberg, Harold, *The Great Pianists*, New York,
     1963
Huneker, James, quoted in Schonberg, ibid.
Rubinstein, Artur, *New York Times*, 1960, quoted in Schonberg, ibid.

Bibliography

Abraham, Gerald, *Chopin's Musical Style*, London, 1939
Ashton Jonson, G. C., *A Handbook to Chopin's Works*, London, 1905
Attwood, William, *The Lioness and the Little One: The Liaison of George Sand and Frédéric Chopin*, New York, 1980
——, ——, *Fryderyck Chopin: Pianist from Warsaw*, New York, 1987
Barea, Ilsa, *Vienna*, New York, 1966
Barzun, Jacques, *Berlioz and His Century*, New York, 1956
Berlioz, Hector, *Les Années romantiques: 1819–1842*, Paris, 1905
——, ——, *Selected Letters* (ed. Humphrey Searle), London, 1966
——, ——, *Memoirs* (trans. David Cairns), London, 1974
Binental, Leopold, *Chopin, Dokumente und Erinnerungen*, Leipzig, 1932
——, ——, *Chopin*, Paris, 1934
Bory, Robert, *La vie de Frédéric Chopin dans l'Image*, Geneva, 1951
Bourniquel, Camille, *Chopin* (trans. Sinclair Road), New York, 1960
Branson, David, *John Field and Chopin*, London, 1972
Castelot, André, *The Turbulent City: Paris 1783–1871* (trans. Denise Folliot), New York, 1962
Cate, Curtis, *George Sand*, New York, 1975
Cobban, Alfred, *A History of Modern France*, vol. 2, London, 1961
Davies, Norman, *God's Playground: A History of Poland*, Oxford, 1981
——, ——, *Heart of Europe: A Short History of Poland*, London, 1984
Delacroix, Eugène, *Correspondance générale* (ed. A. Joulin), Paris, 1936
——, ——, *The Journal of Eugène Delacroix* (trans. L. Norton), London, 1951
Droz, Jacques, *Europe Between Revolutions, 1815–1848*, London, 1967
Eigeldinger, Jean-Jacques, *Chopin vu par ses élèves*, Neuchâtel, 1970
Gottschalk, L. M., *Notes of a Pianist*, London, 1881
Halecki, Oscar, *A History of Poland* (trans. Gardner and Patkaniowska), New York, 1976
Hallé, Charles E. and Marie, *Life and Letters of Sir Charles Hallé*, London, 1896
Haraszowski, Adam, *The Skein of Legends round Chopin*, Glasgow, 1967
Hedley, Arthur, *Chopin*, London, 1947 (rev. 1974)
Hedley, A. (ed. and trans.) *Selected Correspondence of Fryderyk Chopin*, London, 1962
Heine, Heinrich, *Musikalische Berichte aus Paris* (ed. F. Strich), Munich, 1925
Hipkins, E. J., *How Chopin Played*, London, 1937
Huneker, James, *Chopin: The Man and his Music*, New York, 1900
Jordan, Ruth, *Nocturne: A Life of Chopin*, London, 1978
Kobylanska, Krystyna, *Chopin in his Own Land*, Warsaw, 1955
——, —— (ed.), *Korespondencja Fryderyka Chopina z Rodzina*, Warsaw, 1972
Lenz, Wilhelm von, *The Great Piano Virtuosos of Our Time, from Personal*

Acquaintance: Liszt, Chopin, Tausig, Henselt (trans. M. R. Baker), New York, 1899
Liszt, Franz, Frédéric Chopin, Leipzig, 1879
Locke, Ralph P., Music, Musicians and the Saint-Simonians, Chicago, 1986
Loesser, Arthur, Men, Women and Pianos, New York, 1954
Marek, G., and Smith, M., Chopin: A Biography, New York, 1978
Mendelssohn-Bartholdy, Felix, Letters (ed. G. Selden-Goth), London, 1946
Methuen-Campbell, J., Chopin Playing, from the Composer to the Present Day, London, 1981
Moscheles, Charlotte, The Life of Moscheles (trans. Coleridge), London, 1873
Murdoch, William, Chopin: His Life, London, 1934
Murgia, Adelaide, The Life and Times of Chopin, London, 1967
Niecks, Frederick, Frederick Chopin as a Man and Musician, London, 1888
Norwid, Cyprian, Pisma Wybrane (ed. J. W. Gomulicki), Warsaw
Opienski, Henryk (ed.), Chopin's Letters (trans. Ethel Voynich), New York, 1931 (rev. 1971)
Orga, Ates, Chopin: His Life and Times, Tunbridge Wells, 1976
Osborne, G. A., Reminiscences of Frederick Chopin, London, 1879
Radcliffe, Philip, Mendelssohn, London, 1954 (rev. 1976)
Samson, Jim, The Music of Chopin, London, 1985
——, ——, Chopin Studies (ed.), Cambridge, 1988
——, ——, The Cambridge Companion to Chopin (ed.), Cambridge, 1992
Sand, George, Les Majorcains, Paris, 1843
——, ——, Consuelo, Paris, 1844
——, ——, Lucrezia Floriani, Paris, 1846
——, ——, Histoire de ma vie, Paris, 1855
——, ——, Winter in Majorca (trans. Robert Graves), Palma, 1956
Schonberg, H. C., The Great Pianists, New York, 1963
Slonimsky, N., Lexicon of Musical Invective, New York, 1953
Sydow, B. E. (ed.), Korespondencja Fryderyka Chopina, Warsaw, 1955
Walker, Alan, Chopin: Profiles of the Man and the Musician (ed.), London, 1966
——, ——, Franz Liszt: The Virtuoso Years, New York, 1983
Wierzynski, Kasimir, The Life and Death of Chopin, New York, 1949
Zaluski, I. and P., The Scottish Autumn of Frederick Chopin, Edinburgh, 1993
Zamoyski, Adam, Chopin: A Biography, London, 1979

Index